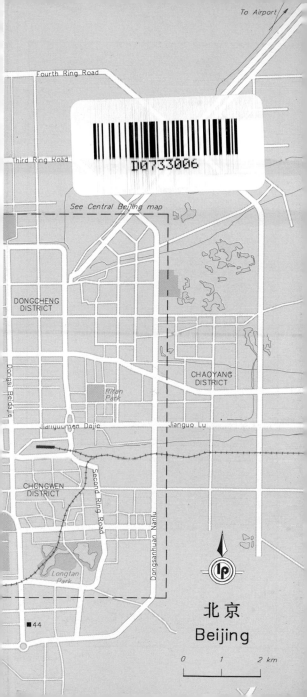

To Airport

Fourth Ring Road

Third Ring Road

D0733006

See Central Beijing map

DONGCHENG DISTRICT

CHAOYANG DISTRICT

Ritan Park

Jianguomen Dajie

Jianguo Lu

Dongsi Beidajie

CHONGWEN DISTRICT

Second Ring Road

Dongsanhuan Nanlu

Longtan Park

■44

北京
Beijing

0   1   2 km

Map 1 Beijing Chinese Key

■ PLACES TO STAY

7 五洲大酒店
9 燕山大酒店
10 友谊大宾馆
14 圆山大酒店
15 华北大酒店
16 四海大宾馆
17 丽都假日饭店
18 燕翔饭店
19 新万寿宾馆
20 中苑宾馆
23 香格里拉饭店
25 奥林匹克饭店
27 上园饭店和西直门饭店
30 新世纪饭店
31 西苑饭店
32 新大都饭店
36 燕京饭店
40 侨园饭店
42 永定门饭店
43 景泰宾馆
44 百乐酒店
45 丽华饭店
46 京华饭店

▼ PLACES TO EAT

33 曲园酒楼
37 麦当劳 II

OTHER

1 颐和园
2 圆明园遗址
3 北京大学
4 中关村
5 清华大学
6 北京语言学院
8 人民大学
10 大钟寺
12 北京师范大学
13 北郊长途汽车站
20 中国剧院
21 中央民族学院
24 北京图书馆
26 五塔寺
28 北京展览馆
29 北京师范学院
34 电视台
35 军事博物馆
38 白云观
39 天宁寺
41 北京南站（永定门站）揪
47 海户屯公共汽车站

Beijing
city guide

Robert Storey

Beijing – city guide
1st edition

Published by
  Lonely Planet Publications
  Head Office: PO Box 617, Hawthorn, Vic 3122, Australia
  Branches: PO Box 2001A, Berkeley, CA 94702, USA
               10 Barley Mow Passage, Chiswick,
               London W4 4PH, UK
               71 bis rue du Cardinal Lemoine,
               75005 Paris, France

Printed by
  Colorcraft Ltd, Hong Kong

Photographs by
  Robert Storey (RS), Chris Taylor (CT), Sonia Berto (SB),
  Richard I'Anson (RI'A), Jo O'Brien (JO) & Alan Samagalski (AS)
                   Front cover: Bas relief of dragon, Beihai Park,
                                courtesy of Herald-Sun newspaper
                                and The Image Bank
           Front cover gatefold: Top: Mutianyu Great Wall (RS)
                                 Bottom: Summer Palace (RS)
           Back cover gatefold: Top: Stone lion (RS)
                                Bottom: Tiananmen (AS)
                    Back cover: Young boy (CT)

First Published
  February 1994

Although the author and publisher have tried to make the
information as accurate as possible, they accept no responsibility for any loss, injury or inconvenience sustained by
any person using this book.

National Library of Australia Cataloguing-in-Publication Data

Storey, Robert
  Beijing city guide

  1st ed.
  Includes index.
  ISBN 0 86442 206 7.

  1. Peking (China) – Guidebooks. I. Title.
  (Series: Lonely Planet city guide)

915.11560459

Text & maps © Lonely Planet 1994
Photos © photographers as indicated 1994
Climate chart compiled from information supplied by Patrick
  J Tyson, © Patrick J Tyson, 1994

Robert Storey

A refugee from the Third World (New York City), Robert escaped to Las Vegas where he became a distinguished slot machine repairman. After graduating from the University of Nevada in Las Vegas with a worthless liberal arts degree, he then went on-the-road and learned to speak Chinese along the way. Today, he is a successful writer, computer hacker, model citizen and a pillar of his community – though no one is quite sure which community that is. His last known address was in Taipei.

From the Author

I'd like to express my gratitude to a number of French foreign residents of Beijing, including Stephane Beccamel, Pierre Sanavio, Pauline Jubert and Catherine Durand-Drouhim. Also special thanks to computer experts Carlos McEvilly (USA) and Ludewijk Kleijn (Netherlands); Tobin Miller and Melanie Straub, two American students in Tianjin; Rupert Winchester (UK) in Hong Kong; to Shane Nunn (USA), now transplanted to South Korea; Richard Flasher (USA), adventure traveller extraordinaire; and to numerous Chinese people I met along the way, who provided helpful advice, companionship, hospitality and some terrific dumplings.

From the Publisher

This first edition of the *Beijing city guide* was edited at the Lonely Planet office in Melbourne, Australia by Vyvyan Cayley. Sally Woodward was responsible for the map-drawing, photograph selection and the overall design of the book.

Thanks also go to: Margaret Jung for the front cover, Tamsin Wilson for the title page illustration and Valerie Tellini, Vicki Beale and Louise Keppie for artistic assistance; Caroline Williamson for editorial support and Katie Cody for proofing the manuscript; Felicia Zhang for help with the Chinese script and Dan Levin for computer assistance.

This Book

This city guide draws on material taken from Lonely Planet's *China - a travel survival kit*, originally written by Michael Buckley and Alan Samalgalski; subsequent editions were updated by Alan, Robert Strauss, Robert Storey, Joe Cummings, Chris Taylor and Clem Lindenmayer. Robert Storey recently revised and updated the Beijing chapter of our guide to China, and it forms the basis of this new book.

Warning & Request

A travel writer's job is never done. Before the ink is dry on a new book, things change, and few places change more quickly than Beijing. At Lonely Planet we get a steady stream of mail from travellers and it all helps – whether it's a few lines scribbled on the back of a used paper plate or a stack of neat typewritten pages spewing forth from our fax machine. Prices go up, new hotels open, old ones degenerate, some burn down, others get renovated and renamed, bus routes change, bridges collapse and recommended travel agents get indicted for fraud. Remember, this book is meant to be a guide, not the oracle – since things go on changing we can't tell you exactly what to expect all the time. Hopefully this book will point you in the right direction and save you some time and money. If you find that China is not identical to the way it's described herein, don't get upset but get out your pen or word processor and write to Lonely Planet. Your input will help make the next edition better. As usual, the writers of useful letters will score a free copy of the next edition, or another Lonely Planet guide if you prefer. We give away lots of books but, unfortunately, not every letter/postcard receives one.

Contents

INTRODUCTION 9

FACTS ABOUT BEIJING 12

History 12	Arts & Culture 17
Orientation 15	Religion 23
Climate 16	Avoiding Offence 23
Population & People 17	Language 25

FACTS FOR THE VISITOR 39

Visas & Embassies 39	Time 71
Documents 43	Electricity 71
Customs 45	Laundry 71
Money 46	Books & Maps 72
When to Go 53	Media 75
What to Bring 53	Film & Photography 79
Tourist Offices 55	Health 81
Business Hours &	Women Travellers 83
Holidays 61	Dangers&Annoyances ..83
Festivals & Events 62	Work 86
Post &	Food 89
Telecommunications 62	Drinks 99

GETTING THERE & AWAY 102

Air 102	International Train 114
Sea 113	Domestic Train.............121
Land 114	Leaving Beijing 126

GETTING AROUND 127

To/From Airport 127	Bicycle 129
Bus 127	Taxi 131
Subway 128	Tours 133

THINGS TO SEE 134

Tiananmen Square 135	Zhongnanhai................144
Tiananmen Gate 136	Summer Palace 144
Qianmen 137	Old Summer Palace 147
Great Hall of the	History Museum &
People 138	Museum of the
Monument to the	Revolution 149
People's Heroes 138	Military Museum 150
Mao Zedong	Natural History
Mausoleum 138	Museum 150
Forbidden City 140	Lu Xun Museum 150

China Art Gallery 151
Xu Beihong Museum .. 151
National Library 151
Capital Museum &
Library 152
Jingshan Park 152
Beihai Park 153
Tiantan Park 157
Grand View Garden 164
Beijing Zoo 164
Lama Temple 165
Confucius Temple &
Imperial College 167
Great Bell Temple 167

Wuta Temple 168
White Dagoba Temple 168
Guangji Temple 168
Niujie Mosque 169
White Cloud Temple ... 169
Black Temple 169
East Cathedral 169
South Cathedral 170
North Cathedral 170
Underground City 170
Ancient Observatory ... 171
Beijing University 172
Blockbuster Bicycle
Tour 173

PLACES TO STAY 179

Places to Stay –
Bottom End 179
Places to Stay –
Middle 183

Places to Stay – Top
End 185
Long Term 189

PLACES TO EAT 191

Cheap Eats 191
Chinese Food 192
Non-Chinese Food 196

Fast Food 198
Self-catering 199

ENTERTAINMENT 202

After Dark 202
Cinema 203

Cultural Shows 204
Sports 208

SHOPPING 210

Where to Shop 210

Shopping Guide 211

EXCURSIONS 220

The Great Wall 220
Ming Tombs 228
Western Qing Tombs .. 231
Eastern Qing Tombs ... 231
Fragrant Hills Park 232
Azure Clouds Temple. 232
Xiangshan Botanical
Gardens 233
Badachu 233
Tanzhe Temple 234

Jietai Temple 234
Marco Polo Bridge 235
Peking Man Site 235
Kangxi Grasslands 237
Miyun Reservoir 237
Haizi Reservoir 238
Shidu 238
Yunshui Caves 239
Longqing Gorge 242
Tianjin 242

MAP INDEX 255

INDEX 256

Introduction

The capital of the People's Republic of China (PRC): home to bureaucrats, generals, political leaders and *laobaixing* (common people); host to reporters, diplomats and tourists; and a labyrinth of doors, walls, tunnels, gates and entrances, temples, pavilions, parks and museums. As far away (4000 km) as Kashgar they run on Beijing's clock; around the country they chortle in *pǔtōnghuà*, the Beijing dialect; in remote Tibet they struggle to interpret the latest directives from the capital. This is where they move the cogs and wheels of the Chinese universe, or try to slow them down if they're moving in the wrong direction.

After the revolution of 1949, China was virtually closed to the outside world. The door creaked open around 1980 and has swung virtually wide open since 1990. This has brought massive economic and social change, with demands for (currently prohibited) political changes. Perhaps nowhere else in China is the generation gap more visible. Appalled by the current drive to 'modernisation', many older people still talk of Chairman Mao and the years of sacrifice for the socialist revolution. But most young people disdain socialism and are more interested in money, motorbikes, fashion, democracy, sex and rock music – not necessarily in that order.

Beijing has the best of everything in China bar the weather: the best food, hotels, the best transport and the best temples. Sometimes the monoliths, militaristic parades, sharply-dressed police, luxury high-rises and tourist armies leave you with the impression that this is China's largest theme park. But sandwiched between the vast squares, boulevards and cavernous buildings are the narrow lanes (called *hutongs*) where traditional Beijing can still be found – street markets offering everything from live ducks to pavement shoe and bicycle repair.

Among the Chinese, Beijing is the promised land. Poor peasants flock to the capital in search of the elusive pot of gold at the end of the rainbow – many wind up camped out on the pavement in front of the railway station. The government tries to encourage them to go home, but the lure of the capital proves too enticing. Meanwhile, down the road at the China World Trade Centre, smartly-attired customers head for a banquet clutching cellular telephones and the same building houses Western-style pubs and discos.

Foreigners certainly seem to enjoy Beijing – the city offers plenty to see and do, and you can't beat the food or shopping. Those who have slugged it out in the ramshackle buses and trains through the poverty-stricken interior of China appreciate the creature comforts of the capital. Other foreigners, having passed their time only in Beijing without seeing the rest of China, come away with the impression that everything is fine in the PRC and that the Chinese are living high. The Chinese they encounter may, in truth, be doing so.

But whatever one says about Beijing, it probably won't be true tomorrow – the city is changing so rapidly it makes you dizzy. In 1981 locals gazed in awe at imported colour TV sets displayed behind plate glass at the Beijing Department Store – no one at that time (except privileged political leaders) could ever hope to own such a machine. These days, street vendors own colour TVs and now the big rage is video tape players and satellite dish antennae. The same street vendors sell everything from steamed bread to rhino horn aphrodisiacs, but not far away you can eat a Big Mac or pizza and buy the latest imported medicines from the West. Whereas bicycles and ox carts were the main form of transport a decade ago, both are prohibited on the new freeways and toll roads which now ring the city.

When the International Olympic Committee rolled into town to check out Beijing's bid for the 2000 Olympics, locals had their heat and hot water turned off – the government didn't want the Committee to see the pollution caused by burning coal. Street urchins were bussed out of town during the three-day visit; workers were stopped and fined for gobbing on the footpath; streets were cleaned, potholes were patched and squatters' shacks were bulldozed; and many were prohibited from driving their vehicles so the Committee would see no traffic jams. For all its seeming liberalism, Beijing keeps an iron-fisted hold on its residents.

Whatever impression you come away with, Beijing is one of the most fascinating places in China. It may be something of a showcase, but what capital city isn't? And with a bit of effort you can get out of the make-up department – Beijing and the surrounding countryside houses some of China's most stunning sights: the Forbidden City, the Summer Palace, Great Wall, Lama Temple, Tiantan, to name just a few. During the Cultural Revolution of the 1960s, these and other historical treasures of China literally took a beating. Now the damage is being repaired, the temples have been restored, everything is being spruced up. Some of this is just window-dressing for the tourists – but the worshippers at the newly opened temples are real.

Group tourists are processed through Beijing in much the same way the ducks are force-fed on the outlying farms – the two usually meet on the first night over the dinner table. But individual travellers will have no trouble getting around. For visitors, Beijing is for the most part 'user-friendly'.

Whatever effort you make to get out and see things will be rewarding. The city offers so much of intrinsic interest that the biggest problem encountered by most visitors is that they simply run out of time before seeing it all.

Facts about Beijing

HISTORY

Beijing is a time-setter for China, but it actually has a short history as Chinese timespans go. Although the area south-west of the city was inhabited by cave dwellers some 500,000 years ago, the earliest records of settlements date from around 1000 BC. It developed as a frontier trading town for the Mongols, Koreans and the tribes from Shandong Province and central China. By the Warring States Period (476-221 BC) it had grown to be the capital of the Yan kingdom and was called Ji, a reference to the marshy features of the area. The town underwent a number of changes as it acquired new warlords, the Khitan Mongols and the Manchurian Jurchen tribes among them. What attracted the conquerors was the strategic position of the town on the edge of the North China Plain. During the Liao Dynasty (907-1125) Beijing was referred to as Yanjing (capital of Yan) – the name now used for Beijing's most popular beer.

History really gets under way in 1215 AD, the year that the great Mongol warrior Genghis Khan thoroughly set fire to the preceding paragraph and slaughtered everything in sight. From the ashes emerged Dadu (Great Capital), alias Khanbaliq, the Khan's town. By 1279 Genghis's grandson Kublai had made himself ruler of most of Asia and Khanbaliq was his capital. Thus was China's Yuan Dynasty (1215-1368) established.

The Mongol emperor was informed by his astrologers that the old city site of Beijing was a breeding ground for rebels, so he shifted it slightly north. The great palace he built no longer remains, but was visited by the great Italian traveller, Marco Polo, who later described what he saw to an amazed Europe. Polo was equally dazzled by the innovations of gunpowder and paper money. These were not without their drawbacks – in history's first case of paper-currency inflation, the last Mongol emperor flooded the country with worthless bills. This, coupled with a large number of natural disasters, provoked an uprising led by the mercenary Zhu Yanhang, who took Beijing in 1368 and ushered in the Ming Dynasty (1368-1644). The city was renamed Beiping (Northern Peace) and for the next 35 years the capital was shifted to Nanjing.

In the early 1400s Zhu's son Yong Le shuffled the court back to Beiping and renamed it Beijing (Northern

Capital). Millions of taels of silver were spent on refurbishing the city. Many of Beijing's famous structures like the Forbidden City and Tiantan were first built in Yong Le's reign. In fact, he is credited with being the true architect of the modern city. The Inner City moved to the area around the Imperial City and a suburban zone was added to the south, a bustle of merchants and street life. The basic grid of present-day Beijing had been laid and history became a question of who ruled the turf.

The first change of government came with the Manchus, who invaded China and established the Qing Dynasty (1644-1911). Under them, and particularly during the reigns of the emperors Kangxi and Qianlong, Beijing was expanded and renovated and summer palaces, pagodas and temples were built.

In the last 120 years of the Manchu Dynasty Beijing and subsequently China were subjected to the afflictions of power struggles, invaders and the chaos created by those who held or sought power: the Anglo-French troops who in 1860 marched in and burnt the Old Summer Palace to the ground; the corrupt regime (1860-1908) of Empress Dowager Wu Cixi; and the disastrous Boxer Rebellion of 1900.

The Manchus were finally trounced in the revolution of 1911 when the Kuomintang Party ostensibly took power and established the Republic of China (ROC) with Sun Yatsen as president. However, real power remained in the hands of warlords. One such warlord, General Yuan Shikai, declared himself emperor in Beijing during 1915.

Yuan died in 1916, but other warlords continued to control most of northern China while the Kuomintang Party held power in the south. The country was badly splintered by private Chinese armies, while foreigners controlled important economic zones (called Concessions) in major ports like Shanghai and Tianjin.

China's continued poverty, backwardness and control by warlords and foreigners were a recipe for rebellion. Beijing University became a hotbed of intellectual dissent, attracting scholars from all over China. Karl Marx's Communist Manifesto was translated into Chinese and became the basis for countless discussion groups. One of the attendees was a library assistant named Mao Zedong (1893-1976). The Communists later established a power base in Shanghai and entered into an uneasy alliance with the Kuomintang Party in order to reunify China.

In 1926, the Kuomintang Party embarked on the Northern Expedition to wrest power from the remaining warlords. Chiang Kaishek (1886-1975) was appointed commander-in-chief by the Kuomintang Party and the Communists. The following year, Chiang turned on his Communist allies and slaughtered them en masse in Shanghai – the survivors carried on a civil war from the countryside. Nevertheless, by the middle of 1928 the Northern Expedition had reached Beijing and a national government was established with Chiang holding both military and political leadership.

In 1937 the Japanese invaded Beijing and by 1939 had overrun eastern China. The Kuomintang government retreated west to the city of Chongqing, which became China's temporary capital during WW II. The Kuomintang Party returned after Japan's defeat in 1945, but their days were numbered – the Chinese civil war was in full swing. The Communists, now under the leadership of Mao Zedong, achieved victory in 1949 – the Kuomintang Party leaders fled to Taiwan, which they control to this day. The People's Liberation Army (PLA) entered Beijing in January, 1949 – on 1 October of the same year, Mao Zedong proclaimed the People's Republic of China (PRC) to an audience of some 500,000 in Tiananmen Square.

After the Revolution

After 1949 came a period of reconstruction. The centre of power has remained in the area around the Forbidden City, but the Communists have significantly altered the face of Beijing. Like the emperors of bygone eras they wanted to leave their mark. Down came the commemorative arches, and blocks of buildings were reduced to rubble to widen Chang'an Jie and Tiananmen Square. From 1950 to 1952 the outer walls were levelled in the interests of traffic circulation. Soviet experts and technicians poured in, which may explain the Stalinesque features on the public structures that went up. Meanwhile industry, negligible in Beijing until this time, was rapidly expanded (with pollution to match).

Progress of all kinds came to a halt in 1966 when Mao launched what became known as the Cultural Revolution. Seeing his powerbase eroding, Mao officially sanctioned wall posters and criticisms of party members by university staff and students, and before long students were being issued with red armbands and taking to the streets. The Red Guards *(hongweibing)* had been born. By August 1966 Mao was reviewing mass parades of the Red Guards in Tiananmen Square, who were chanting and waving copies of his famous 'little red book'.

There was nothing sacred enough to be spared the brutal onslaught of the Red Guards as they went on the rampage through the country. Universities and secondary schools were shut down; intellectuals, writers and artists were dismissed, killed, persecuted or sent to labour in the countryside; publication of scientific, artistic, literary and cultural periodicals ceased; temples were ransacked and monasteries disbanded; and many physical reminders of China's 'feudal', 'exploitative' or 'capitalist' past, including temples, monuments, and works of art were destroyed. Beijing was not spared, and many priceless cultural treasures were lost.

China was to remain in the grip of chaos for the next decade. It wasn't until around 1979 that Deng Xiaoping – a former protégé of Mao who had emerged as a pragmatic leader – launched a 'modernisation' drive. The country opened up and Westerners were finally given a chance to see what the Communists had been up to for the past 30 years.

Beijing saw considerable change during the 1980s – private businesses, once banned by the Communists, were allowed again. Repair work started on the temples, monuments and libraries wrecked during the Cultural Revolution. Unfortunately, the decade ended on a sour note in June, 1989, when PLA troops brutally suppressed a student-led pro-democracy protest. China found itself shunned by most of the world, and it has only been in the past couple of years that Beijing has re-emerged as a popular destination for travel and investment.

ORIENTATION

Though it may not appear so in the shambles of arrival, Beijing is a place of very orderly design. Long, straight boulevards and avenues are crisscrossed by a network of lanes. Places of interest are either very easy to find if they're on the avenues, or impossible to find if they're buried down the narrow alleys.

This section refers to the chessboard of the downtown core, once a walled enclosure. The symmetry folds on an ancient north-south axis passing through Qianmen (Front Gate). The major east-west road is Chang'an (Avenue of Eternal Tranquillity).

As for the street names: Chongwenmenwai Dajie means 'the avenue (dajie) outside (wai) Chongwen Gate (Chongwenmen)'; whereas Chongwenmennei Dajie means 'the avenue inside (nei) Chongwen Gate' (that is, inside the old wall). It's an academic exercise since the gate and the wall in question no longer exist.

Streets are also split along compass points; Dongdajie (East Avenue), Xidajie (West Avenue), Beidajie (North Avenue) and Nandajie (South Avenue). These streets head off from an intersection, usually where a gate once stood.

A major boulevard can change names six or eight times along its length, so intersections become important. The buses are also routed through these points. It therefore pays to study your gates and intersections, and familiarise yourself with the high-rise buildings (often hotels) which serve as useful landmarks to gauge your progress along the chessboard. Other streets are named after bridges, also long gone, like the Bridge of Heaven (Tianqiao), and after features such as old temples which are still there.

Officially, there are three 'ring roads' around Beijing, circumnavigating the city centre in three concentric circles. The first (innermost) ring road is fiction – just part of the grid around the Forbidden City. However, the second ring road (*èrhuán*) and third (*sānhuán*) should be taken seriously – multilane freeways which serve as rapid transit corridors (by taxi) if you avoid rush hour. Construction of a fourth ring road (*sìhuán*) is underway.

The city limits of Beijing extend some 80 km, including the urban, the suburban, and the nine counties under its administration. With a total area of 16,800 sq km, Beijing municipality is roughly the size of Belgium.

CLIMATE

Beijing gets a lot of it – the city is not blessed with congenial weather. Autumn (September to October) is the best time to visit: there's little rain, it's not dry or humid, and the city wears a pleasant cloak of foliage. Winter can be interesting if you don't mind the cold; although the temperature can dip as far as -20°C and the northern winds cut like a knife through bean curd, parts of the capital appear charming in this season. The subdued winter lighting renders the place very photogenic – the cold, dry air makes for good visibility. You also won't have to worry about encountering large armies of tourists, and hotels typically offer a 20% discount. Winter clothing is readily available – the locals wear about 15 layers.

Spring is short, dry and dusty. From April to May a phenomenon known as 'yellow wind' plagues the capital – fine dust particles blown from the Gobi Desert in the north-west sandpaper everything in sight, including your face. The locals run around with mesh bags

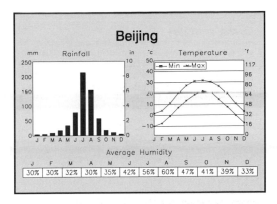

over their heads. In the 1950s the government ordered the extermination of the city's birds, which led to an insect uprising. They then ordered the insects' habitats (grass and other greens) to be dug up, which led to even more dust being set loose. In summer (June to August) the average temperature is 26°C – hot with sticky humidity, plus heavy afternoon thundershowers and mosquitoes in July.

POPULATION & PEOPLE

The population of Beijing is approximately 10 million souls. The vast majority of Beijingers (over 95%) are Han Chinese. The rest of China's 55 official ethnic minorities are scattered about, but a few have established little enclaves – Uigurs from Xinjiang have their own little neighbourhood in north-west Beijing, for example. As China has opened up to the outside world, the capital has acquired a small but fast-growing foreign community.

ARTS & CULTURE

Acrobatics (tèjì biǎoyǎn)

Acrobats are pure fun and they're China's true ambassadors. Donating pandas may have soothed relations but it's the acrobats who capture the international imagination. Some people find the animal acts a bit sad,

Opera (píngjú)

Beijing opera is usually regarded as the **crème de la crème** of all the opera styles prevalent in China. Traditionally it's been the opera of the masses. The themes are usually inspired by disasters, natural calamities, intrigues or rebellions. Many have their source in the fairy tales and stock characters and legends of classical literature. Titles like **The Monkey King, A Drunken Beauty** and **A Fisherman's Revenge** are typical.

The music, singing and costumes are products of the opera's origins. Formerly, opera was performed mostly on open-air stages in markets, streets, teahouses or temple courtyards. The orchestra had to play loudly and the performers had to develop a piercing style of singing which could be heard over the throng. The costumes are a garish collection of sharply contrasting colours because the stages were originally lit by oil lamps.

The movements and techniques of the dance styles of the Tang Dynasty are similar to those of today's opera. Provincial opera companies were characterised by their dialect and style of singing, but when these companies converged on Beijing they started a style of musical drama called **kunqu**. This developed during the Ming Dynasty, along with a more popular variety of play-acting with pieces based on legends, historical events and popular novels. These styles gradually merged by the late 18th and early 19th centuries into the opera we see today.

The musicians usually sit on the stage in plain clothes and play without written scores. The **erhu** is a two-stringed fiddle which is tuned to a low register, has a soft tone and generally supports the **huqin**, another two-stringed fiddle tuned to a high register. The **yueqin**, a sort of moon-shaped four-stringed guitar, has a soft tone and is used to support the erhu. Other instruments are the **sheng** (reed pipes) and the **pipa** (lute), as well as drums, bells and cymbals. Last but not least is the **ban**, a time-clapper which virtually directs the band, beats time for the actors and gives them their cues.

but in general foreigners have reacted to the shows enthusiastically. Sometimes performing tigers and pandas (not together) show up as an added bonus.

Circus acts go back 2000 years in the Middle Kingdom. Effects are obtained using simple props: sticks, plates, eggs and chairs; and apart from the acrobatics there's magic, vaudeville, drama, clowning, music, conjuring, dance and mime thrown into a complete performance. Happily it's an art which gained from the Communist takeover and which did not suffer

There are four types of actors' roles: the **sheng, dan, jing** and **chou**. The sheng are the leading male actors and they play scholars, officials, warriors, etc. They are divided into the **laosheng** who wear beards and represent old men, and the **xiaosheng** who represent young men. The **wensheng** are the scholars and the civil servants. The **wusheng** play soldiers and other fighters, and because of this are specially trained in acrobatics.

The dan are the female roles. The **laodan** are the elderly, dignified ladies such as mothers, aunts and widows. The **qingyi** are aristocratic ladies in elegant costumes. The **huadan** are the ladies' maids, usually in brightly coloured costumes. The **daomadan** are the warrior women. The **caidan** are the female comedians. Traditionally, female roles were played by male actors.

The jing are the painted-face roles, and they represent warriors, heroes, statesmen, adventurers and demons. Their counterparts are the **fujing**, ridiculous figures who are anything but heroic. The chou is basically the clown. The **caidan** is sometimes the female counterpart of this male role.

Apart from the singing and music, the opera also uses acrobatics and mime. Few props are used, so each move, gesture or facial expression is symbolic. A whip with silk tassels indicates an actor riding a horse. Lifting a foot means going through a doorway. Language is often archaic Chinese, music is ear-splitting (bring some cotton wool), but the costumes and make-up are magnificent. The only action that really catches the Western eye is a swift battle sequence – the female warriors involved are trained acrobats who leap, twirl, twist and somersault into attack.

There are numerous other forms of opera. The Cantonese variety is more 'music hall', often with a 'boy meets girl' theme. Gaojia opera is one of the five local opera forms from Fujian province and is also popular in Taiwan, with songs in the Fujian dialect but influenced by the Beijing opera style. ∎

during the Cultural Revolution. Performers used to have the status of gypsies, but now it's 'people's art'.

Most of the provinces have their own performing troupes, sponsored either by government agencies, industrial complexes, the army or rural administrations. About 80 troupes are active in China, they're much in demand and scalpers make huge profits. You'll also see more bare leg, star-spangled costumes and rouge in one acrobat show than you'll see anywhere else in China.

Acts vary from troupe to troupe. Some traditional acts

haven't changed over the centuries, while others have incorporated roller skates and motorcycles. A couple of time-proven acts that are hard to follow include the 'balancing in pairs' with one man balanced upside down on the head of another mimicking every movement of the partner below, mirror image, even drinking a glass of water! Hoop-jumping is another. Four hoops are stacked on top of each other; the human chunk of rubber going through the very top hoop may attempt a backflip with a simultaneous body-twist.

The 'Peacock Displaying its Feathers' involves an array of people balanced on one bicycle. According to the Guinness Book of Records a Shanghai troupe holds the record at 13, though apparently a Wuhan troupe has done 14. The 'Pagoda of Bowls' is a balancing act where the performer, usually a woman, does everything with her torso except tie it in knots, all the while casually balancing a stack of porcelain bowls on foot, head or both – and perhaps also balancing on a partner.

Taijiquan & Gongfu

Previously spelled 'taichi', *taijiquan* or *taiji* (slow motion shadow boxing) has in recent years become quite trendy in many countries. It has been popular in China for centuries. It is basically a form of exercise, but it's also an art and is one form of Chinese martial arts. *Gongfu* (previously spelled 'kungfu') differs from taiji in that the former is performed at much higher speed, can employ weapons and it intended to do bodily harm. While taiji is not a form of self-defence, the movements are similar to gongfu.

There are different styles of taiji, such as Chen and Yang. It's popular with young and old alike – the movements are supposed to develop the breathing muscles, promote digestion, improve muscle tone and keep you looking young.

A modern innovation is to perform taiji movements to the thump of disco music. It's customary to practice this form of exercise in the park at the crack of dawn.

Qigong

As much an art form as a traditional Chinese medicine, *qigong* cannot easily be described in Western terms but it's rather like faith healing. *Qi* represents life's vital energy, and *gong* is from gongfu. Practitioners try to project their qi to perform various miracles, including driving nails through boards as well as healing others.

It's interesting to watch them do it. Typically, they

place their hands above or next to the patient's body without actually making physical contact. To many foreigners this looks like a circus act, and indeed even many Chinese suspect that it's nothing but quackery. However, there are many who claim that they have been cured of serious illness without any other treatment than qigong, even after more conventional doctors have told them that their condition is hopeless.

Denounced as another superstitious link to the bourgeois past, rampaging Red Guards nearly obliterated qigong and its practitioners during the Cultural Revolution. Now it's staging a comeback, but many of the highly skilled practitioners are no longer alive. In China, you are most likely to see qigong in the ever-popular movies (mainly imported from Hong Kong), where mortally wounded heroes are miraculously revived with a few waves of the hands.

Does it work? It's not easy to say, but there is a theory in medicine that all doctors can cure a third of their patients regardless of what method is used. So perhaps qigong gets this cure rate too.

Music

Traditional Traditional Chinese musical instruments include the two-stringed fiddle *(èrhú)*, three-stringed flute *(sānxúan)*, four-stringed banjo *(yùeqín)*, two-stringed viola *(húqín)*, vertical flute *(dòngxiāo)*, horizontal flute *(dízi)*, piccolo *(bāngdí)*, four-stringed lute *(pípá)*, zither *(gǔzhēng)*, ceremonial trumpet *(sǔonà)*, and ceremonial gongs *(dàlúo)*.

Temple musicians (JO)

Modern China's music market is heavily influenced by the already well established music industries in Taiwan and Hong Kong. The advent of satellite TV and the popularity of MTV – broadcast via Hong Kong's Star TV network – is also having an impact.

Real culture shock strikes when East meets West over the music score. China's leadership has had a hard time deciding how to react – in the beginning, Western music was vehemently denounced by the government as another form of dangerous 'spiritual pollution'. China's first concert featuring a foreign rock group was in April, 1985, when the British group 'Wham' was allowed to perform. The audience remained sedate – music fans who dared to get up and dance in the aisles were hauled off by the PSB. Since then, things have become more liberal and China has produced some notable bands.

The hip young urban Chinese like disco music. On the popular music front, Taiwanese love songs have been enormously successful in China, and Mandarin versions (the original songs are Cantonese) of Hong Kong popular hits produced for the Taiwan and China markets are frequently chart hits. While Chinese tastes generally run towards soft melodies, Beijing has a nascent heavy metal and punk scene. There are dance halls in all the major hotels, generally alternating between disco, live music and a karaoke session.

The older generation got a jolt with the release of *Rock & Roll for the New Long March* by Cui Jian. More jolts came with heavy metal sounds by the bands, Tang Dynasty and Black Panther. The cassette tape *Rock & Roll Beijing*, released in 1993, impressed many foreigners – the quality of the music could compete with some of the best offerings in the West. One feature of the recording was an all-female rock group. In the past, talented Chinese rock groups have had to scrounge to get the equipment they need, but it seems that some are now getting donations from Western rock groups and Overseas Chinese.

In an attempt to show that the geriatric leadership is also hip, government officials authorised a disco version of *The East is Red*. There are orchestras organised on western lines which substitute Chinese for Western instruments. Western fads like break dancing and Brazil's erotic dance, the 'lambada', have come and gone – clear cases of 'spiritual pollution' according to the government. Exactly where all this is leading no one knows.

Art Objects

Foreigners struggling to read street signs might not be

so impressed, but calligraphy has traditionally been regarded in China as the highest form of visual art.

The Chinese are also famous for their fine watercolour paintings, jade stone, porcelain and ceramic teaware.

RELIGION

While minority religions (mainly Islam and Christianity) exist in large areas of China and even a few pockets in Beijing, Chinese religion is dominated by Taoism, Confucianism and Buddhism.

The Cultural Revolution had a devastating effect on Chinese religion – it has yet to recover fully. Temples were closed or destroyed, monks were sent to labour in the countryside where they often perished, and believers were prohibited from worship. But slowly the temples are being restored and worshippers are returning. Chinese religion has largely been kept alive in Hong Kong, Macau and Taiwan – donations from Overseas Chinese have become a significant source of funding for temple reconstruction. While freedom of religion is now legally permitted in China, it's worth noting that membership in the Chinese Communist Party is not permitted for anyone found to be actively practising religion.

AVOIDING OFFENCE

Face

Face can be loosely considered as status and many Chinese people will go to great lengths to avoid 'losing face'. For example, a foreigner may front up to a hotel desk and have a furious row with the receptionist because the foreigner believes that the hotel has vacant rooms while the receptionist firmly denies all knowledge of the fact. The staff may in fact be saving the vacant rooms for friends, or else they might not want to rent what they consider a 'substandard' room to a foreigner. Regardless of who is right or wrong, the receptionist is even less likely to admit the truth (and 'lose face') if the foreigner throws a fit.

In such situations, you can accomplish a great deal more with smiles, talking about other things for a while ('Where did you learn such good English?'), showing some of your photos from your trip, etc, before pushing your case in a quiet manner.

Avoid direct criticisms of people. If you have to complain about something, like the hot water not working, do so in a fairly quiet tone. Confrontation causes loss of

Traditional calligraphy (SB)

face and that leads to trouble. Venting your rage in public and trying to make someone lose face will cause the Chinese to dig in their heels and worsen your situation. A lot of Westerners really blow it on this point.

Speaking Frankly

Related to the issue of face is the issue of speaking frankly. People often don't say what they think, but rather what they think you want to hear. Certain issues like death and divorce are avoided altogether. Someone might ask you if you're married, but if you're divorced or your spouse is dead, just say you're 'unmarried' (or 'married' if you prefer) and let it go at that.

Personal Questions

Chinese people will often strike up a conversation with a total stranger with opening questions about your marriage, the number of children you have, how much money you make, and (oddly) your blood-type. To ask a total stranger such questions in the West would be most unsettling, but it is quite normal in China.

How do you respond if you don't wish to reveal your blood-type, how much money you make or your personal family history to a complete stranger? Simply make up whatever answer you feel comfortable with. No need to say how much money you make, just make up a figure. But don't blow up and yell, 'None of your business!'. That would be a major faux pas on your part.

Deadly Chopsticks

A pair of chopsticks sticking vertically into the rice bowl resembles incense sticks in a bowl of ashes. This is considered a death sign in China and many other countries of the Orient – it's rude and should be avoided.

Red Ink

Don't write a note in red ink. If you want to give someone your address or telephone, write in any colour but red. Red ink conveys a message of unfriendliness. If you're teaching in China it's OK to use red ink to correct students' papers, but if you write extensive comments or suggestions on the back of the paper, use some other colour besides red.

Passion Prohibited

The Chinese are not nearly as innocent as they pretend to be when it comes to sexual matters. However, the Communist regime is one of the most prudish in the world. Walking around hand in hand with a member of the opposite sex or otherwise getting passionate in public can be considered scandalous behaviour – even if there are 20 prostitutes living in your hotel! It should also go without saying that any type of public nudity – toplessness at the beach and so on – is asking for big trouble.

LANGUAGE

The official language of the PRC is the Beijing dialect, usually referred to in the West as 'Mandarin Chinese'.

The official name of Mandarin in China is *pǔtōnghuà*, or 'common speech', but it is variously referred to as *hànyǔ* (Han language), *zhōngwén* and *zhōngguóhuà*, both of which mean simply 'Chinese'.

The word 'Mandarin' derives from the use of the Beijing dialect as a standard language by the scholar class in centuries past. The widespread promulgation of a national language based on the Beijing dialect has its origins in the Kuomintang period.

Lonely Planet publishes a *Mandarin Chinese Phrasebook*. A small dictionary with English, romanisation and Chinese characters is also immensely helpful.

Grammar

Chinese grammar is far simpler than the grammars of European languages. For a start, there are no articles (a, the), no tenses and no plurals. This immediately does away with biggest hurdles facing students of, say, German or French. Many travellers are intimidated by Chinese but, once they latch onto the basic principle that constructing a Chinese sentence is basically a matter of stringing words together, a great deal of progress can be made quickly.

The basic point to bear in mind is that, like English, Chinese is a subject-verb-object language. So the English sentence 'I love you' can be translated literally word for word into Chinese.

Tones

Chinese is a language with a large number of homonyms (words of different meaning but identical pronunciation), and if it were not for its tonal quality it probably would not work very well as a language. Mandarin has four tones; the following provides an example of how tone can change the meaning:

high tone	*mā*	mother
rising tone	*má*	hemp or numb
falling-rising tone	*mǎ*	horse
falling tone	*mà*	to scold or swear

Pinyin

In 1958 the Chinese officially adopted a system known as *pīnyīn* as a method of writing their language using the Roman alphabet. Since the official language of China is the Beijing dialect, this pronunciation is used. The original idea was to eventually do away with characters completely and just use pinyin. However, tradition dies hard and the idea has gradually been abandoned.

Pinyin is often used on shop fronts, street signs and advertising billboards. Don't expect Chinese people to be able to use pinyin, however. There are also indications in China that adherence to the pinyin system is breaking down.

In the countryside and the smaller towns you may not see a single pinyin sign anywhere, so unless you speak Chinese you'll need a phrasebook with Chinese characters if you're travelling in these areas. Though pinyin is helpful, it's not an instant key to communication, since Westerners often don't get the pronunciation and intonation of the romanised word correct.

Since 1979 all translated texts of Chinese diplomatic documents and Chinese magazines published in foreign languages have used the pinyin system of spelling names and places. The system replaces the old Wade-Giles and Lessing systems of romanising Chinese script. Thus under pinyin, 'Mao Tse-tung' becomes *Mao Zedong*; 'Chou En-lai' becomes *Zhou Enlai*; and 'Peking' becomes *Beijing*. The name of the country remains as it has been generally written: 'China' in English and German, and 'Chine' in French – in pinyin it's 'Zhongguo'. When Hong Kong (an English version of Cantonese for 'fragrant harbour') goes over to China in 1997 it will become Xianggang.

Pronunciation The letter **v** is not used in Chinese. The trickiest sounds in pinyin are **c**, **q** and **x**. Most letters are pronounced as in English, except for the following description of the sounds produced in spoken Mandarin.

Vowels

a	like the 'a' in 'father'
ai	like the 'i' in 'I'
ao	like the 'ow' in 'cow'
e	like the 'u' in 'blur'
ei	like the 'ei' in 'weigh'
i	like the 'ee' in 'meet' or the 'oo' in 'book'
ian	like in 'yen'
ie	like the English word 'yeah'
o	like the 'o' in 'or'
ou	like the 'oa' in 'boat'
u	like the 'u' in 'flute'
ui	like 'way'

uo	like 'w' followed by an 'o' like in 'or'
yu	like German umlaut 'ü' or French 'u' in 'union'
ü	like German umlaut 'ü'

Consonants

c	like the 'ts' in 'bits'
ch	like in English, but with the tongue curled back
h	like in English, but articulated from the throat
q	like the 'ch' in 'cheese'
r	like the 's' in 'pleasure'
sh	like in English, but with the tongue curled back
x	like the 'sh' in 'shine'
z	like the 'ds' in 'suds'
zh	like the 'j' in 'judge' but with the tongue curled back

Consonants (except for **n, ng**, and **r**) never end syllables. In pinyin, apostrophes can separate syllables – writing *(ping'an)* prevents pronounciation as *(pin'gan)*.

To confuse matters, Beijingers have their own distinct accent sometimes referred to as 'r-hua' because every word ends with an 'r' sound. The 'Qiaoyuan Hotel' becomes the 'Qiaoyuar'. The Chinese word for tea *(cha)* becomes *char*. And so on.

Gestures

Hand signs are frequently used in China. The 'thumbs-up' sign has a long tradition as an indication of excellence or, in Chinese, *gūa gūa jiào*. Another way to indicate excellence is to gently pull your own earlobe between thumb and index finger.

The Chinese have a system for counting on their hands. If you can't speak the language, it would be worth your while to at least learn Chinese finger counting. The symbol for number 10 is to form a cross with the index fingers, but in many locations the Chinese just show a fist.

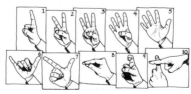

Finger counting

The Written Language

Chinese characters look like so many little pictures, and hence is often referred to as a language of 'pictographs'. Many of the basic Chinese characters are in fact highly stylised pictures of what they represent, but this element is only part of the story in what is a highly complex system.

Chinese linguists divide characters into six groups according to their composition. The first group is the pictogram, which is what most Westerners call to mind when they think of Chinese characters. It is a character which is a stylised picture of what it represents; a horse, say, or the moon. The second group, the ideogram, represents its object in abstract terms; thus the word for 'middle' is a vertical line cutting through the centre of a rectangle. The third group, the compound ideogram, is a combination of two or more ideograms to denote an idea or object; thus the combination of two tree ideograms creates the word *sēn*, or 'forest'. The fourth group, the phonogram, is a combination of a meaning element and a phonetic element, and is the most common kind of Chinese character (around 90% of Chinese characters are phonograms). The other two groups, the phonetic loan and derivative character, claim fewer members.

Just how many Chinese characters are there? Including ancient writings, it's possible to verify the existence of some 56,000 characters, but the vast majority of these are obsolete and others were variations of the same characters in times before national standards had been imposed. It is commonly felt that a well educated contemporary Chinese might know and use between 6000 and 8000 characters. Students looking at getting through a Chinese newspaper will need to know around 1200 to 1500 characters to get the gist of what's going on, but will probably need between 2000 and 3000 before the going starts to get easy.

The question of how many characters you need to read certain Chinese texts is, however, a little misleading. While the building block of the Chinese language is the monosyllabic Chinese character, Chinese words are usually made up of two or more characters in combination. A student of Chinese, for example, might know the characters for 'look' (*kàn*), 'home' (*jiā*) and 'dog' (*gǒu*), but would probably have to look up a dictionary to find out that all three in combination (*kànjiāgǒu*) mean 'watchdog'. A classic example of a less obvious character compound is the combination of *wēi*, meaning 'dangerous' and *jī*, meaning 'opportunity', to create the word 'crisis' (*wēijī*).

Simplification In the interests of promoting universal literacy, in 1954 the Committee for Reforming the Chinese Language was set up by the Beijing Government. Around 2200 Chinese characters have been simplified.

The reforms were implemented successfully in the PRC, but Chinese communities outside China (notably Taiwan and Hong Kong) continue to use traditional full-form characters. The last few years, probably as a result of large scale Overseas Chinese investment and tourism, has seen a return of the full-form characters to China, mainly in advertising (where the traditional characters are considered more attractive) and restaurant, hotel and shop signs. What this means in the long term is difficult to say. The government insists that simplified characters are here to stay, but the increased usage of traditional characters will probably mean that the two systems will come into competition in China.

Greetings & Civilities

hello
    nǐ hǎo   你好！
good-bye
    zàijiàn   再见
thank you
    xièxie   谢谢
you're welcome
    búkèqi   不客气
I'm sorry
    duìbùqǐ   对不起
no, don't have
    méiyǒu   没有
no, not so
    búshì   不是
I am a foreign student.
    wǒ shì liúxuéshēng   我是留学生
What's to be done now?
    zěnme bàn?   怎么办？
It doesn't matter.
    méishì   没事
I want...
    wǒ yào...   我要 . . . . .
No, I don't want it.
    búyào   不要
I don't understand.
    wǒ tīngbudǒng   我听不懂
I do understand.
    wǒ tīngdedǒng   我听得懂

Do you understand?
 dǒng ma? 懂吗？

Pronouns

I
 wǒ 我
you
 nǐ 你
he, she, it
 tā 他／她／它
we, us
 wǒmen 我们
you (plural)
 nǐmen 你们
they, them
 tāmen 他们

Toilets

toilet (restroom)
 cèsuǒ 厕所
toilet paper
 wèishēng zhǐ 卫生纸
bathroom (washroom)
 xǐshǒu jiān 洗手间

Money

How much is it?
 duōshǎo qián? 多少钱？
Is there anything cheaper?
 yǒu piányì yìdiǎn de ma? 有便宜一点的吗？
That's too expensive.
 tài guìle 太贵了
Bank of China
 zhōngguó yínháng 中国银行
FEC (foreigners' money)
 wàihuìjuàn 外汇券
RMB (people's money)
 rénmínbì 人民币
change money
 huàn qián 换钱
travellers' cheque
 lǚxíng zhīpiào 旅行支票

Accommodation

Hotel
 lǚguǎn 旅馆

small hotel
    lǚshè   旅社
hostel
    zhāodàisuǒ   招待所
tourist hotel
    bīnguǎn, fàndiàn, jiǔdiàn   宾馆，饭店，酒店
dormitory
    duōrénfáng   多人房
single room
    dānrénfáng   单人房
double room
    shuāngrénfáng   双人房
bed
    chuángwèi   床位
economy room
    jīngjìfáng   经济房
economy room (with bathroom)
    jīngjì tàofáng   经济套房
standard room (with bathroom)
    biāozhǔnjiān   标准套房
luxury room (with bathroom)
    háohuá tàofáng   豪华套房
hotel namecard
    lǚguǎn de míngpiàn   旅馆的名片
wash clothes
    xǐ yīfú   洗衣服
book a whole room
    bāofáng   包房

Post & Telecommunications

post office
    yóujú   邮局
letter
    xìn   信
envelope
    xìnfēng   信封
package
    bāoguǒ   包裹
air mail
    hángkōng xìn   航空信
surface mail
    píngyóu   平邮
stamps
    yóupiào   邮票
postcard
    míngxìnpiàn   明信片
aerogramme
    hángkōng xìnjiàn   航空邮件

poste restante
   cúnjú hòulǐnglàn   存局候领栏
telephone
   diànhuà   电话
telephone office
   diànxùn dàlóu   电讯大楼
telephone card
   diànhuà kǎ   电话卡
international call
   guójì diànhuà   国际电话
collect call
   duìfāng fùqián diànhuà   对方付电话
direct-dial call
   zhíbō diànhuà   直通电话
fax
   chuánzhēn   传真

Bicycle

bicycle
   zìxíngchē   自行车
I want to hire a bicycle.
   wǒ yào zu yíliàng zìxíngche   我要租一辆自行车
How much is it per day?
   yìtiān duōshǎo qián?   一天多少钱?
How much is it per hour?
   yíge xiǎoshí duōshǎo qián?   一个小时多少钱?
deposit
   yājīn   押金

Transport

I want to go to...
   wǒ yào qù...   我要去 . . .
I want to get off
   wǒ yào xiàchē   我要下车
luggage
   xíngli   行李
left-luggage room
   jìcún chù   寄存处
one ticket
   yìzhāng piào   一张票
I want to depart at...(time)
   wǒ yào...diǎn zǒu   我要 . . . . .点开
Could you buy a ticket for me?
   kěyǐ tì wǒ mǎi yìzhāng piào mā?   可以替我买一张票吗?
What time does it depart?
   jǐdiǎn kāi?   几点开?
What time does it arrive?
   jǐdiǎn dào?   几点到?

How long does the trip take?
zhècì lǚxíng yào duōcháng shíjiān? 这次旅行要花多少时间

buy a ticket
mǎi piào 买票

refund a ticket
tuì piào 退票

taxi
chūzū chē 出租车

Bus

bus
gōnggòng qìchē 公共汽车

minibus
xiǎo gōnggòng qìchē 小公共汽车

long-distance bus station
chángtú qìchē zhàn 长途汽车站

bus map
jiāotōng dìtú 交通地图

When is the first bus?
tóubān qìchē jǐdiǎn kāi? 头班汽车几点开？

When is the last bus?
mòbān qìchē jǐdiǎn kāi? 末班汽车几点开？

When is the next bus?
xià yìbān qìchē jǐdiǎn kāi? 下一班几点开？

Train

train
huǒchē 火车

ticket office
shòupiào chù 售票处

advance train ticket office
huǒchē piào yùshòu chù 火车票预售处

railway station
huǒchē zhàn 火车站

main railway station
zhǔyào huǒchē zhàn 主要火车站

hard-seat
yìngxí, yìngzuò 硬席，硬座

soft-seat
ruǎnxí, ruǎnzuò 软席，软座

hard-sleeper
yìngwò 硬卧

soft-sleeper
ruǎnwò 软卧

platform ticket
zhàntái piào 站台票

Which platform?
dìjǐhào zhàntái 第几号站台？

upgrade ticket (after boarding)
  bǔpiào 补票
1st class waiting room
  tóu děng hòuchēshì 头等候车楼
subway (underground)
  dìxiàtiě 地下铁路
subway station
  dìtiě zhàn 地铁站

Air Transport

airport
  fēijīchǎng 飞机场
CAAC
  zhōngguó mínháng 中国民航
charter flight
  bāojī 包机
one-way ticket
  dānchéng piào 单程票
round-trip ticket
  láihuí piào 来回票

Emergency

police
  jǐngchá 警察
Fire!
  huǒzāi! 火灾
Help!
  jiùmìng a! 救命
Thief!
  xiǎotōu! 小偷！

Medical

I'm sick.
  wǒ shēngbìngle 我生病了
I'm injured.
  wǒ shòushāngle 我受伤了
hospital
  yīyuàn 医院
pharmacy
  yàodiàn 药店
diarrhoea
  lādùzi 拉肚子
anti-diarrhoeal drug
  húangliǎnsù 黄连素
laxative
  xièyào 泻药

fever
   fāshāo   发烧

Time

What is the time?
   jǐ diǎnle?   几点了？
...hour...minute
   ...diǎn...fēn   点 . . . 分 . . .
now
   xiànzài   现在
today
   jīntiān   今天
When?
   shénme shíhòu?   什么时候？
tomorrow
   míngtiān   明天
the day after tomorrow
   hòutiān   后天
three days ahead
   dà hòutiān   大后天
in the morning
   zǎochén   早晨
daytime
   báitiān   白天
afternoon
   xiàwǔ   下午
night, evening
   wǎnshàng   晚上
Wait a moment.
   děng yīxià   等一下

Numbers

0	*líng*	零
1	*yī, yāo*	一
2	*èr, liǎng*	二
3	*sān*	三
4	*sì*	四
5	*wǔ*	五
6	*liù*	六
7	*qī*	七
8	*bā*	八
9	*jiǔ*	九
10	*shí*	十
11	*shíyī*	十一
12	*shí'èr*	十二
20	*èrshí*	二十
21	*èrshíyī*	二十一
100	*yìbǎi*	一百

200	*liǎngbǎi*	二百
1000	*yìqiān*	一千
2000	*liǎngqiān*	两千
10,000	*yíwàn*	一万
20,000	*liǎngwàn*	两万
100,000	*shíwàn*	十万
200,000	*èrshíwàn*	二十万

Directions

map
    dìtú   地图
Where is the...?
    ...*zài nǎlǐ?* ... . 在哪里？
I'm lost.
    wǒ mílùle   我迷路了
turn right
    yòu zhuǎn   右转
turn left
    zuǒ zhuǎn   左转
go straight
    yìzhí zǒu   一直走
turn around
    xiàng huí zǒu   向回走

Geographical Terms

road, trail
    lù   路
street
    jiē, dàjiē   街，大街
boulevard
    dàdào   大道
alley
    xiàng, hútong   巷，胡同
north
    běi   北
south
    nán   南
east
    dōng   东
west
    xī   西
cave
    dòng   洞
hot spring
    wēnquán   温泉
lake
    hú   湖

mountain
>   *shān* 山

river
>   *hé, jiāng* 河，江

valley
>   *gǔ, gōu* 谷，沟

waterfall
>   *pùbù* 瀑布

Studying Chinese

Beijing is a good place to study Chinese, but prices and quality of instructions varies widely. A bottom-end price quote for four hours of instruction per day, five days a week is US$250 per month for the first month, US$50 per week thereafter if you stay a long time. Dormitory housing starts at around US$4.50 a day for private room, or half that amount to share the room. There have been complaints from students that universities try to hit foreigners with all sorts of various hidden surcharges – 'study licences' and so on. It's probably to your advantage to sign up for a one-month course, and if you like it you can extend later.

As China continues to experiment with capitalism, universities have found it increasingly necessary to raise their own funds and not depend so much on State largess. For this reason, almost all universities welcome fee-paying foreign students. One place popular with foreign language students is Beijing Language Institute (BLI) *(yǔyán xuéyuán)*, east of Qinghua University. Another place worth trying is the Central College of Nationalities *(zhōngyāng mínzú xuéyuàn)*.

Facts for the Visitor

VISAS & EMBASSIES

Visa Requirements

Visas for travel in China are easiest to get in Hong Kong and Macau. If you aren't going to Hong Kong, then inquire first at the nearest Chinese Embassy.

The cheapest visas can be obtained from the Visa Office of the Ministry of Foreign Affairs of the PRC (☎ 585 1794, 585 1700), 5th Floor, Low Block, China Resources Building, 26 Harbour Rd, Wanchai, Hong Kong Island. You'll have to queue, but you're saving a few dollars. The office is open from Monday to Friday, 9 am to 12.30 pm and 2 to 5 pm, Saturday 9 am to 12.30 pm. You pay in Hong Kong dollars (HK$) here; HK$90 for 2½ day service, HK$240 for same day (exchange rate approximately US$1=HK$7.7).

Numerous travel agencies in Hong Kong also can obtain your Chinese visa. Besides saving you the hassle of visiting the visa office and queueing, a few travel agents can get you more time than the usual 30 days. For a standard single-entry tourist visa of one or two months' validity, issued in two working days, expect to pay around HK$120 to HK$140. For a visa issued in 24 hours, HK$180; issued the same day, HK$280. Dual-entry visas cost double.

In Macau, you can obtain a Chinese visa the same day from China Travel Service (☎ 70 0888), Xinhua Building, Rua de Nagasaki. Visa applications require two pass-port-size photos. Your application must be written in English.

Multiple-entry visas are available through some travel agencies. These cost approximately HK$750 and are valid for six months' duration, allowing an unlimited number of border crossings during this time. But there is a catch – you can only stay in China for 30 days at a time and getting this extended is nearly impossible. Another minor catch is that these are in fact business visas, and normally will only be issued if you've been to China at least once before and have a stamp in your passport to prove it.

Certain ports of entry such as Shenzhen issue five-day

visas at the border for HK$250. Chinese residents of Hong Kong, Macau and Taiwan can apply for a permit which entitles them to multiple visa-free entry.

One-month single-entry visas are valid from the date of entry that you specify on the visa application. But all other visas are valid from the date of issue, *not* from the date of entry, so there's no point in getting such a visa far in advance of your planned entry date. There are seven types of visas, as follows:

L	Travel *(Lüxing)*
F	Business *(Fangwen)*
D	Resident *(Dingju)*
G	Transit *(Guojing)*
X	Student *(liu Xue)*
Z	Working *(ren Zhi)*
C	Stewardess *(Chengwu)*

Visa Extensions

Visa extensions are handled by the Foreign Affairs Section of the local PSB (the police force). The general rule is that if you entered on a one-month visa you can get one extension of one month's duration. You may be able to wangle more, especially with cogent reasons like illness (except AIDS) or transport delays, but second extensions are usually only granted for one week with the understanding that you are on your way out of China. Similarly, if you entered on a three-month visa, you'll probably only get a one-week extension.

Re-entry Visas

Most foreign residents of China have multiple-entry visas and don't need a re-entry visa. However, there might be other requirements (tax clearance, vaccinations, etc) – if in doubt, check with the PSB before departing.

Chinese Embassies

Some of the addresses of Chinese embassies and consulates in major cities overseas include:

Australia
 15 Coronation Drive, Yarralumla, ACT 2600 (☎ (06) 273 4780, 273 4781)
 Consulate: Melbourne (☎ (03) 822 0604)
Austria
 Meternichgasse 4, 1030 Wien (☎ (06) 75 3149, 713 6706)

Belgium
    443-445, Aavenue de Tervuren, 1150 Bruxelles
    (☎ 771 3309, 771 2681)
Canada
    515 St Patrick St, Ottawa, Ontario KIN 5H3   (☎ 234 2706,
    234 2682)
Denmark
    Oregards alle 25, 2900 Hellerup, Copenhagen (☎ 62 5806,
    61 1013)
France
    11 Ave George V, 75008 Paris (☎ 472 33677, 473 67790)
Germany
    Kurfislrstenallee 12, 5300 Bonn 2 (Bad Godesberg)
    (☎ 36 1095, 36 2350)
Italy
    56 Via Bruxelles, 56-00198 Roma Italia
    (☎ 841 3458, 841 3467)
Japan
    3-4-33, Moto-Azabu, Minato-ku, Tokyo (106)
    (☎ 340 33380, 340 33065)
Netherlands
    Adriaan Goekooplaan 7, 2517 JX Den Haag (☎ 355 1515,
    355 9209)
New Zealand
    2-6 Glenmore St, Wellington (☎ 472 1382, 472 1384)
Spain
    C/Arturo Soria, 113 28043 Madrid (☎ 519 4242, 519 3651)
Sweden
    Lidovagen 8 115 25, Stockholm (☎ 783 6739, 783 0179)
Switzerland
    Kalecheggweg 10, 3006 Berne Suisse (☎ 44 7333, 43 4593)
UK
    49-51 Portland Place, London WIN 3AH (☎ 636 2580,
    636 1835)
USA
    2300 Connecticut Ave NW, Washington, DC 20008
    (☎ 328 2500, 328 2517)
    Consulates: 3417 Montrose Blvd, Houston, Texas 77006;
    104 South Michigan Ave, Suite 1200, Chicago, Illinois
    60603; 1450 Laguna St, San Francisco, CA 94115; 520 12th
    Ave, New York, NY 10036.

Foreign Embassies in China

In Beijing there are two main embassy compounds –
Jianguomenwai and Sanlitun. Map Nos 18 and 19 at the
back of the book give details of the location of the
embassies in these two areas. The following embassies
are in Jianguomenwai:

Austria
    5 Xiushui Nanjie (☎ 532 2061; fax 532 1505)
Bangladesh
    42 Guanghua Lu (☎ 532 2521)

Bulgaria
    4 Xiushui Beijie (☎ 532 2232)
Czech & Slovak
    Ritan Lu (☎ 532 1531; fax 532 4814)
India
    1 Ritan Donglu (☎ 532 1908; fax 532 4684)
Ireland
    3 Ritan Donglu (☎ 532 2691)
Israel
    Room 405, West Wing, China World Trade Centre,
    1 Jianguomenwai Dajie (☎ 505 0328)
Japan
    7 Ritan Lu (☎ 532 2361)
Mongolia
    2 Xiushui Beijie (☎ 532 1203)
New Zealand
    1 Ritan Dong 2-Jie (☎ 532 2731; fax 532 4317)
North Korea
    Ritan Beilu (☎ 532 1186)
Philippines
    23 Xiushui Beijie (☎ 532 2794)
Poland
    1 Ritan Lu (☎ 532 1235; fax 532 5364)
Romania
    corner of Ritan Dong 2-Jie and Ritan Donglu (☎ 532 3315)
Singapore
    1 Xiushui Beijie (☎ 532 3926; fax 532 2215)
Sri Lanka
    3 Jianhua Lu (☎ 532 1861; fax 532 5426)
Thailand
    40 Guanghua Lu (☎ 532 1903; fax 532 3986)
UK
    11 Guanghua Lu (☎ 532 1961)
USA
    Embassy: 3 Xiushui Beijie (☎ 532 3831 ext 274);
    Consulate: Bruce Building, 2 Xiushui Dongjie
    (☎ 532 3431 ext 225)
Vietnam
    32 Guanghua Lu (☎ 532 1125)

The Sanlitun compound in Beijing is home to the following embassies:

Australia
    21 Dongzhimenwai Dajie (☎ 532 2331; fax 532 4605)
Belgium
    6 Sanlitun Lu (☎ 532 1736; fax 532 5097)
Cambodia
    9 Dongzhimenwai Dajie (☎ 532 1889; fax 532 3507)
Canada
    19 Dongzhimenwai Dajie (☎ 532 3536; fax 532 4072)
Denmark
    1 Sanlitun Dong 5-Jie (☎ 532 2431)

Finland
Tayuan Diplomatic Building, 14 Liangmahe Nanlu
(☎ 532 1817; fax 532 1884)
France
3 Sanlitun Dong 3-Jie (☎ 532 1331)
Germany
5 Dongzhimenwai Dajie (☎ 532 2161; fax 532 5336)
Hungary
10 Dongzhimenwai Dajie (☎ 532 1431)
Italy
2 Sanlitun Dong 2-Jie (☎ 532 2131; fax 532 4676)
Malaysia
13 Dongzhimenwai Dajie (☎ 532 2531; fax 532 5032)
Myanmar (Burma)
6 Dongzhimenwai Dajie (☎ 532 1584; fax 532 1344)
Nepal
1 Sanlitun Xi 6-Jie (☎ 532 1795)
Netherlands
1-15-2 Tayuan Building, 14 Liangmahe Nanlu (☎ 532 1131;
fax 532 4689)
Norway
1 Sanlitun Dong 1-Jie (☎ 532 2261; fax 532 2392)
Pakistan
1 Dongzhimenwai Dajie (☎ 532 2504)
Portugal
Bangonglou 2-72 (☎ 532 3497; fax 532 4637)
Russia
4 Dongzhimen Beizhongjie, west of the Sanlitun Compound in a separate compound (☎ 532 2051; fax 532 4853)
Spain
9 Sanlitun Lu (☎ 532 1986; fax 532 3401)
Sweden
3 Dongzhimenwai Dajie (☎ 532 3331; fax 532 3803)
Switzerland
3 Sanlitun Dong 5-Jie (☎ 532 2736; fax 532 4353)

DOCUMENTS

Foreign Documents

Business name cards are essential, even if you don't do
business – exchanging name cards with someone you've
just met goes down well with the locals. It's particularly
good if you can get your name translated into Chinese
and have that printed just next to your English name.
You can get name cards made cheaply in China, but it's
better to have some in advance of your arrival.

Carry your old expired passport if you have one.
Some hotels also require you to hand over your passport
as security, even if you've paid in advance – an expired
passport is useful for these situations. Ditto for bicycle
renters who want your passport as security, though they
will often take a cash deposit.

As for your real passport, if yours is within a few months of expiry, get a new one now – many countries will not issue a visa if your passport has less than six months of validity remaining. Be sure that your passport has at least a few blank pages for visas and entry and exit stamps. It could be embarrassing to run out of blank pages when you are too far away from an embassy to get a new passport issued or extra pages added.

Losing your passport is very bad news indeed. Getting a new one takes time and money. However, if you will be staying in China or any foreign country for a long period of time, it helps tremendously to register your passport with your embassy. This will eliminate the need to send telexes back to your home country to confirm that you really exist.

If you lose your passport, you should certainly have some ID card with your photo. Many embassies require this before issuing a new passport. Some embassies will accept a driver's licence but others will not – again, an old expired passport will often save the day.

If you're travelling with your spouse, a photocopy of your marriage licence might come in handy should you become involved with the law, hospitals or other bureaucratic authorities.

Useful, though not required, is an International Health Certificate to record your vaccinations.

If you're thinking about working or studying in China or anywhere else along the way, photocopies of college diplomas, transcripts and letters of recommendation could prove helpful.

The International Student Identity Card (ISIC) is of no real use in China, but you can sometimes use it to obtain cheap air fares in other parts of Asia. It helps to back up the ISIC with a regular student card and an official-looking letter from your college head. The extra back-up documents are necessary because there's quite a world-wide trade in fake ISIC cards. Additionally, there are maximum age limits (usually 26) for some concessions, and the fake-card dealers have been clamped down on. Nevertheless, fake cards are widely available and usable, but some are quite poor quality.

Chinese Documents

Foreigners who live, work or study in China will be issued with a number of documents, and some of these can be used to obtain substantial discounts for trains, flights, hotels, museums and tourist sites.

Most common and least useful is the so-called 'white card', a simple student ID card with pasted-on photo and usually kept in a red plastic holder (some call it a 'red card' for this reason). Having one of these supposedly allows you to pay for train tickets in RMB – it works about 50% of the time. A white card is easily forged – you could reproduce one with a photocopy machine – and the red plastic holders are on sale everywhere. For this reason, you might be approached by touts wanting to sell you a fake one. The fact is that outside of major cities like Beijing, railway clerks really have no idea what a white card is supposed to look like – fake ones sometimes work when real ones don't! One French student had a knock-down drag-out battle in Zhengzhou station with a smug booking clerk who threw her absolutely genuine white card into the rubbish bin and told her it was a fake.

The so-called 'yellow card' (really orange) is not so much a card as a small booklet. The cover is orange and the pages are white. Except for the cover, the book can be easily forged with a photocopier, but there do not seem to be too many fakes around – yet. The value of the yellow card is that it allows foreigners to pay in RMB rather than FEC. These do seem to work better than white cards.

The 'green card' is a residence permit, issued to English teachers, foreign experts and students who live in the PRC. It's such a valuable document that you'd better not lose it if you have one, or the PSB will be all over you. Foreigners living in China say that if you lose your green card, you might want to leave the country rather than face the music. A green card will permit you to pay Chinese prices in hotels, on flights, trains and elsewhere. In addition, many hotels offer major discounts to green card holders (even five-star hotels!). The green card is not really a card but resembles a small passport – it would be very difficult to forge without modern printing equipment and special paper. Green cards are issued for one year and must be renewed annually.

Travel Permit *(tōngxíngzhèng)*

Most of China is open except for certain remote border areas. You don't need a travel permit for Beijing, but if you're contemplating travel in remote spots, inquire at the PSB to learn the latest regulations.

CUSTOMS

Chinese border crossings have gone from being severely traumatic to exceedingly easy. While there seems to be lots of uniformed police around, the third degree at Customs seems to be reserved for pornography-smuggling Hong Kongers rather than the stray foreign tourist.

There are clearly marked 'green channels' and 'red channels', the latter reserved for those with such everyday travel items as refrigerators and colour TV sets.

You're allowed to import 600 cigarettes or the equivalent in tobacco products, two litres of alcoholic drink and one *pint* of perfume. Importation of fresh fruit is prohibited.

It's illegal to import any printed material, film, tapes, etc which are 'detrimental to China's politics, economy, culture and ethics'. But don't be too concerned about what you take to read. As you leave China, any tapes, manuscripts, books, etc 'which contain state secrets or are otherwise prohibited for export' can be seized. Cultural relics, handicrafts, gold and silver ornaments, and jewellery purchased in China have to be shown to Customs on leaving. You'll also have to show your receipts; otherwise the stuff may be confiscated. Don't get paranoid – foreigners are seldom searched.

MONEY

The basic unit of Chinese currency is the *yuan* – designated in this book by a capital 'Y'. In spoken Chinese, the word *kuai* or *kuaiqian* is often substituted for *yuan*. Ten *jiao* make up one *yuan* – in spoken Chinese, it's pronounced *mao*. Ten *fen* make up one *jiao*, but these days *fen* are becoming rare because they are worth so little.

Absurdly, there are two types of currency in use in China: Renminbi and Foreign Exchange Certificates.

Currency

Renminbi (RMB) Renminbi or 'People's Money' is issued by the Bank of China. Paper notes are issued in denominations of one, two, five, 10, 50 and 100 *yuan*; one, two and five *jiao*; and one, two and five *fen*. Coins are in denominations of one *yuan*; five *jiao*; and one, two and five *fen*. The one-*fen* note is small and yellow, the two-*fen* note is blue, and the five-*fen* note is small and green – all are next to worthless.

Foreign Exchange Certificates (FEC) How many countries can you name that have two currencies? The three letters most hated by foreigners and loved by Chinese are FEC. Foreign Exchange Certificates, or 'tourist money', are issued in China for use by foreigners and for compatriots from Hong Kong, Macau and Taiwan.

FEC create numerous hassles. FEC and RMB are supposed to be worth the same, but in fact they are not. FEC are worth more, but when you pay in FEC you will often receive change in RMB. When you ask for change in FEC, the people you're dealing with will often say that they don't have it. You cannot exchange RMB (legally) when you leave China. If you want to pay for everything in RMB (most foreigners try), you will face constant arguments. The wearisome battles over FEC and the constant solicitations from the 'change money' people can detract from your enjoyment of travelling in China. Some conspiracy theorists speculate that the government invented FEC just to prevent foreigners from becoming friendly with Chinese people.

FEC come in seven denominations: 100 *yuan*, 50 *yuan*, 10 *yuan*, five *yuan*, one *yuan*, five *jiao* and one *jiao*. There are no coins. It's good to keep lots of small bills in FEC to avoid the situation where you must accept change in RMB.

You're meant to use FEC for all hotels, train and air transport, as well as international telephone calls or faxes. The government does not require that you pay for buses, taxis, postage stamps or food in FEC. In practice, the rules get bent both ways – some hotels and railway stations accept RMB from foreigners, while taxi drivers, restaurants and even some street vendors have got into the habit of demanding payment in FEC. There is no legitimate reason why you must pay in FEC for goods which are made in the PRC, but expect continuous vehement arguments if you stand up for your rights. Some people seem to think it's illegal for foreigners to have RMB – it's not.

Some foreign visitors have managed to pay for their whole stay in Beijing using only RMB, but this requires stamina and an official Chinese student ID card (genuine or otherwise). You'll probably need a mixture of both RMB and FEC.

Some shops and hotels operate a 'price differential'. You may be asked if you want to pay a given price in FEC or pay about 50% more in RMB. Most hotels simply will *not* accept payment in RMB no matter how hard you plead, cry or rant. The Beijing railway station has a separate booking offices for foreigners which insists on payment in FEC, and air tickets can only be bought in FEC, unless you have the magic green card.

On the other hand, in smaller towns and in the countryside where few foreigners go you'll probably find that the locals have never seen FEC, and you'll have to pay in RMB.

The FEC versus RMB battles can occupy much of your time and energy. In many youth hostels, travellers have a tendency to sit around all day and talk about FEC and changing money.

It is likely that FEC will be done away – it antagonises China's trading partners who have erected trade barriers in retaliation. The Chinese government says that FEC will be eliminated but refuses to say when. But even if FEC get the axe, other rules might be arbitrarily imposed – like forcing foreigners to pay with US$, or pay triple-price in RMB, and so on.

Exchange Rates

Australia	A$1	=	Y3.86
Britain	UK£1	=	Y8.72
Canada	C$1	=	Y4.49
France	Ffr1	=	Y1.03
Germany	DM1	=	Y3.45
Hong Kong	HK$1	=	Y0.75
Japan	Y100	=	Y4.00
Netherlands	g1	=	Y3.05
New Zealand	NZ$1	=	Y2.71
Switzerland	Sfr1	=	Y3.91
USA	US$1	=	Y5.75

Changing Money

Foreign currency and travellers' cheques can be changed at border crossings, main branches of the Bank of China, CITIC, tourist hotels, the Friendship Store and some other big department stores. You'll be issued with FEC and small change will be made up of RMB one, two and five-*fen* notes and coins. Hotels usually give the official rate, but some will add a small commission. A bigger problem is that a few upmarket hotels only change money for their own guests – you can try lying and making up a false room number, but they sometimes check the registration records.

Hong Kong dollars, Japanese Yen and most West European currencies can be exchanged at major banks, but US dollars are still the easiest to change.

Whenever you (legally) change foreign currency into Chinese currency you'll be given a money-exchange voucher recording the transaction. If you've got any leftover FEC when you leave the country and want to reconvert them to hard currency you *must* have those vouchers – not all of them, but at least equal to *double* the amount of FEC you want to re-exchange. In other words, only 50% of what you originally exchanged can be re-exchanged on departure – the government is saying that you must spend the rest while in China.

FEC can be taken in and out of the country as you please.

Black Market

Having two currencies and unrealistic official exchange rates has caused the black market to boom. The black market is interested in FEC, Hong Kong and US dollars.

The rate fluctuates wildly, but at the time of this writing you could easily gain 50% by purchasing RMB on the black market. Unfortunately, the reports of cheating and outright theft have become so common that it cannot be recommended that you change on the street. Indeed, it would be fair to say that 90% of all street exchanges result in attempted rip-offs.

You might think that you're good at changing money on the street, but we assure you that the rip-off artists are also very good at what they do. There are different techniques. If you are so foolish as to hand over your money first, you're finished – you will be short-changed and nothing short of outright violence will get your money back. But even if you demand that they hand over their cash first, you can still get cheated. In this case, they may claim that *you short-changed them* and demand their money back, and create a very ugly scene (often with the help of accomplices) if you refuse. So you give them back theirs and they give you back yours, but in the process they've removed some large denomination bills and replaced them with small ones (they are skilled magicians!). A crude but effective technique is simply to grab the cash out of your hands and run off.

It seems to be the experience of most travellers that female moneychangers are less likely to use threats, intimidation, violence or grab the cash out of your hands. However, female moneychangers have been known to often short-change customers. The very worst thing to do is change with a group of young men on the street – if there's just one of you versus three young men, you might as well hang a sign around your neck saying 'Rob me'.

Many people have found it fairly easy to change money in small shops, especially in areas where travellers congregate. Indeed, in some of the budget hotels, you can often simply change with the people at the reception desk or the money-exchange counter! The rate in the hotel might not be as good as the moneychangers offer, but it beats getting robbed. If you need RMB, you can always get it from banks, but they'll only exchange it on a one for one basis (a rotten deal for you, but a great deal for them).

Another possibility is to buy RMB at black-market rates in Hong Kong. Some moneychangers in Tsimshatsui deal in RMB, though the biggest market seems to be concentrated in Sheung Wan near the Macau Ferry Pier. The 'black market' is perfectly legal in Hong Kong – the illegal part is carrying the money across the border. It is strictly prohibited to take RMB into or out of China, and big signs at the border crossings warn you about this. We aren't going to advise you to break the law, but we know damn well that most travellers do it. However, if you do decide to carry RMB across the Chinese border, keep it well hidden even though you aren't likely to be strip-searched.

As for bringing things to Beijing to sell, you'll probably find that the Chinese strike too much of a hard bargain to make it worth the trouble.

Travellers' Cheques

Besides the advantage of safety, travellers' cheques are useful to carry in China because the exchange rate is actually more favourable than the rate you get for cash. Cheques from most of the world's leading banks and issuing agencies are acceptable in Beijing – stick to the major companies such as Thomas Cook, American Express and Bank of America, and you'll be OK.

The American Express office in Beijing, due to government regulations, cannot provide the Emergency Cheque Cashing service, but it is provided by four Chinese banks. For inquiries, contact American Express in Beijing at W115D China World Tower, China World Trade Centre, Jianguomenwai Dajie.

Credit Cards

Plastic is gaining more acceptance in Beijing. Useful cards include Visa, MasterCard, American Express, JCB and Diners Club. It's even possible to get a cash advance against your card.

Telegraphic Transfers

Getting money sent to you while you're in Beijing can be a real drag – try to avoid it. On the average, it takes about five weeks for your money to arrive. If you have high-placed connections in the banking system it can take considerably less time, but most travellers are not so fortunate. If you must have money sent to you, try to get it sent to CITIC – the Bank of China appears to be hopeless. At CITIC it is even possible to send money out of China, but only if you have hard currency.

Bank Accounts

Foreigners can indeed open bank accounts in China, both RMB and US dollar accounts (the latter only at special foreign-exchange banks). You do not need to have resident status – a tourist visa is sufficient. Virtually every foreigner working in Beijing will tell you that CITIC is far better to do business with than the Bank of China. Automatic-teller machines have been introduced at the Bank of China, but payment is only in RMB.

Costs

Costs in Beijing are rising, and no matter what you do, it's not going to be as cheap as Jakarta or Bombay. How much it actually costs you largely depends on the degree of comfort you desire. Hotels are going to be the biggest expense, but food and transport can add up quickly too. Excluding the cost of getting to Beijing, you can survive on US$10 per day. This means you must stay in dormitories, travel by bus or bicycle rather than taxi, eat from street stalls or small cafés, and refrain from buying anything.

Travelling, however, is something to be enjoyed. Staying in some dump and slugging it out on Beijing's hopelessly overcrowded buses can make your trip not worth the trouble. You'll have to make these judgments yourself, but bear in mind that your journey can be a miserable experience if you're constantly worried about how far the money is going to stretch and if you force yourself to live in perpetual discomfort.

On the opposite end of the spectrum, rooms at five-star hotels can be over US$100 per day and meals at posh restaurants can be US$50. And there are an increasing number of classy department stores charging Western prices. If you're looking for ways to blow a lot of money, Beijing can accommodate you.

Price Hikes

Foreigners will inevitably be charged more for most things in Beijing. This situation certainly exists in many other developing countries, but the big difference is that in China, it's official policy. All businesses from the airlines and railways to museums and parks are told *by the government* to charge foreigners more. With such official support, many Chinese view ripping off foreigners as their patriotic duty. Sometimes the charge is just a little bit more than a local would pay, but at other times it's 20 times more than the Chinese price.

The blatant overcharging has caused more than a few foreigners to get disgusted and hop on the first flight out of the country. But sometimes, the opposite happens – some total stranger in a restaurant pays for your meal; a passenger you met on the bus offers you a free place for the night and lets you borrow the family bicycle; a young student works as your personal tour guide for the entire day and wants nothing in return but a chance to practise English. Such moments are especially touching in China, because most Chinese are still poor and can hardly afford to be so generous.

These individual acts of kindness help to restore your faith in humanity – it's a pity that not everyone is like that. Try not to go around Beijing feeling constantly ripped off, but on the other hand, keep your guard up when necessary. To avoid problems, always ask the price first before you get the goods or services rendered. If you can't speak Chinese, write it down.

Tipping

As some compensation for being frequently over-charged, China is at least one of those wonderful countries where tipping is not done and almost no one asks for it. When tips are offered in China, they are offered *before* you get the service, not after – that will ensure (hopefully) that you get better service. All things considered, tipping isn't a good idea because it will make it rough for foreigners who follow you.

Bargaining

In large stores where prices are clearly marked, there is usually no latitude for bargaining. In small shops, bargaining is sometimes possible, especially when buying touristy souvenir stuff. At street stalls, bargaining is expected. In all cases, there is one important rule to follow – be polite. There is nothing wrong with asking for a discount, if you do so with a smile. The worst they can say is 'no'. Some foreigners seem to think that bargaining should be a screaming and threatening contest. This is not only unpleasant for all concerned, it seldom results in you getting a lower price – indeed, in 'face-conscious' China, intimidation is likely to make the vendor more recalcitrant and you'll be overcharged.

You should keep in mind that entrepreneurs are in business to make money; they aren't going to sell anything to you at a loss. Your goal should be to pay the Chinese price, as opposed to the foreigners' price – if you can do that, you've done well.

Consumer Taxes

Although big hotels and fancy restaurants may add a tax or 'service charge' of 10% or more, all other consumer taxes are included in the price tag.

WHEN TO GO

China's peak season for tourism is summer – if you can tolerate the cold of winter, you can avoid the crowds. However, you need to pay careful attention to major public holidays – the Chinese New Year in particular is a horrible time to travel.

WHAT TO BRING

As little as possible. It's much better to buy things as you need them than to throw things away because you've got too much to carry.

That advice having been given, there are some things you will want to bring from home. But the first thing to consider is what kind of bag you will use to carry all your goods.

Backpacks are the easiest type of bag to carry if you need to do much walking – a frameless or internal-frame pack is the easiest to manage on buses and trains. The 'expandable' type are most convenient – a clever arrangement of straps causes these packs to shrink or expand according to how much is inside. Packs that close with a zip can be secured with a padlock. Any pack can be slit open with a razor blade, but a lock will usually prevent pilfering by hotel staff and baggage handlers at airports.

If you don't want to use a backpack, a shoulder bag is much easier to carry than a suitcase. Some cleverly designed shoulder bags can also double as backpacks by re-arranging a few straps. Forget suitcases.

Chinese-made luggage looks good but is generally rotten quality. Zips are the biggest problem – some don't last a day! The stitching also has a tendency to disintegrate. The only good thing about Chinese backpacks is that they're cheap and won't attract as much attention as Western models.

Whatever you bring, make it small and light. A daypack or small shoulder bag is useful. A beltpack is OK for maps, extra film and other miscellanea, but don't use it for valuables such as your travellers' cheques and passport – it's an easy target for pickpockets.

Inside? Lightweight and compact are two words that should be etched in your mind when you're deciding what to bring. Drill holes in the handle of your toothbrush if you have to – anything to keep the weight down! In theory, you only need two sets of clothes, one to wear and one to wash. Dark-coloured clothing is preferable because it doesn't show the dirt; white clothes will force you to do laundry daily. You will, no doubt, be buying clothes in Beijing where prices are ridiculously low. However, don't believe sizes – 'large' in China is often equivalent to 'medium' in the West.

If you're travelling to Beijing at the height of winter, prepare yourself for severe cold. You can buy excellent down or quilt jackets in Beijing's department stores; the khaki-green PLA models make a functional souvenir. You might want to bring a stocking (ski) cap with you. They can be bought in Beijing but are hard to find and often too small or poorly-made. By contrast, good sweaters are a bargain in China. You might want to bring fur-lined boots and mittens. Mediocre ones can be bought in China but large (Western) sizes are difficult to find. Western long johns are more comfortable and warmer than the Chinese variety. Chinese raingear is functional but poor quality, except for the rain boots which are excellent.

The usual standards of Asian decorum apply. While shorts are less acceptable for women, plenty of Chinese women wear them and you shouldn't get any unpleasant reactions. In Beijing, miniskirts are in vogue and many young women wear skin-hugging tights. However, bikinis have still not made their debut in China, so if you're heading for the beach or the pool, bring conservative swimwear.

The Chinese place little importance on what foreigners wear, as long as they remain within an acceptable level of modesty; casual clothes are always acceptable.

Absolutely essential is a good pair of sunglasses – Beijing's sunshine is often brilliant, especially during winter. A bottle of sunscreen (UV lotion) can prove useful.

The following is a checklist of things you might consider packing. You can delete whatever you like from this list.

Passport, visa, documents (International Health Certificate, college certificates, marriage licence photocopy, student ID card), money, money belt or vest, air ticket, address book, reading matter, pen, notepad, gluestick, namecards, visa photos (about 20), Swiss army knife, camera & accessories, extra camera battery, colour slide film, video camera & blank tapes, radio, personal stereo & rechargeable batteries, small battery recharger (220 volt), electrical conversion plug, padlock, cable lock (to secure luggage on trains), earplugs, sunglasses, contact lens solution, alarm clock, leakproof water bottle, torch (flashlight) with batteries & bulbs, comb, compass, daypack, long pants, short pants, long shirt, T-shirt, nylon jacket, sweater (only in winter), raincover for backpack, umbrella or rain poncho, razor, razor blades, shaving cream, sewing kit, spoon, sunhat, sunscreen (UV lotion), toilet paper, tampons, toothbrush, toothpaste, dental floss, deodorant, shampoo, laundry detergent, underwear, socks, thongs (flip-flops), nail clipper, tweezers, mosquito repellent, vitamins, laxative, contraceptives including condoms, special medications you use and a medical kit.

TOURIST OFFICES

Local Tourist Offices

There are basically three local tourist offices in Beijing, as follows:

China International Travel Service (CITS)

CITS deals with China's foreign tourist hordes, and mainly concerns itself with organising and making travel arrangements for group tours. CITS existed as far back as 1954, yet the organisation still does not have its act together.

CITS can buy train and plane tickets for you (and some boat tickets), reserve hotel rooms, organise city tours, and even get you tickets for the cinema, opera, acrobatics and other entertainment, as well as organise trips to communes and farms, and provide vehicles (taxis, minibuses) for sightseeing or transport. Solo travellers will rarely have to deal with them.

Service varies. Some CITS people are friendly and full of useful information! There are others who are downright rude and only interested in squeezing money out of foreigners. Beijing CITS stands out as a glaring example of the latter.

The main travel office is at the Beijing Tourist Building (☎ 515 8570; fax 515 8603), 28 Jianguomenwai Dajie, buried behind the New Otani Hotel near the Friendship Store (see Map No 10 at the back of this book). The other important branch office is in the Beijing International Hotel (☎ 512 0509; fax 512 0503), north of the railway station at 9 Jianguomennei Dajie (also shown on Map No

10, of Central Beijing). There are many other smaller branch offices in some of the large hotels – these plug Great Wall tours and do not offer the full range of CITS services.

China Travel Service (CTS)

CTS was originally set up to handle tourists from Hong Kong, Macau and Taiwan, and foreign nationals of Chinese descent (Overseas Chinese).

These days it makes little difference – CTS has now become a keen competitor with CITS and will gladly book tours for Westerners. Service varies from excellent to unrestrained avarice. The main Beijing office of CTS (☎ 512 9933; fax 512 9008) is at 8 Dongjiaomin Xiang, Dongcheng District.

China Youth Travel Service (CYTS)

The name of this service implies that this is some sort of student organisation, but these days CYTS performs essentially the same services as CITS and CTS. Being a smaller organisation, CYTS seems to try harder to compete against the big league. This could result in better service, but not necessarily lower prices. The Beijing office (☎ 512 7770) is at 23B Dongjiaomin Xiang, Dongcheng District.

Overseas Reps

CITS The main office of CITS in Hong Kong (Tsimshatsui East) can book air tickets to China and has a good collection of English-language pamphlets. The main office and central branch office are open Monday to Friday from 9 am to 5 pm and from 9 am to 1 pm on Saturday; the Mongkok branch office keeps longer hours (9 am to 6.30 pm on Saturday and a half-day on Sunday).

Outside of China and Hong Kong, CITS is usually known as the China National Tourist Office.

Australia
> China National Tourist Office, 11th Floor, 55 Clarence St, Sydney NSW 2000 (☎ (02) 299 4057; fax 290 1958)

France
> China National Tourist Office, 51 Rue Saint-Anne, 75002, Paris (☎ 429 69548; fax 426 15468)

Germany
> China National Tourist Office, Eschenheimer Anlage 28, D-6000 Frankfurt am Main-1 (☎ (069) 55 5292; fax 597 3412)

Top: Young boy (CT)
Bottom: Temple courtyard scene (JO)

Hong Kong
　　Main Office, 6th Floor, Tower Two, South Seas Centre, 75 Mody Rd, Tsimshatsui East, Kowloon (☎ 732 5888; fax 721 7154)
　　Central Branch, Room 1018, Swire House, 11 Chater Rd, Central (☎ 810 4282; fax 868 1657)
　　Mongkok Branch, Room 1102-1104, Bank Centre, 636 Nathan Rd, Mongkok, Kowloon (☎ 388 1619; fax 385 6157)
　　Causeway Bay Branch, Room 1104, Causeway Bay Plaza, 489 Hennessy Rd, Causeway Bay (☎ 836 3485; fax 591 0849)
Japan
　　China National Tourist Office, 6F Hachidal Hamamatsu-cho Building, 1-27-13 Hamamatsu-cho Minato-ku, Tokyo (☎ (03) 343 31461; fax 343 38653)
UK
　　China National Tourist Office, 4 Glentworth St, London NW1 (☎ (071) 935 9427; fax 487 5842)
USA
　　China National Tourist Office, Los Angeles Branch, 333 West Broadway, Suite 201, Glendale CA 91204 (☎ (818) 545 7505; fax 545 7506)
　　New York Branch, Lincoln Building, 60E, 42nd St, Suite 3126, New York, NY 10165 (☎ (212) 867 0271; fax 599 2892)

CTS Many foreigners make use of the CTS offices in Hong Kong and Macau to obtain visas and book trains, planes, boats and other transport to China. CTS can sometimes get you a better deal on hotels booked through their office than you could obtain on your own (of course, this doesn't apply to backpackers' dormitories). CTS has 19 branch offices in Hong Kong, and the Kowloon, Mongkok and Wanchai offices are open on Sundays and public holidays. These offices can be crowded – avoid this by arriving at 9 am when the doors open. CTS representatives include the following:

Australia
　　Ground Floor, 757-759 George St, Sydney, NSW 2000 (☎ (02) 211 2633; fax 281 3595)
Canada
　　556 West Broadway, Vancouver, BC V5Z 1E9 (☎ (604) 872 8787; fax 873 2823)
France
　　10 Rue de Rome, 75008, Paris (☎ (1) 452 29272; fax 452 29279)
Germany
　　Düsseldorfer Strasse 14 6000, Frankfurt/M 1 (☎ (69) 25 0515; fax 23 2324)
Hong Kong
　　Central Branch, 2nd Floor, China Travel Building, 77 Queen's Road, Central (☎ 521 7163; fax 525 5525)

Kowloon Branch, 1st Floor, Alpha House, 27-33 Nathan Rd, Tsimshatsui (☎ 721 4481; fax 721 6251)
Mongkok Branch, 62-72 Sai Yee St, Mongkok (☎ 789 5970; fax 390 5001)
Wanchai Branch, Ground Floor, Southern Centre, 138 Hennessy Rd, Wanchai (☎ 832 3888)
China Hong Kong City Branch, 10-12 China Hong Kong City, 33 Canton Rd, Tsimshatsui (☎ 736 1863)

Indonesia
PT Cempaka Travelindo, Jalan Hayam Wuruk 97, Jakarta-Barat (☎ (21) 629 4256; fax 629 4836)

Japan
Nihombashi-Settsu Building, 2-2-4, Nihombashi, Chuo-Ku, Tokyo (☎ (03) 3273 5512; fax 3273 2667)

Macau
Xinhua Building, Rua de Nagasaki (☎ 70 0888; fax 70 6611)

Malaysia
Yuyi Travel Sdn Bhd, 1st Floor, Sun Complex, Jalan Bukit Bintang 55100, Kuala Lumpur (☎ (03) 242 7077; fax 241 2478)

Philippines
489 San Fernando St, Binondo, Manila (☎ 47-41-87; fax 40-78-34)

Singapore
Ground Floor, SIA Building, 77 Robinson Rd, Singapore, 0106 (☎ 224 0550; fax 224 5009)

Thailand
559 Yaowaraj Rd, Bangkok 10500 (☎ (2) 226 0041; fax 226 4712)

UK
24 Cambridge Circus, London WC2H 8HD (☎ (071) 836 9911; fax 836 3121)

USA
2nd Floor, 212 Sutter St, San Francisco, CA 94108 (☎ (800) 332 2831, (415) 398 6627; fax 398 6669)
Los Angeles Branch, Suite 138, 223 East Garvey Ave, Monterey Park, CA 91754 (☎ (818) 288 8222; fax 288 3464)

USEFUL ORGANISATIONS

Public Security Bureau (PSB)

The Public Security Bureau (*gōng'ān jú*) is the name given to China's police, both uniformed and plain-clothed. Its responsibilities include suppression of political dissidence, crime detection, preventing foreigners and Chinese from having sex with each other (no joke), mediating family quarrels and directing traffic. A related force is the Chinese People's Armed Police Force (CPAPF), which was formed several years ago to absorb cuts in the PLA. The Foreign Affairs Branch (*wài shì kē*) of the PSB deals with foreigners. This branch is responsible for issuing visa extensions.

The PSB is responsible for introducing and enforcing regulations concerning foreigners. So, for example, they bear responsibility for exclusion of foreigners from certain hotels. If this means you get stuck for a place to stay, they can offer advice. Don't pester them with trivia or try to 'use' them to bully a point with a local street vendor. Do turn to them for mediation in serious disputes with hotels, restaurants, taxi drivers, etc. This often works since the PSB wields God-like power – especially in remote areas.

The Foreign Affairs Branch office of the Beijing PSB (☎ 512 2471) is at 85 Beichizi Dajie, the street running north-south at the east side of the Forbidden City – see Map No 12 of the Wangfujing Area, given at the back of the book. It's open from 8.30 to 11.30 am and 1 to 5 pm Monday to Friday; from 8.30 to 11.30 am Saturday;

Security officers (RS)

closed on Sunday. Visa extensions cost Y25 for most nationalities, but others pay Y50 while some get it free.

BUSINESS HOURS & HOLIDAYS

Banks, offices, government departments and PSB offices are open from Monday to Saturday. As a rough guide only, they open at around 8 to 9 am, close for two hours in the middle of the day, then re-open until 5 or 6 pm. Sunday is a public holiday.

Many museums, parks, zoos and monuments have similar opening hours, and are also open on Sunday but close on Monday to compensate.

Out in the free market, business hours are long – you can grab breakfast at 7 am or dinner at 8 pm with no problem. Around the railway station, you can find people peddling food nearly 24 hours a day, seven days a week.

The PRC has nine national holidays during the year:

New Year's Day
: 1 January

Spring Festival
: Usually in February. This is otherwise known as Chinese New Year and starts on the first day of the first moon according to the traditional lunar calendar. Although officially lasting only three days, many people take a week off work. Be warned: this is China's biggest holiday and unless you have booked a month or two in advance, this is definitely *not* the time to visit. Although the demand for accommodation skyrockets, many hotels close down at this time and all transport is chock-a-block. If you must stay anywhere in China at this time, book your room in advance and sit tight until the chaos is over!

International Working Women's Day
: 8 March

International Labour Day
: 1 May

Youth Day
: 4 May – commemorates the student demonstrations in Beijing on 4 May 1919, when the Versailles Conference decided to give Germany's 'rights' in the city of Tianjin to Japan

Children's Day
: 1 June

Anniversary of the Founding of the Communist Party of China
: 1 July

Anniversary of the Founding of the PLA
: 1 August

National Day
: 1 October – celebrates the founding of the PRC on 1 October 1949

FESTIVALS & EVENTS

Beijing is probably at its prettiest on May Day (1 May), a 'religious holiday' for Communists officially known as International Labour Day. During this time, the whole city (especially Tiananmen Square) is decorated with flowers.

Beijing also rolls out its marching bands and militaristic displays on National Day (1 October).

Special prayers are held at Buddhist and Taoist temples on days when the moon is either full or just the thinnest sliver. According to the Chinese lunar calendar, these days fall on the 14th and 15th days of the lunar month and on the last (29th or 30th) day of the month just ending and the first day of the new month.

The Lantern Festival (*yuánxiāo jié*) is not a public holiday, but it's a relatively colourful time to visit Beijing. It falls on the 15th day of the 1st moon according to the lunar calendar. People take the time to make (or buy) paper lanterns and walk around the streets in the evening holding them.

Guanyin is the goddess of mercy. Her birthday falls on the 19th day of the 2nd moon and is a good time to visit Taoist temples.

Tomb Sweep Day (*qīng míng jié*) is a day for worshipping ancestors; people visit the graves of their departed relatives and clean the site. They often place flowers on the tomb and burn ghost money for the departed. It falls on 5 April in the Gregorian calendar in most years, and on 4 April in leap years.

The Mid-Autumn Festival (*zhōngqiū jié*) is also known as the Moon Festival. This takes place on the 15th day of the 8th moon. Gazing at the moon and lighting fireworks are popular activities, and this is also the time to eat tasty moon cakes.

POST & TELECOMMUNICATIONS

Postal Rates

Letters Rates for international surface mail are shown in the table. Add Y0.50 for air mail.

Postcards International postcards cost Y1.10 by surface mail and Y1.60 by air mail to anywhere in the world.

Aerogrammes These are Y1.90 to anywhere in the world.

Printed Matter Rates for international surface mail
are shown in the table. Each additional kg above 2000
grams costs Y11. For air mail add Y0.40 to these figures.

Small Packets Rates for international surface mail are
given in the table. For air mail add Y0.40 to these figures.

Parcels Rates vary depending on the country of destination. The charge for a one-kg parcel sent surface mail
from China to the UK is Y52, to the USA Y30.60, and to
Germany Y35.60. The charge for a one-kg parcel sent air
mail to the UK is Y82, to the USA Y77, and to Germany
Y70.60.

Post offices are very picky about how you pack things;
don't finalise your packing until the thing has got its last
Customs clearance. Most countries impose a maximum
weight limitation (10 kg is typical) on packages received.
This rate varies from country to country but the Chinese
post office should be able to tell you what the limitation
is. If you have a receipt for the goods, then put it in the
box when you're mailing it, since it may be opened again
by Customs further down the line.

Postal Rates

Letters

Weight	Rate
0-20 grams	Y1.50
20-50 grams	Y2.90
50-100 grams	Y4.50
100-250 grams	Y8.80
250-500 grams	Y17.90
500-1000 grams	Y34.90
1000-2000 grams	Y49.40

Printed Matter

Weight	Rate
0-20 grams	Y1
20-50 grams	Y1.50
50-100 grams	Y2.80
100-250 grams	Y5.30
250-500 grams	Y9.90
500-1000 grams	Y15.80
1000-2000 grams	Y26.10

Small Packets

Weight	Rate
0-100 grams	Y3.50
100-250 grams	Y7
250-500 grams	Y12.60
500-1000 grams	Y20.90
1000-2000 grams	Y39

EMS International express mail service charges vary according to country, and whether you are sending documents for parcels. For documents, EMS to Hong Kong and Macau costs Y50; to Japan, Korea and South-East Asia, Y70; South Asia, Y80; Europe, Canada and the USA, Y95; Middle East and Africa, Y105; and to South America, Y115. EMS is not available to every country.

Registration Fees The registration fee for letters, printed matter and packets is Y1. Acknowledgement of receipt is Y0.80 per article.

Domestic Mail Within the same city, mail delivery for a letter (20 grams and below) costs Y0.10, postcards also Y0.10. Out of town, letters are Y0.20, postcards Y0.15. The fee for registration is Y0.30.

Sending Mail

The international postal service seems efficient, and air-mailed letters and postcards will probably take around five to 10 days to reach their destinations. If possible, write the country of destination in Chinese, as this should speed up the delivery. Domestic post is amazingly fast, perhaps one or two days from Beijing to Shanghai. Within Beijing it may be delivered the same day that it's sent.

You can post letters at the reception desks of all major hotels. Even at cheap hotels you can do this – reliability varies but in general it's OK. There is a small but convenient post office in the CITIC building. Another useful post office is in the basement of the China World Trade Centre.

Overseas parcels must be posted from the International Post & Telecommunications Building on Jianguomen Beidajie, not far from the Friendship Store. A counter inside sells wrapping paper, string, tape and glue.

Private Carriers United Parcel Service (☎ 499 4100, 467 2278), otherwise known as UPS, has several service centres for posting express documents and parcels abroad. Most convenient is their office on the ground floor of the Scite Tower on Jianguomenwai (opposite CITIC building). Express service is also offered by DHL (☎ 466 2211), Federal Express (☎ 501 1017), TNT Skypak (☎ 465 2227). None of these private carriers are cheap, but they're fast and secure.

Receiving Mail

All letters and parcels marked 'Poste Restante, Beijing Main Post Office' will wind up at the International Post & Telecommunications Building on Jianguomen Beidajie, not far from the Friendship Store. Hours are from 8 am to 7 pm. The staff even file poste restante letters in alphabetical order, a rare occurrence in China, but you pay for all this efficiency – there is a Y1 fee charged for each letter received!

Some major tourist hotels will hold mail for their guests, but this doesn't always work.

Officially, the PRC forbids several items from being mailed to it – the regulations specifically prohibit 'reactionary books, magazines and propaganda materials, obscene or immoral articles'. You also cannot mail Chinese currency abroad, or receive it by post. Like elsewhere, mail-order hashish and other recreational chemicals will not amuse the authorities.

Telephone

China's creaky phone system is being overhauled. Whereas just a few years ago calling from Beijing to Shanghai could be an all-day project, now you can just pick up a phone and dial direct. International calls have also become much easier.

Many hotel rooms are equipped with phones from which local calls are free. Local calls can be made from public pay phones (there are some around but not many). Beijing's budding entrepreneurs try to fill the gap – people with private phones run a long cord out the window and stand on street corners, allowing you to use their phone to place local calls for around Y0.50 each. Long-distance domestic and international calls are not always possible on these phones, but ask. A few restaurants and hotels use the same system – free calls for guests, Y0.50 for non-guests, and long-distance calls are charged by the minute.

You can place both domestic and international long-distance phone calls from main telecommunications offices. The advantage of doing so is that you can pay in RMB rather than FEC, a substantial savings if you're using black-market cash. On the other hand, these offices are a nuisance – you have to fill out forms in Chinese, pay for the call in advance, wait for perhaps 30 minutes and finally someone gestures to you indicating that you've been connected so you should pick up the phone and start talking.

Domestic long-distance rates in China vary according

to distance, but are cheap. By contrast, international calls are expensive. Rates for station-to-station calls to most countries in the world are Y18 per minute. Hong Kong is slightly cheaper at Y12 per minute. There is a minimum charge of three minutes. Reverse-charge calls are often cheaper than calls paid for in China. Time the call yourself, because the operator will not break in to tell you that your minimum period of three minutes is approaching. After you hang up, the operator will ring back to tell you how much it cost. There is no call cancellation fee.

If you are expecting a call – either international or domestic – try to advise the caller beforehand of your hotel room number. The operators frequently have difficulty understanding Western names, and the hotel receptionist may not be able to locate you. If this can't be done, then try to inform the operator that you are expecting the call and write down your name and room number – this increases your chances of success.

Direct Dialling

Domestic direct dialling (DDD) and international direct dialling (IDD) calls are cheapest if you can find a phone which accepts magnetic cards. These phones are usually available in the lobbies of major hotels, and the hotel's front desk should also sell the phone cards. These cards come in two denominations, Y20 and Y100; for an international call, you'll need the latter.

If card phones aren't available, you can usually dial direct from the phones in the business centres found in most luxury hotels. You do not have to be a guest at these hotels, but equip yourself with a sufficient supply of FEC before dialling, since RMB is almost never accepted for international calls.

If your hotel lacks card phones or a business centre, you should be able to dial direct from your hotel room. You'll have to ask the staff at your hotel what's the dial-out code for a direct line (usually a '7' on most switchboards, or sometimes a combination like '78'). Once you have the outside line, dial 00 (the international access code – the same throughout China) followed by the country code, area code and the number you want to reach. If the area code begins with zero (like '03' for Melbourne, Australia) omit the first zero.

There are a few things to be careful about. The equipment used on most hotel switchboards is not very sophisticated. It's often a simple timer and it begins charging you starting from 30 seconds after you dial '7' (or '78' or whatever). The timer does not know if your call succeeds or not so you get charged if you stay on the line over 30 seconds, even if you just let the phone ring repeatedly or get a busy signal! On the other hand, if you complete your conversation within 30 seconds and hang up, you don't get charged at all. The hotel switchboard timer keeps running until you hang up, not when the other party hangs up, so replace the receiver as soon as the conversation ends.

The usual procedure is that you make the call and someone comes to your room five or 10 minutes later to collect the cash. If the hotel does not have IDD, you can usually book calls from your room through the switchboard and the operator calls you back, but this procedure will be more expensive.

With domestic direct dialling, it's useful to know the area codes of China's cities. These all begin with zero, but if you're dialling into China from abroad, omit the first zero from each code. China's country code is 86. The codes for provincial capitals and major cities are as follows, listed in alphabetical order:

Anhui		Heilongjiang	
Hefei	(0551)	Harbin	(0451)
Beijing	(01)	Mudanjiang	(0453)
Fujian		Henan	
Fuzhou	(0591)	Kaifeng	(0378)
Quanzhou	(0595)	Luoyang	(0379)
Xiamen	(0592)	Zhengzhou	(0371)
Gansu		Hubei	
Lanzhou	(0931)	Wuhan	(027)
Guangdong		Yichang	(0717)
Canton	(020)	Hunan	
Foshan	(0757)	Changsha	(0731)
Shantou	(0754)	Yueyang	(0730)
Shenzhen	(0755)	Inner Mongolia	
Zhanjiang	(0759)	Baotou	(0472)
Zhuhai	(0756)	Hohhot	(0471)
Guangxi		Xilinhot	(0479)
Beihai	(0779)	Jiangsu	
Guilin	(0773)	Lianyungang	(0518)
Nanning	(0771)	Nanjing	(025)
Guizhou		Suzhou	(0512)
Guiyang	(0851)	Xuzhou	(0516)
Zunyi	(0852)	Jiangxi	
Hainan		Jiujiang	(0792)
Haikou	(0750)	Lushan	(07010)
Sanya	(0899)	Nanchang	(0791)
Hebei		Jilin	
Chengde	(0314)	Changchun	(0431)
Shijiazhuang	(0311)	Jilin	(0432)
Qinhuangdao	(0335)		

Liaoning		Shanxi	
Dalian	(0411)	Datong	(0352)
Dandong	(0415)	Taiyuan	(0351)
Shenyang	(024)	Sichuan	
Ningxia		Chengdu	(028)
Guyuan	(0954)	Chongqing	(0811)
Yinchuan	(0951)	Leshan	(0833)
Qinghai		Tianjin	(022)
Golmud	(0979)	Tibet	
Xining	(0971)	Lhasa	(0891)
Shaanxi		Xinjiang	
Xi'an	(029)	Ürümqi	(0991)
Yan'an	(0911)	Yunnan	
Shandong		Kunming	(0871)
Ji'nan	(0531)	Simao	(0879)
Qingdao	(0532)	Zhejiang	
Qufu	(05473)	Hangzhou	(0571)
Weihai	(05451)	Ningbo	(0574)
Yantai	(0535)	Wenzhou	(0577)
Shanghai	(021)		

Essential Numbers

The person answering the phone will likely be Chinese-speaking only, so if you're looking to practise your Chinese, this is one way to do it.

local directory assistance	114
long-distance directory assistance	113, 173
HK & Macau directory assistance	115
police hot line	110
fire hot line	119
phone repair	112

Telecommunication for Expats

Short-term visitors needn't bother reading this, but those planning to do business, work or study in the PRC have several telecommunication options not available to tourists.

Getting a private telephone installed in your hotel room or apartment is possible in large cities like Beijing or Shanghai, but there are long waiting lists and costs are high. Foreigners are expected to pay their phone bills in FEC (and therefore get priority over locals) but installation can still take months and costs approximately US$2000. To get your own phone line, a residence permit is required.

Though considered a luxury in the West, pagers are far more common in China than telephones – even street vendors have them! This is due to the fact that the number of telephone lines available is inadequate to

Opera performance (CT)

meet demand, but no such problem exists with pagers. Those with a residence permit can obtain a pager in just a couple of weeks, and the cost is low at around Y25 per month.

Those living on a budget, such as foreign students, may well find pagers a more realistic option than having a phone installed.

Cellular telephones are all the rage with status-conscious urban Chinese with money to burn. Despite initial costs of over US$2000 and monthly fees of around US$200, demand easily outstrips the supply of available channels and year-long waiting lists are common in Beijing. On the other hand, those who already have a cellular line can sell it to others at a profit, because buying a second-hand line allows one to jump the queue. Indeed, applying for a cellular phone line only to resell it later has become a lucrative business.

Computer buffs may be interested in electronic mail (Email). Chinapac (CNPAC) – China's packet-switching network – has a node in Beijing but nowhere else (yet). To get online requires a Y300 initial hook-up fee, plus Y50 per month service charge. Transferring data is billed by 64-byte segments, plus time calculated at Y0.8 per minute. Compared to most countries, these charges are reasonable. Getting hooked up only takes a couple of days, but finding the person at the phone company who knows anything about it can be a major hassle. The place to go is the Network Management Centre of CNPAC (☎ 601 0518), Ministry of Post & Telecommunications, 11 Xi Chang'an Jie, Beijing – good luck trying to explain to the sleepy receptionists just what you want. If it helps, the Chinese name for Email is *diànzi yóujiàn*. It's customary for the telecom personnel to give new customers free telecommunication software – don't accept it unless you want to wind up with a computer virus.

Fax, Telex & Telegraph

Major hotels usually operate a business centre complete with telephone, fax and telex service, not to mention photocopying and perhaps the use of typewriters and word processors. As a rule, you do not have to be a guest at the hotel to use these services, but you certainly must pay. Prices seem to be pretty uniform regardless of how fancy the hotel is, but it's still not a bad idea to ask the rates first.

Hotels demand payment in FEC – you'll save substantially by faxing from a telecom office and paying with black-market RMB. However, not all telecom offices offer a fax service.

International fax and telexes (other than those to Hong Kong or Macau) cost Y23 per minute with a three-minute minimum charge, which is absurdly expensive to send a one-page fax! International telegram rates are usually around Y3.50 per word, and more for the express service. Rates to Hong Kong and Macau are less.

TIME

All of China runs on Beijing's clock, which is set eight hours ahead of Greenwich Mean Time. When it's noon in Beijing the time in cities around the world is:

Frankfurt	5 am
Hong Kong	12 noon
London	4 am
Los Angeles	8 pm
Melbourne	2 pm
Montreal	11 pm
New York	11 pm
Paris	5 am
Rome	5 am
Wellington	4 pm

The government experimented with daylight savings time from 1986 until 1992, when it was suddenly abandoned.

ELECTRICITY

Electricity is 220 volts, 50 cycles AC. Plugs come in at least four designs – three-pronged angled pins (like in Australia), three-pronged round pins (like in Hong Kong), two flat pins (American-style but without the ground wire) or two narrow round pins (European-style). Conversion plugs are easily purchased in Hong Kong but are damn near impossible to find in China. Battery chargers are widely available, but these are generally the bulky style which are not suitable for travelling – buy a small one in Hong Kong or elsewhere.

LAUNDRY

Each floor of just about every hotel in China has a service desk. The attendant's job is to clean the rooms, make the beds, and collect and deliver laundry. Almost all tourist hotels have a laundry service, and if you hand in clothes one day you should get them back a day or two later. If the hotel doesn't have a laundry, the staff can usually direct you to one. Hotel laundry service tends to be expensive and you might wind up doing what many travellers do – hand-washing your own clothes. If you plan on doing this, dark clothes are better since the dirt doesn't show up so clearly.

Laundry service (RS)

BOOKS & MAPS

There is enough literature on China to keep you reading for the next 5000 years of their history, but relatively little dealing with Beijing exclusively.

People & Society

Classics & Fiction If you want to read a weighty Chinese classic, you could try *Journey to the West*, available in English in a four-volume set in Beijing and from some Hong Kong bookstores.

The Dream of the Red Chamber (also known as *The Story of the Stone*) by Cao Xueqin, is a Chinese classic written in the late 18th century. Published in five volumes by Penguin, it's not an easy read. An abridged edition is available in China.

The third great Chinese classic is *Outlaws of the Marsh*. This is also available in abridged form.

The best-known English fiction about China is *The Good Earth* by Pearl S Buck.

Peking (Pan Books) by Anthony Grey is your standard blockbuster by the author of *Saigon*. Not bad.

George Orwell's *1984* was ahead of its time in predicting the political trends in the Communist world. *Animal Farm* is perhaps a closer approximation to post-1949 China and its bloated cadres.

Recent Accounts *The Search for Modern China* by Jonathan D Spence is the definitive work, often used as a textbook in college courses. If you want to understand the PRC, this is the book to read.

An intriguing and popular book is *The New Emperors* by Harrison E Salisbury. The 'emperors' he refers to are Mao Zedong and Deng Xiaoping.

A moving and now popular book is *Wild Swans* by Jung Chang. The author traces the lives of three Chinese women – the author's grandmother (an escaped concubine with bound feet), her mother and herself.

Tiananmen-Inspired If nothing else, the 1989 killings at Tiananmen Square forced foreign journalists to take off the rose-coloured glasses and produce a few hard-hitting books.

Tiananmen, the Rape of Peking (Doubleday) by Michael Fathers and Andrew Higgins is probably the best book on the protests.

Beijing Spring (Asia 2000) by David and Peter Turnley is a good pictorial history of the Tiananmen events.

Tiananmen Diary (Unwin Paperbacks) by Harrison Salisbury and *Tiananmen Square* (Douglas & McIntyre) by Scott Simmie and Bob Nixon outline the same story.

Beijing Jeep (Simon & Schuster) by Jim Mann is about the short unhappy romance of American business in China.

History

The Dragon Wakes (Penguin) by Christopher Hibbert is a good history from 1793 to 1911.

The Chinese People Stand Up (BBC) by Elizabeth Wright examines China's turbulent history from 1949 up to the brutal suppression of pro-democracy demonstrators in 1989.

The Soong Dynasty (Sidgwick and Jackson) by Sterling Seagrave is one of the most popular books on the corrupt Kuomintang period. Unfortunately, the author severely damaged his credibility when he later published *The Marcos Dynasty* which contains more rumour than fact.

Travel Guides

You hold in your hands what is, we hope, the definitive guide to Beijing. However, if you really want to delve into the history and culture of this remarkable city, the Chinese themselves produce some detailed guides in English.

Beijing – Old & New by New World Press (1984) provides infinite details of nearly every pagoda, park, pavilion, brick and stone in China's capital. It's rather dry reading.

Places of Interest in Beijing (China Travel & Tourism Press) is far more readable than the former. The guide includes all the major and minor attractions, but also some unusual 'sights' such as the Changping Highway, China-Japan Friendship Hospital and the Beijing No 3 Cotton Textile Mill. Nevertheless, there's over 300 pages of usable information here.

Bookshops

Beijing's bookstores stock a limited selection of reading material, but it's still much better than anywhere else in China. The best two places to look are the book section of the Friendship Store on Jianguomenwai Dajie, and the Foreign Languages Bookstore on Wangfujing Dajie. These are shown on Map Nos 10 and 12 respectively, which you'll find in the map section at the back of the book. Some hotel giftshops carry a decent assortment of English-language paperbacks.

Hong Kong is an excellent place to stock up on books, so take advantage of the opportunity if you're passing through there. You'll find more reading material about China in Hong Kong than you will in China itself. Recommended bookstores include:

Joint Publishing Company 9 Queen Victoria St, opposite the Central Market (☎ 525 0102) – good books for Chinese-language study

Peace Book Company 35 Kimberley Rd, Tsimshatsui (☎ 896 7832) – official outlet for PRC books & magazines

Swindon Books 13-15 Lock Rd, Tsimshatsui (☎ 366 8033) – large selection

Time Books Granville & Nathan Rds, Tsimshatsui (☎ 721 7138)
– lots of glossy bestsellers
Wanderlust Books 30 Hollywood Rd, Central (☎ 523 2042) –
excellent collection of travel books & knowledgeable,
English-speaking staff

Maps

English-language maps of Beijing are handed out for
free at the big hotels, often part of an advertising supple-
ment for various companies whose locations are, of
course, also shown on the map. These maps usually
have no Chinese characters but are still very useful for
getting around.

It's better to fork out a few RMB for a bilingual map
which shows bus routes. These are available from the
Friendship Store and hotel giftshops.

If you can deal with Chinese character maps, you'll
find a wide variety to choose from. It's impossible for us
to say which one is best because new editions printed by
different companies are issued every couple of months.
Street vendors hawk these maps near the subway stations, entrances to parks and other likely places.

The *Beijing Shiqutu* is a huge wall map in Chinese
characters. It's great for decorating your wall, but isn't
too convenient to carry around on the street.

If you want fine detail in portable form, the best
solution is to carry an atlas. The *Beijing Street Directory
& Map (běijīng shìqū xiángtú)* is excellent – everything is
in English and Chinese. This is available from the
Foreign Languages Bookstore. The Xinhua Bookstore on
Wangfujing Dajie sells an even more detailed atlas called
Beijing Shenghuo Dituce, but this one has Chinese charac-
ters only.

Most maps of Beijing which are published in China
use the simplified characters (unless they are published
for Overseas Chinese tourists). If you have a fondness
for the traditional form, buy a Beijing map in Hong
Kong.

MEDIA

News Agencies

China has two news agencies, the Xinhua News Agency
and the China News Service. The Xinhua (New China)
Agency is a national agency with its headquarters in
Beijing and branches in each province as well as in the
army and many foreign countries. It provides news for

the national, provincial and local papers and radio stations, transmits radio broadcasts abroad in foreign languages, and is responsible for making contact and exchanging news with foreign news agencies. In Hong Kong, Xinhua acts as the unofficial embassy.

The main function of the China News Service is to supply news to Overseas Chinese newspapers and journals, including those in Hong Kong and Macau. It also distributes Chinese documentary films abroad.

Chinese-Language Publications

There are nearly 2000 national and provincial newspapers in China. The main one is Renmin Ribao (People's Daily), with nationwide circulation. It was founded in 1946 as the official publication of the Central Committee of the Communist Party. Most editions tend to be exceedingly boring though they do provide a brief rundown of world events.

At the other end of the scale there is China's version of the gutter press – several hundred 'unhealthy papers' and magazines hawked on street corners and at bus stations in major cities with nude or violent photos and stories about sex, crime, witchcraft, miracle cures and UFOs. These have been severely criticised by the government for their obscene and racy content, but they are also extremely popular. There are also about 40 newspapers for the minority nationalities.

Foreign-Language Publications

China publishes various newspapers, books and magazines in a number of European and Asian languages. The only English-language newpaper (and one which you are most likely to come across during your travels) is *China Daily*. First published in June 1981, it now has two overseas editions (Hong Kong and USA). Overseas subscriptions can be obtained from the following sources:

Hong Kong
    Wen Wei Po, 197 Wanchai Rd (☎ 572 2211; fax 572 0441)
USA
    China Daily Distribution Corporation, Suite 401, 15 Mercer St, New York, NY 10013 (☎ 212-219 0130; fax 210 0108)

Although you might stumble across some of the English-language magazines in luxury hotels and Friendship Stores, they are most readily available by subscription. These can be posted to you overseas. The place to subscribe is not in China itself, but in Hong Kong. If interested, contact Peace Book Company (☎ 896 7382; fax 897 6251), 17th Floor, Paramount Building, 12 Ka Yip St, Chai Wan, Hong Kong. You can write, fax or call in at the office for their catalogue. A rundown of what's available in English and other foreign languages follows, in alphabetical order:

Beijing Review, a weekly magazine on political and current affairs. Useful for learning about China's latest political policies. The magazine is published in English, French, Spanish, German and Japanese.

China Medical Abstracts, a special-interest quarterly magazine in English.

China Philately, a bimonthly magazine in English for stamp collectors.

China Pictorial, a monthly large-format glossy magazine with good photos, cultural and historical stuff. Available in English, French, Spanish, German and Japanese.

China Screen, a quarterly magazine in English or Chinese with a focus on the Chinese motion-picture industry.

China Sports, an English-language monthly which helps demonstrate the superiority of Chinese athletes over foreigners.

China Today, a monthly magazine. The magazine was founded in 1952 by Song Qingling (the wife of Sun Yatsen) and used to be called *China Reconstructs*. The name was changed in 1989 because – as one official said – '37 years is a hell of a long time to be reconstructing your country'.

China's Foreign Trade, a monthly publication in English, French, Spanish or Chinese, with a self-explanatory title.

China's Patents & Trademarks, a quarterly magazine in Chinese and English. The title is self-explanatory.

China's Tibet, a quarterly magazine in Chinese or English. Its chief purpose is to convince overseas readers that China's historical claim to Tibet is more than just hot air. Some of the articles about Tibetan culture and religion might prove interesting.

Chinese Literature, a quarterly magazine in English or French. Topics include poetry, fiction, profiles of Chinese writers and so on.

El Popola Cinio, a monthly magazine in Esperanto – good if you want to familiarise yourself with this language.

Kexue Tongbao, a semi-monthly publication in English with a focus on the sciences.

Nexus, a quarterly magazine in English. It is claimed that this is China's first non-government funded magazine in English (who knows?). Articles cover various aspects of Chinese culture and society.

Shanghai Pictorial, a bimonthly magazine available in Chinese or English. Photos of fashionable women dressed in the latest, as well as container ships, cellular telephones and other symbols of Shanghai's developing economy.

Social Sciences in China, a quarterly publication in English. The
magazine covers topics like archaeology, economics, phi-
losophy, literature and a whole range of academic pur-
suits by Chinese scholars.

Women of China, a monthly magazine in English designed to
show foreigners that Chinese women are not treated as
badly as they really are.

Imported Publications

It's easy to score copies of popular imported English-
language magazines like *Time*, *Newsweek*, *Far Eastern
Economic Review* and *The Economist*. Occasionally you
might find European magazines in French or German.
Foreign newspapers like the *Asian Wall Street Journal*,
International Herald-Tribune and Hong Kong's *South
China Morning Post* are also available. Imported periodicals are most readily available from the big tourist
hotels and the Friendship Store.

Discarded Reading Matter

When the Communist Party committee of Beijing investi-
gated the bustling black market for foreign books, magazines and newspapers they discovered that hotel staff and
garbage collectors are well-placed intermediaries for this
business. Foreign hotel guests regularly leave behind
several tonnes of foreign publications every month, but
resident foreigners throw out nearly 20 tonnes.

The Beijing committee analysed printed matter left
behind at the Xinqiao Hotel and was pleased to discover
that nearly half of the publications had good or relatively
good contents. The remaining items contained 'partly
erroneous' or 'problematic' material such as 'half-naked
advertisements'. When the courageous committee delved
into diplomatic dustbins, they discovered that 15% of their
haul was 'anti-communist, anti-Chinese, obscene and
pornographic' – definitely bottom of the barrel. ■

Radio & TV

Domestic radio broadcasting is controlled by the Central
People's Broadcasting Station (CPBS). Broadcasts are
made in *pǔtōnghuà*, the standard Chinese speech, as well
as in local Chinese dialects and minority languages.

Music buffs can listen to Chinese classical, opera,
foreign violin concertos, piano solos, etc on AM radio at
640 kHz, 720 kHz, or FM stereo at 94.5 MHz and 98.2
MHz.

If you want to hear world news broadcasts in English, a short-wave radio receiver would be worth bringing with you. You can buy these in China, but the ones from Hong Kong are usually more compact and better quality.

The Chinese Central Television (CCTV) began broadcasting in 1958, and colour transmission began in 1973. Beijing boasts a second local channel, Beijing Television (BTV). Unless you want to practise your Chinese, you'll probably find most of the local stuff boring.

But the situation is not hopeless – satellite TV has taken the country by storm. Hong Kong's Star TV is particularly popular because it broadcasts in Chinese and does not require a decoder (advertising revenues pay the bill) to receive it. Star TV also has an English channel, available at many of the better hotels. Some upmarket hotels also offer in-house video. If you can't live without TV shows, you should inquire at a hotel before checking in to see just what's available.

FILM & PHOTOGRAPHY

Beijing is a very photogenic city, and there are 10 billion potential human portraits as well. Some Chinese shy away from having their photo taken, and even duck for cover. Others are proud to pose and will ham it up for the camera – and they're especially proud if you're taking a shot of their kid. Nobody expects any payment for photos, so don't give any or you'll set a precedent. What the Chinese would go for is a copy of a colour photo, which you could mail to them.

There are three basic approaches to photographing people. One is the polite 'ask for permission and pose it' shot, which is sometimes rejected. Another is the 'no-holds barred and upset everyone' approach. The third is surreptitious, standing half a km away with a metre-long telephoto lens. Many Chinese will disagree with you on what constitutes good subject matter; they don't really see why anyone would want to take a street scene, a picture of a beggar or a shot of an old man driving a donkeycart.

The Chinese are obsessed with photos of themselves standing in front of something. A temple, waterfall, heroic statue or important vintages of calligraphy are considered suitable backgrounds. At amusement parks, Mickey Mouse and Donald Duck get into nearly every photo, while Ronald McDonald and the Colonel of Kentucky Fried fame are favourite photo companions in Beijing. If you hang around these places you can sometimes clip off a few portrait photos for yourself, but don't be surprised if your photo subjects suddenly drag you into the picture as an exotic prop!

Imported film is expensive, but Japanese companies like Fuji and Konica now have factories in China and this has brought prices of colour print film down to what you'd pay in the West, sometimes less. While colour print film is available almost everywhere, it's almost always 100 ASA (21 DIN).

Posing for the camera (RS)

Genuine Chinese brands of film are a big unknown – some are good and some are trash, so you'll just have to experiment if you want to use the stuff. Another big unknown is whether or not these films will work with fully-automatic cameras which need to sense the film speed. The letters 'DX' printed on a box of film indicates that it is suitable for automatic cameras, but we have yet to see a Chinese brand carrying this designation.

Black & white film can be found at a few select photo shops, but its use is not common as colour photos are now the big thing. Colour slide film is seldom used by the Chinese, but can be bought in Beijing at speciality shops. It's cheapest at the Friendship Store and photo shops on Wangfujing Dajie. Major hotels also sell it, but at a significant mark-up.

Polaroid film is rumoured to exist, but if you know you'll need it, bring your own supply. Finding the special lithium batteries used by many cameras is also hit or miss and you'd be wise to bring a spare. Video cameras were once subject to shaky regulations but there seems to be no problem now.

Big hotels and stores along Wangfujing are equipped with the latest Japanese photoprocessing machines. Quality colour prints can be turned out in one or two hours at reasonable cost.

It's a different situation with colour slides. Ektachrome and Fujichrome can be processed in Beijing, but this is normally slow and expensive and quality is not assured. If you don't want to risk your slides being scratched, covered with fingerprints or over-developed, save the processing until you get home.

Undeveloped film can be sent out of China and, going by personal experience only, the dreaded X-ray machines do not appear to be a problem.

Prohibited Subjects

Religious reasons for avoiding photographs are absent among the Han Chinese. Some guy isn't going to stick a spear through you for taking a picture of his wife and stealing part of her soul.

On the other hand, photography from planes and photographs of airports, military installations, harbour facilities and train terminals are prohibited; bridges may also be a touchy subject.

These rules get enforced if the enforcers happen to be around. One traveller, bored at the airport, started photographing the X-ray procedure in clearance. PLA men promptly pounced on her and ripped the film out of her camera.

Taking photos is not permitted in most museums, at archaeological sites and in many temples, mainly to protect the postcard and colour slide industry. It prevents Westerners from publishing their own books about these sites and taking business away from the Chinese-published books. It also prevents valuable works of art from being damaged by countless flash photos, but in most cases you're not allowed to take even harmless natural light photos or time exposures. The Chinese are not alone in imposing such restrictions, which can be frustrating at times.

Monks can be vigorous enforcers of this rule in temples. They can rip film out of cameras faster than you can cock the shutter – must be some special martial arts training.

HEALTH

Beijing is a reasonably healthy city – the cold climate means you needn't fear tropical bugs like malaria. Water supplies are fairly good, but it's still recommended that you only drink boiled or bottled water. Tea should be no problem.

The most likely illness to befall you in Beijing is influenza. China is notorious for outbreaks of nasty strains of flu, especially during winter and spring. Pneumonia is a possible complication. The situation is exacerbated by the Chinese habit of spitting anywhere and everywhere, which spreads respiratory illnesses. You can protect yourself up to a limited extent with a flu vaccine, but 100% protection would require that you live in total quarantine or give up breathing.

It's very likely that a health insurance policy purchased in your home country will *not* cover you in China – if unsure, ask your insurance company. If you're not covered, it would be prudent to purchase travellers' health insurance.

Medical Facilities

The Sino-German Policlinic (☎ 501 1983) (*zhōngdé zhěnsuǒ*) has Western-trained doctors and is one of the most popular medical clinics with foreigners. Emergency service is available 24 hours a day, but there are regular office hours and it's often a good idea to call first for an appointment – the staff speak good English. This clinic is a good place to get those odd vaccinations like rabies and hepatitis B, and a dental service is also available. The clinic is downstairs in Landmark Tower B-1, adjacent to the Sheraton Great Wall Hotel.

Beijing Union Medical College (*xiéhé yīyuàn*) has a 24-hour emergency room (*jízhěn shì*) (☎ 512 7733 ext 217) and a foreigners' clinic (*wàishìbàn gōng shì*) (☎ 512 7733 ext 251). The address is 1 Shifuyuan, Wangfujing.

There is a foreigners' clinic at the Friendship Hospital (*yǒuyí yīyuàn*) (☎ 422 1122), 95 Yongan Lu. The hospital is on the west side of Tiantan Park in the Tianqiao area. Normal outpatient business hours are from 8 to 11.30 am and 2.30 to 5 pm.

Asia Emergency Assistance is for those really big emergencies. The service is not cheap, but this place can even dispatch a small aircraft to evacuate injured persons from remote areas. There are several branch offices – the Beijing Alarm Centre (☎ 505 3521; fax 505 3526) is in room 1010 of the China World Trade Centre (*guómào dàshà*) at 1 Jianguomenwai Dajie. The Hong Kong Alarm Centre (☎ (852) 810 7881; fax 845 0395) can also be contacted for medevac services. The service is available 24 hours a day.

Sexually Transmitted Diseases

The Cultural Revolution may be over but the sexual revolution is booming in China, and STDs are spreading rapidly. It pays to be cautious, therefore, in sexual activity, particularly as you could be unlucky enough to catch herpes or, worse still, AIDS, for neither of which is there any cure. Apart from sexual abstinence, condoms provide the most effective protection and they are available in China. The word for condom is *bǎoxiǎn tào* which literally translates as 'insurance glove'.

As most people know by now, AIDS can also be spread through infected blood transfusions, and by dirty needles – vaccinations, acupuncture, ear piercing and tattooing can potentially be as dangerous as intravenous drug use if the equipment is not clean. You may choose to buy your own acupuncture needles, which are widely available in Beijing, if you're intending having that form of treatment. Medical clinics which cater to foreigners all use disposable needles and syringes.

WOMEN TRAVELLERS

In general, foreign women are unlikely to suffer serious sexual harassment in China. There have been reports of foreign women being harassed by Chinese men in Beijing's parks or while cycling alone at night, but rape (of foreign women) is not common. This doesn't mean it cannot happen, but most Chinese rapists appear to prefer Chinese victims. The police tend to investigate crimes against foreigners much more closely and more severe penalties (like execution) are imposed if the perpetrator is caught. This provides foreign women with a small but important aura of protection.

Wearing see-through blouses, short shorts, skimpy bikinis and going topless at the beach is asking for trouble. While Beijingers are hip to the latest fashions (including miniskirts), the countryside is much more conservative. If you're going far afield from the city, it would be worthwhile to dress a bit conservatively – wear trousers or a below-the-knee skirt, with a shirt that covers your shoulders. For outdoor wear, sandals are acceptable but thongs are not.

DANGERS & ANNOYANCES

Crime & Punishment

Fictional stories from the official Chinese press paint a picture of exemplary honesty, including the Beijing shop

Health billboard (RS)

assistant who inadvertently shortchanged a foreign
tourist and finally managed to track him down in Lhasa
through an advertisement she inserted in the *China
Daily*. Another legend involves a foreign businessman
who decided to discard a pair of trousers in his hotel
room before catching a taxi to the airport. Just as his
flight was called, a breathless room-attendant came
racing into the airport carrying the trousers. Attempts to
jettison used razor blades often meet with the same
defeat.

The reality is different. Though your chance of being
attacked on the street is small, there is crime in China.
Pickpocketing is the most common form of theft and one
you need to carefully guard against. In back alleys, a
thief might try to grab your bag and run away, but far
more common is razoring of bags and pockets in
crowded places like buses and railway stations. If you
want to avoid opening wallets or bags on the bus, keep
a few coins or small notes ready in an accessible pocket
before launching yourself onto the crowd.

Hotels are usually safe places to leave your stuff; each
floor has an attendant watching who goes in and out. If
anything is missing from your room then they're going
to be obvious suspects since they've got keys to the
rooms. Don't expect them to watch over your room like
a hawk, though, because they don't.

Dormitories could be a problem; there have been a
few reports of thefts by staff, but the culprits are more
likely to be other foreigners! There are at least a few
people who subsidise their journey by ripping off their
fellow travellers. Most hotels have storage rooms where
you check your bags in; some insist that you do. Leaving

your stuff in the dormitory is a good way to get it pilfered. Don't leave your valuables (passport, travellers' cheques, money, air tickets) lying around anywhere.

A money belt is the safest way to carry valuables, particularly when travelling on buses and trains. During the cooler weather, it's more comfortable to wear a vest (waistcoat) with numerous pockets, but you should wear this under a light jacket or coat since visible pockets invite wandering hands even if sealed with zips.

Perhaps the best way to avoid getting ripped off is to not bring a lot of junk you don't need – personal stereos, video cameras, expensive specs and jewellery all invite theft.

If something of yours is stolen, you should report it immediately to the nearest Foreign Affairs Branch of the PSB. They will ask you to fill in a loss report before investigating the case and sometimes even recovering the stolen goods.

If you have travel insurance (recommended), it is essential to obtain a loss report so you can claim compensation.

Spitting

The national sport, spitting, is practised by everyone regardless of how well-dressed or sophisticated they look. All venues are possible – on board buses and trains, in restaurants, etc. Never walk too closely alongside a stationary bus full of passengers, and try not to get caught in the crossfire elsewhere!

In Beijing, it is technically illegal. Anti-spitting campaigns with fines for violators are periodically launched, usually to coincide with a visit by an important foreign dignitary.

Queues

Basically, there are none. People tend to 'huddle' rather than queue, resembling American-style football but without the protective gear. You're most likely to encounter the situation when trying to board a bus. Good luck.

The Sex Police

Beijing is the most xenophobic of all Chinese cities. While the Beijing PSB doesn't necessarily try to cause trouble with foreigners, they can and will create international incidents over trivial nonsense if you cross them.

Avoiding trouble is usually straightforward, if you understand what the rules are.

The most important rule is that Western men cannot 'insult' Chinese women – 'insult' seems to be a Chinese idiom meaning 'have sex with'. It's not even necessary to actually touch the woman; just the appearance of being 'too intimate' can lead to problems. If a Westerner rides in a taxi with a Chinese woman, there is a good chance that the taxi will be pulled over, ID cards checked and, if the woman is a Chinese national, she will probably be arrested and the man may have his passport confiscated. We personally know one Westerner who was beaten by the police when he tried to prevent them from hauling away his girlfriend, who in fact was a Hong Kong Chinese. China is a very male-oriented society – cases of Western women getting involved with Chinese men are viewed far less seriously and seldom cause problems with the PSB.

Beijing has far more police than you at first realise, since most are dressed in plain clothes. One of the prime duties of the plain-clothes PSB is to follow journalists and interrogate everyone the journalists talk to. There are also video cameras placed at strategic locations all over Beijing. You can spot them up in the trees along major boulevards. The video tapes were used as evidence to prosecute student activists and sympathisers after the 1989 protests at Tiananmen Square.

There are also civilian 'snitch squads' who watch foreigners and report suspicious activities to the police. This had led to some spectacular blunders, like the police bursting into a foreigner's hotel room and dragging the man and his screaming female companion naked from their bed – only to discover that the 'Chinese' woman being 'insulted' was Japanese and the couple were married.

WORK

There are opportunities to teach English and other foreign languages, or even other technical skills if you're qualified. Teaching in Beijing is not a way to get rich – pay is roughly US$180 a month, payable in RMB rather than hard currency. This is about four times what the average urban Chinese worker earns. There are usually some fringe benefits like free or low-cost housing and special ID cards that get you discounts on trains and flights. As a worker in China, you will be assigned to a 'work unit', but unlike the locals you'll be excused from political meetings and the God-like controls over your life that the typical Chinese has to endure.

It's become fairly common for universities to pressure foreigners into working excessive hours. A maximum teaching load should be 20 hours per week, and even this is a lot; you can insist on no more than 15. Chinese professors teach far fewer hours than this. Some hardly show up for class at all since they often have outside business interests.

The main reason to work in China is to experience the country at a level not ordinarily available to travellers. Unfortunately, just how close you will be able to get to the Chinese people depends on what the PSB allows. In Beijing, where the local PSB is almost hysterical about evil foreign 'spiritual pollution', your students may be prohibited from having any contact with you beyond the classroom, though you may secretly meet them far away from the campus. Foreign teachers are usually forced to live in separate apartments or dormitories. Chinese students wishing to visit you at your room may be turned away at the reception desk; otherwise they may be required to register their name, ID number and purpose of visit. Since many people are reluctant to draw attention to themselves like this (and they could be questioned by the PSB later), they may be unwilling to visit you at all.

In other words, teaching in Beijing can be a lonely experience, unless you spend all your free time in the company of other expats, but this deprives you of the 'foreign experience' you may be seeking.

Two topics which cannot be discussed in the classroom are politics and religion. Foreigners teaching in Beijing have reported spies being placed in their classrooms. Other teachers have found microphones hidden in their dormitory rooms (one fellow took revenge by attaching his personal stereo to the microphone wires and blasting the snoops with punk music!).

Rules change – Beijing is less paranoid now than it was in the immediate aftermath of Tiananmen. So things might have improved by the time you read this. If you are interested in working in Beijing or other cities in China, contact a Chinese embassy or the universities directly.

Doing Business

In bureaucratic China, even simple things can be made difficult. Renting property, getting a telephone installed, hiring employees, paying taxes, etc, can generate mind-boggling quantities of red tape. Many foreign business people who have worked in China say that success is usually the result of dogged persistence and finding cooperative officials.

If you have any intention of doing business in China, be it buying, selling or investing, it's worth knowing that most towns and – in large cities – many neighbourhoods, have a Commerce Office *(shāngyè jú)*. If you approach one of these offices for assistance, the reaction you get can vary from enthusiastic welcome to bureaucratic inertia. In case of a dispute (the goods you ordered are not what was delivered, etc) the Commerce Office could assist you, provided that they are willing.

Buying is simple, selling is more difficult, but setting up a business in Beijing is a whole different can of worms. If yours is a high-technology company, you can go into certain economic zones and register as a wholly foreign-owned enterprise. In that case you can hire people yourself without going through the government, enjoy a three-year tax holiday, obtain long-term income tax advantages and import duty-free personal items for corporate and expat use (including a car!). The alternative is listing your company as a representative office, which does not allow you to sign any contracts in China – these must be signed by the mother company. The Foreign Service Company (FESCO) is where you hire employees. FESCO currently demands around US$325 per month per employee, 75% of which goes to the government.

It's easier to register as a representative office. First find out where you want to set up (a city or special economic zone), then go through local authorities (there are no national authorities for this). Go to the local Commerce Office, Economic Ministry, Foreign Ministry, or any ministry that deals with foreign economic trade promotion. In Beijing, the Haidian High-Technology Zone is recommended if you can qualify, but where you register depends on what type of business you're doing. Contact your embassy first – they can advise you.

The most important thing to remember when you go to register a company is not to turn away when you run into a bureaucratic barrier. Bureaucrats will tell you that everything is 'impossible'. In fact, anything is possible – it all depends on your *guanxi* (relationships). Whatever you have in mind is negotiable, and all the rules are not necessarily rules at all.

Tax rates vary from zone to zone, authority to authority. It seems to be negotiable but 15% is fairly standard in economic zones. Every economic zone has a fairly comprehensive investment guide, available in English and Chinese – ask at your embassy, whose economic council might have copies of these. These investment

guides are getting to be very clear, although even all their
printed 'rules' are negotiable!

FOOD

You can put your mind at ease about food shortages,
because despite China's long history of famines the
country is not short of food. Famines have resulted from
natural disasters (droughts, floods, typhoons) and
human disasters (wars, the Cultural Revolution, etc).
Barring an earthquake (natural or political), food supplies should be more than adequate.

In 1949 Beijing had an incredible 10,000 snack bars
and restaurants; by 1976 that number had dwindled to
less than 700. Restaurants, a nasty bourgeois concept,
were all to have been phased out and replaced with
revolutionary dispensaries dishing out rice. However,
the newly-permitted free enterprise system has generated an explosion of privately-owned eateries.

Eating out in the capital is a true adventure, one that
should be seized with both chopsticks. But first, you'll
have to learn how to use them.

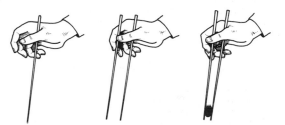

How to use chopsticks

Main Dishes

Naturally enough, cooking styles vary considerably
around China and most of the regional and minority
styles are represented in the capital. There is certainly
ample variety for the average gastronome and there's no
way you'll get through them all.

Beijing & Shandong Beijing and Shandong cuisines
come from the cold northland of China. Since this is

China's wheat belt, steamed bread, dumplings and noodles figure prominently rather than rice.

The most famous speciality is Beijing Duck, served with pancakes and plum sauce. Another local dish is beggar's chicken, supposedly created by a beggar who stole the emperor's chicken and had to bury it in the ground to cook it. The dish is wrapped in lotus leaves and baked all day in hot ashes.

A warning: the ducks get their revenge. Many foreigners tucking into Beijing Duck for the first time have a tendency to get very ill from the experience. It's uncertain whether this is caused by some sinister plot hatched by the ducks themselves or simple overeating. Nevertheless, go easy the first time. Your initial duck dinner should be a small one, and if you don't wind up in the emergency room then you might consume more the second time around.

Another northern speciality is Mongolian hotpot, composed of assorted meats and vegetables cooked in a burner right on the dining table – it's so good in China that it's hard to believe it can be so bad in Mongolia. Hotpot is usually eaten during winter. Mongolian barbecue is a variation featuring a slowly-roasted goat or lamb carcass along with a hotpot full of spicy vegetables. If you've eaten the Korean dish *bulgogi*, you've got the idea. A warning, though: the price of hotpot depends entirely on the ingredients. It can cost Y20 or Y200 depending on what's thrown into the pot, so ask first to avoid indigestion when the bill arrives.

Due to Beijing's substantial Muslim minority population, Muslim barbecues are also popular. Muslim barbecues use lamb, and shish kebabs are called *shashlik*.

Bird's nest soup is a speciality of Shandong cooking. Another is sweet-and-sour Yellow River carp; the fish is singed on the outside while still alive and served while still breathing! Not surprisingly, it isn't a big hit with foreigners.

Shanghainese Of all Chinese cuisines, this one gets the poorest reviews by foreigners. Shanghainese cooking is noted for its use of seafoods, but it's heavy and oily. Many Westerners say it's greasy, tasteless and disgusting, but liberal use of spices can make it almost palatable. Eels are popular, as is drunken chicken, cooked in *shaoxing* (a potent Chinese firewater a bit like warm sherry). Other things to try are some of the cold-meat-and-sauce dishes, ham-and-melon soup, bean curd (tofu) and brown sauce, braised meat balls, deep-fried chicken, and pork ribs with salt and pepper.

Sichuan & Hunan Sichuan food is the hottest of the four major categories. It's great stuff if you like spicy food, but keep the drinking water handy! Specialities include frogs' legs and smoked duck; the duck is cooked in peppercorns, marinated in wine for 24 hours, covered in tea leaves and cooked again over a charcoal fire. Other dishes to try are shrimps with salt and garlic; dried chilli beef; bean curd with chilli; bear paws braised in brown sauce; fish in spicy bean sauce and aubergines in garlic.

Hunan food is a variation, often hot and spicy like Sichuan cuisine. The Hunanese give new meaning to the words 'hot dogs', since spicy canines are often on the menu. For those who prefer Fido with his tail wagging, Hunan chefs do similar things with ducks, chickens and seafood.

Cantonese & Chaozhou This is southern Chinese cooking – lots of steaming, boiling and stir-frying. It's the healthiest if you're worried about cholesterol and coronaries, as it uses the least amount of oil. It's lightly cooked and not as highly spiced as the other three, with lots of seafood, vegetables, roast pork, chicken, steamed fish and fried rice.

Dim sum is a snack-like variation, served for breakfast and lunch (but never dinner) and consisting of all sorts of little delicacies served from pushcarts wheeled around the restaurant. It's justifiably famous and highly addictive stuff.

The Cantonese are renowned for making just about anything palatable: specialities are abalone, dried squid, 1000-year eggs (made by soaking eggs in horses' urine), shark's fin soup, snake soup and dog stew. Other culinary exotica include anteaters, pangolins (a sort of armadillo), cats, rats, owls, monkeys, turtles and frogs. One saying is that the Cantonese eat everything with four legs but the table. Another Chinese joke is that the Cantonese are industrious people, capable of doing any job except zookeeper.

Despite the unusual ingredients, Cantonese food has long been a favourite of Westerners. Chinese restaurants around the world often include a rich selection of Cantonese dishes on the menu.

Dealing with Menus

Some restaurants are cafeteria-style and you can just point to what you want, but in most places you have to order. A few restaurants have English menus, but most don't. If the language barrier proves impassable, it's possible to order a meal by pointing at something that somebody else already has. However, the following menu should be sufficient to get you started.

Restaurant Vocabulary

restaurant
  cāntīng 餐厅
I'm vegetarian.
  wô chī sù 我吃素
menu
  cài dān 菜单
bill (cheque)
  zhàng dān 帐单
set meal (no menu)
  tàocān 套餐
to eat/let's eat
  chī fàn 吃饭
chopsticks
  kuàizi 筷子
knife and fork
  dāochā 刀叉
spoon
  tiáogēng 调羹

Sample Menu

Rice

plain white rice
  mǐfàn 米饭
watery rice porridge
  xīfàn 稀饭
rice noodles
  mǐfěn 米粉

Bread, Buns & Dumplings

fried roll
  yínsī juǎn 银丝卷
steamed buns
  mántóu 馒头
steamed meat buns
  bāozi 包子
fried bread stick
  yóutiáo 油条
boiled dumplings
  jiǎozi 饺子
prawn cracker
  lóngxiā piàn 龙虾片

Vegetable Dishes

fried rice with vegetables
shūcài chǎofàn 蔬菜炒饭
fried noodles with vegetables
shūcài chǎomiàn 蔬菜炒面
spicy peanuts
wǔxiāng huāshēng mǐ 五香花生米
fried peanuts
yóuzhà huāshēng mǐ 油炸花生米
spiced cold vegetables
liángbàn shíjǐn 凉拌什锦
Chinese salad
jiācháng liángcài 家常凉菜
fried rape in oyster sauce
háoyóu pácài dǎn 蚝油扒菜胆
fried rape with mushrooms
dōnggū pácài dǎn 冬菇扒菜胆
fried bean curd in oyster sauce
háoyóu dòufu 蚝油豆腐
spicy hot bean curd
mápó dòufu 麻婆豆腐
bean curd casserole
shāguō dòufu 沙锅豆腐
bean curd & mushrooms
mógū dòufu 磨菇豆腐
garlic & morning glory
dàsuàn kōngxīn cài 大蒜空心菜
fried garlic
sù chǎo dàsuàn 素炒大蒜
fried eggplant
sùshāo qiézi 素烧茄子
fried beansprouts
sù chǎo dòuyá 素炒豆芽
fried green vegetables
sù chǎo qīngcài 素炒青菜
fried green beans
sù chǎo biǎndòu 素炒扁豆
fried cauliflower & tomato
fānqié càihuā 炒蕃茄菜花
broiled mushroom
sù chǎo xiānme 素炒鲜蘑
black fungus & mushroom
mù'ěr huákǒu mó 木耳滑口蘑
fried white radish patty
luóbo gāo 萝卜糕
assorted hors d'oeuvre
shíjǐn pīnpán 什锦拼盘
assorted vegetarian food
sù shíjǐn 素什锦

Egg Dishes

preserved egg
    sōnghuā dàn   松花蛋
fried rice with egg
    jīdàn chǎofàn   鸡蛋炒饭
fried tomatoes & eggs
    xīhóngshì chǎo jīdàn   西红柿炒鸡蛋
egg & flour omelette
    jiān bǐng   煎饼

Beef Dishes

fried rice with beef
    niúròu chǎofàn   牛肉丝炒饭
noodles with beef (soupy)
    niúròu tāng miàn   牛肉汤面
spiced noodles with beef
    niúròu gān miàn   牛肉干面
fried noodles with beef
    niúròu chǎomiàn   牛肉炒面
beef with white rice
    niúròu fàn   牛肉饭
beef platter
    niúròu tiěbǎn   牛肉铁板
beef with oyster sauce
    háoyóu niúròu   蚝油牛肉
beef braised in soy sauce
    hóngshāo niúròu   红烧牛肉
beef with tomatoes
    fānqié niúròu piàn   蕃茄牛肉片
beef with green peppers
    qīngjiāo niúròu piàn   青椒牛肉片
beef curry & rice
    gālǐ jīròu fàn   咖哩牛肉饭
beef curry & noodles
    gālǐ jīròu miàn   咖哩牛肉面

Chicken Dishes

fried rice with chicken
    jīsī chǎofàn   鸡丝炒饭
noodles with chicken (soupy)
    jīsī tāng miàn   鸡丝汤面
fried noodles with chicken
    jīsī chǎomiàn   鸡丝炒面
chicken leg with white rice
    jītuǐ fàn   鸡腿饭
spicy hot chicken & peanuts
    gōngbào jīdīng   宫爆鸡丁

fruit kernal with chicken
  guǒwèi jīdīng 果味鸡丁
sweet & sour chicken
  tángcù jīdīng 糖醋鸡丁
sauteed spicy chicken pieces
  làzi jīdīng 辣子鸡丁
sauteed chicken with green peppers
  jiàngbào jīdīng 酱爆鸡丁
chicken slices & tomato sauce
  fānqié jīdīng 蕃茄鸡丁
mushrooms & chicken
  cǎomó jīdīng 草蘑鸡丁
chicken pieces in oyster sauce
  háoyóu jīdīng 蚝油鸡丁
chicken braised in soy sauce
  hóngshāo jīkuài 红烧鸡块
sauteed chicken with water chestnuts
  nánjiè jīpiàn 南芥鸡片
sliced chicken with crispy rice
  jīpiàn guōbā 鸡片锅巴
chicken curry
  gālí jīròu 咖哩鸡肉
chicken curry & rice
  gālí jīròu fàn 咖哩鸡肉饭
chicken curry & noodles
  gālí jīròu miàn 咖哩鸡肉面

Duck Dishes

Beijing Duck
  běijīng kǎoyā 北京烤鸭
duck with white rice
  yāròu fàn 鸭肉饭
duck with noodles
  yāròu miàn 鸭肉面
duck with fried noodles
  yāròu chǎomiàn 鸭肉炒面

Pork Dishes

pork chop with white rice
  páigǔ fàn 排骨饭
fried rice with pork
  ròusī chǎofàn 肉丝炒饭
fried noodles with pork
  ròusī chǎomiàn 肉丝炒面
pork & mustard greens
  zhàcài ròusī 榨菜肉丝

noodles, pork & mustard greens
  zhàcài ròusī miàn 榨菜肉丝面
pork with crispy rice
  ròupiàn guōbā 肉片锅巴
sweet & sour pork pieces
  tángcù zhūròu piàn 糖醋猪肉片
sweet & sour pork fillet
  tángcù lǐjī 糖醋里肌
pork fillet with white sauce
  huáliū lǐjī 滑溜里肌
shredded pork fillet
  chǎo lǐjī sī 炒里肌丝
soft pork fillet
  ruǎnzhá lǐjī 软炸里肌
spicy hot pork pieces
  gōngbào ròudīng 宫爆肉丁
fried black pork pieces
  yuánbào lǐjī 尤爆里肌
sauteed diced pork & soy sauce
  jiàngbào ròudīng 酱爆肉丁
spicy pork cubes
  làzi ròudīng 辣子肉丁
pork cubes & cucumber
  huánggguā ròudīng 黄瓜肉丁
golden pork slices
  jīnyín ròusī 金银肉丝
sauteed shredded pork
  qīngchǎo ròusī 清炒肉丝
shredded pork & hot sauce
  yúxiāng ròusī 鱼香肉丝
shredded pork & green peppers
  qīngjiāo ròusī 青椒肉丝
shredded pork & bamboo shoots
  dōngsǔn ròusī 冬笋肉丝
shredded pork & green beans
  biǎndòu ròusī 扁豆肉丝
pork with oyster sauce
  háoyóu ròusī 蚝油肉丝
boiled pork slices
  shǔizhǔ ròupiàn 水煮肉片
pork, eggs & black fungus
  mùxū ròu 木须肉
pork & fried onions
  yángcōng chǎo ròupiàn 洋葱炒肉片
fried rice (assorted)
  shíjǐn chǎofàn 什锦炒饭
fried rice Canton-style
  guǎngzhōu chǎofàn 广州炒饭

Seafood Dishes

fried rice with shrimp
  xiārén chǎofàn 虾仁炒饭
fried noodles with shrimp
  xiārén chǎomiàn 虾仁炒面
diced shrimp with peanuts
  gōngbào xiārén 宫爆虾仁
sauteed shrimp
  qīngchǎo xiārén 清炒虾仁
deep-fried shrimp
  zhà xiārén 炸虾仁
fried shrimp with mushroom
  xiānmó xiārén 鲜蘑虾仁
squid with crispy rice
  yóuyú guōbā 鱿鱼锅巴
sweet & sour squid roll
  suānlà yóuyú juàn 酸辣鱿鱼卷
fish braised in soy sauce
  hóngshāo yú 红烧鱼
braised sea cucumber
  hóngshāo hǎishēn 红烧海参
clams
  gé 蛤
crab
  pángxiè 螃蟹
lobster
  lóngxiā 龙虾

Soup

three kinds of seafood soup
  sān xiān tāng 三鲜汤
squid soup
  yóuyú tāng 鱿鱼汤
sweet & sour soup
  suānlà tāng 酸辣汤
tomato & egg soup
  xīhóngshì dàn tāng 西红柿蛋汤
corn & egg thick soup
  fènghuáng lìmǐ gēng 凤凰粟米羹
egg & vegetable soup
  dànhuā tāng 蛋花汤
mushroom & egg soup
  mógu dànhuā tāng 蘑菇蛋花汤
fresh fish soup
  shēng yú tāng 生鱼汤
vegetable soup
  shūcài tāng 蔬菜汤

cream of tomato soup
  nǎiyóu fānqié tāng 奶油蕃茄汤
cream of mushroom soup
  nǎiyóu xiānmó tāng 奶油鲜蘑汤
pickled mustard green soup
  zhàcài tāng 榨菜汤
bean curd & vegetable soup
  dòufǔ cài tāng 豆腐菜汤
wanton soup
  húndùn tāng 馄饨汤
clear soup
  qīng tāng 清汤

Miscellanea & Exotica

kebab
  ròu chuàn 肉串
goat, mutton
  yáng ròu 羊肉
dogmeat
  gǒu ròu 狗肉
deermeat (venison)
  lùròu 鹿肉
snake
  shé ròu 蛇肉
ratmeat
  lǎoshǔ ròu 老鼠肉
pangolin
  língli 穿山甲
frog
  qīngwā 青蛙
eel
  shàn yú 鳝鱼
turtle
  hǎiguī 海龟
Mongolian hotpot
  huǒguō 火锅

Condiments

garlic
  dàsuàn 大蒜
black pepper
  hújiāo 胡椒
hot pepper
  làjiāo 辣椒
hot sauce
  làjiāo jiàng 辣椒酱

ketchup
fānqié jiàng 蕃茄酱
salt
yán 盐
MSG
wèijīng 味精
soy sauce
jiàng yóu 酱油
vinegar
cù 醋
sesame seed oil
zhīmá yóu 芝麻油
butter
huáng yóu 黄油
sugar
táng 糖
jam
guǒ jiàng 果酱
honey
fēngmì 蜂蜜

DRINKS

Non-alcoholic Drinks

Tea is the most commonly served brew in the PRC; it
didn't originate in China but in South-East Asia. Indian
tea is not generally available in restaurants, but if you
need the stuff, large supermarkets stock Lipton and
Twinings. Coffee addicts will find a plentiful supply of
Maxwell House and Nescafe in all the shops, but seldom
in restaurants.

Coca-Cola, first introduced into China by American
soldiers in 1927, is now produced in Beijing. Fanta and
Sprite are widely available, both genuine and copycat
versions. Sugary Chinese soft drinks are cheap and sold
everywhere – some are so sweet they'll turn your teeth
inside out. *Jianlibao* is a Chinese soft drink made with
honey rather than sugar, and is one of the better brands.
Lychee-flavoured carbonated drinks are unique to
China and get rave reviews from foreigners. Fresh milk
is rare but you can buy imported UHT milk at high
prices from Western-style supermarkets.

A surprising treat is fresh sweet yoghurt, available
from street stalls and shops everywhere. It's usually sold
in what look like small milk bottles and is consumed by
drinking with a straw rather than eating with a spoon.
This excellent stuff would make a great breakfast if you
could find some decent bread to go with it.

Alcohol

If tea is the most popular drink in the PRC then beer must be number two. By any standards the top brands are great stuff. The best known is *Tsingtao* (*Qingdao*), made with a mineral water which gives it its sparkling quality. It's really a German beer since the town of Qingdao (formerly spelled 'Tsingtao') where it's made was once a German concession and the Chinese inherited the brewery. Experts in these matters claim that draft Tsingtao tastes much better than the bottled stuff.

Beijing has a number of local brews – the best is reputed to be *Yanjing*. Another brand, simply called *Beijing Beer*, tastes much like coloured water. San Miguel is brewed in Canton and is available from some shops in Beijing. Real Western imports are sold in Friendship Stores and five-star hotels at five-star prices.

China has probably cultivated vines and produced wine for over 4000 years, but Westerners give them mixed reviews. The word 'wine' gets rather loosely translated; many Chinese 'wines' are in fact spirits. Rice wine – a favourite with Chinese alcoholics due to its low price – is intended mainly for cooking rather than drinking. *Hejie Jiu* (lizard wine) is produced in the southern province of Guangxi; each bottle contains one dead lizard suspended perpendicularly in the clear liquid. Wine with dead bees or pickled snakes is also desirable for its alleged tonic (or aphrodisiac) properties. In general, the more poisonous the creature, the more potent are the alleged tonic effects.

Maotai, a favourite of the Chinese, is a spirit made from sorghum (a type of millet) and is used for toasts at banquets. It tastes rather like rubbing alcohol and makes a good substitute for petrol or paint thinner.

Chinese women don't drink (except beer) in public; women who hit the booze are regarded as prostitutes. However, Western women can easily violate this social taboo without unpleasant consequences, since the Chinese expect weirdness from Westerners anyway. As a rule Chinese men are not big drinkers, but toasts are obligatory at banquets. If you really can't drink, fill your wine glass with tea and say you have a bad stomach. In spite of all the toasting and beer drinking, public drunkenness is strongly frowned upon.

Imported alcohol – like XO, Johnny Walker, Kahlua, Napoleon Augier Cognac, etc – is highly prized by the Chinese for its prestige value rather than exquisite taste. The snob appeal plus steep import taxes translates into absurdly high prices, so don't walk into a hotel bar and order this stuff unless you've brought a wheelbarrow full of cash. If you can't live without Western spirits, take advantage of your two-litre duty-free allowance on entry to China.

Drinks Vocabulary

beer
   píjiǔ　啤酒
whisky
   wēishìjì jiǔ　威士忌酒
vodka
   fútèjiā jiǔ　伏特加酒
fizzy drink (soda)
   qìshuǐ　汽水
Coca-Cola
   kěkǒu kělè　可口可乐
tea
   chá　茶
coffee
   kāfēi　咖啡
water
   kāi shuǐ　开水
mineral water
   kuàng quán shuǐ　矿泉水
red grape wine
   hóng pútáo jiǔ　红葡萄酒
white grape wine
   bái pútáo jiǔ　白葡萄酒
rice wine
   mǐ jiǔ　米酒
ice cold
   bīngde　冰的

Getting There & Away

AIR

Tickets to Hong Kong are generally cheaper than tickets directly to Beijing, but a Hong Kong to Beijing flight will probably eat up the savings. While Hong Kong is a great place to find cheap air fares, Beijing is not – this reflects the lack of free-market competition. In fact, most tickets purchased outside China will be cheaper; a London to Beijing ticket is likely to be less than half the price of a Beijing to London ticket, for example.

When you're looking for cheapie fares you have to go to a travel agent rather than directly to the airline which can only sell fares at full list price.

There are numerous discount tickets which are valid for 12 months, allowing multiple stopovers with open dates. These tickets allow for a great deal of flexibility. Just be sure that you check the ticket carefully – some are only valid for six months or even 60 days.

Off-season discounts are available. The 'low season' is winter, except during the Chinese New Year. The 'shoulder season' is spring and autumn. Summer is the 'peak season', when peak prices are charged and seat availability can be a problem, but there are still ways to get discounts even at this time. If you're flying from the southern hemisphere, seasons are reversed. Some off-season round-trip discount tickets require that you both arrive at and depart from your destination during low season, so that if you arrive in China during low season and later change the departure date to peak season, you might have to pay a penalty.

APEX (Advance Purchase Excursion) tickets are sold at a discount but will lock you into a rigid schedule. Such tickets must be purchased two or three weeks ahead of departure, do not permit stopovers and may have minimum and maximum stays as well as fixed departure and return dates. Unless you definitely must return at a certain time, it's best to purchase APEX tickets on a one-way basis only. There are stiff cancellation fees if you decide not to use your APEX ticket.

Some airlines offer student discounts on their tickets to student card holders, of up to 25%. Besides having an International Student Identity Card (ISIC), an official-looking letter from the college is also required by some airlines. Many airlines also require you to be aged 26 or younger to qualify for a discount.

Frequent flyer deals are common. The way it works is that you fly frequently with one airline, and eventually you accumulate enough mileage to qualify for a free ticket. You must first apply to the airline for a frequent flyer account number; some airlines will issue these on the spot or by telephone if you call their head office. Every time you buy an air ticket and/or check in for your flight, you must inform the clerk of your frequent flyer account number, or you won't get credit. Save your tickets and boarding passes, since it's not uncommon for the airlines to fail to give proper credit. You should receive monthly statements by post informing you how much mileage you've accumulated. Once you've accumulated sufficient mileage to qualify for freebies, you're supposed to receive vouchers by mail. Many airlines have 'black-out periods', or times when you cannot fly for free (Christmas and the Chinese Lunar New Year are good examples). The worst thing about frequent flyer programmes is that these tend to lock you into one airline while another airline might be offering a cheaper fare or more convenient flight schedule.

Airlines usually carry babies up to two years of age at 10% of the relevant adult fare; a few may carry them free of charge. For children aged four to 12 years the fare on international flights is usually 50% of the full fare or 67% of a discounted fare.

The attitude of the Chinese government has always been to keep lucrative business for itself. Foreigners are just thrown a few scraps, and even this is done grudgingly. This attitude certainly applies to the airline business. Very few foreign carriers are permitted to fly into China, and even this was only reluctantly conceded so that China's own airlines could gain access to foreign markets. Fortunately, Beijing is the grand exception. It's the only Chinese city where many foreign carriers have been permitted routes.

The China Aviation Administration of China (*zhōngguó mínháng*), also known as CAAC, is the official flag carrier of the PRC. Officially CAAC has been broken up into smaller airlines. This doesn't mean that CAAC is out of business, but it now assumes the role of 'umbrella organisation' for its numerous subsidiaries. The seven major divisions of CAAC are Air China, China Eastern, China Southern, China Northern, China Southwest, China Northwest, and Xinjiang Airlines. In addition to the CAAC network, there are some domestic private lines in China such as Shanghai Airlines.

In its role as 'umbrella organisation', CAAC publishes a comprehensive international and domestic timetable in both English and Chinese, which comes out in April and November each year. These can be bought at some CAAC offices in China, but are easier to get from the CAAC office in Hong Kong.

To/From Hong Kong

CAAC and Dragonair have this route pretty much sewn up. Many foreign airlines would like to fly on this lucrative route, but the Chinese government won't allow them in.

In Hong Kong, travel agents cannot book you into a CAAC flight; for this, you need to go directly to the airline office. There are two such offices in Hong Kong, as follows:

Central, Ground Floor, 17 Queen's Rd (☎ 840 1199)
Kowloon, Ground Floor, Mirador Mansion, 54-64B Nathan
  Rd, Tsimshatsui (☎ 739 0022)

Dragonair (*gǎnglóng hángkōng*) is a joint-venture airline between Hong Kong's Cathay Pacific and CAAC. If you fly on Dragonair, you can book through Cathay Pacific's offices around the world. If you're a member of Cathay's frequent flyer programme (known as the 'Marco Polo Club'), flights on Dragonair can be credited to your mileage total.

Any travel agent with a computer can book you onto a Dragonair flight but you can directly contact the ticketing offices of Dragonair (☎ 736 0202), Room 1843, Swire House, 9 Connaught Rd, Central; and 12th Floor, Tower 6, China Hong Kong City, 33 Canton Rd, Tsimshatsui.

There is virtually no discounting on flights into China and Dragonair's prices are identical to CAAC charges except in business class. The price is fixed by the Chinese government; currently, the one-way economy fare is US$240 and a round-trip costs exactly double.

Hong Kong is a good place to pick up cheap air tickets to almost anywhere in the world. Remember that prices of cheap tickets change and bargains come and go rapidly, and that some travel agents are more reliable than others. Travel agents advertise in the classified sections of the newspapers. Some agents with good recommendations include:

Traveller Services, Room 1012, Silvercord Tower 1, 30 Canton
  Rd, Tsimshatsui, Kowloon (☎ 375 2222; fax 375 2233). The
  efficient staff give fast, reliable and cheap service.

Phoenix Services, Room B, 6th Floor, Milton Mansion, 96 Nathan Rd, Tsimshatsui, Kowloon (☎ 722 7378; fax 369 8884). This is one of Hong Kong's longest-running and most reliable operators.

Shoestring Travel, Flat A, 4th Floor, Alpha House, 27-33 Nathan Rd, Tsimshatsui (☎ 723 2306; fax 721 2085) – maybe not the friendliest, but cheap and reliable.

Hong Kong Student Travel Bureau or HKSTB, Room 1021, 10th Floor, Star House, Salisbury Rd, Tsimshatsui, Kowloon (☎ 721 3269, 369 3804). Their service is reliable, though they are no longer the cheapest place.

To/From Australia

Australia is not a cheap place to fly out of. Among the cheapest regular tickets available in Australia are the APEX fares. The cost of these tickets depends on your departure date from Australia. Peak season in Australia is from December to January.

It's possible to get reductions on the cost of APEX and other fares by going to the student travel offices and/or some of the travel agents in Australia that specialise in cheap air tickets

The cheapest way into China is via Hong Kong. A one-way fare from Australia to Hong Kong is likely to cost from about A$750 (A$1100 return); for Beijing, reckon on A$980 (A$1770).

The cheapest return tickets to Beijing are with MAS (Malaysian Air Systems) from Melbourne or Sydney. The fare is A$1305/A$1410 low season/high season, but you will have to stay overnight at your own expense in Kuala Lumpur. China Airlines flies direct from Sydney to Beijing for A$1450 return.

Travel agents advertise in the travel sections of the Saturday papers, such as the Melbourne *Age* and the *Sydney Morning Herald*. Also look in *Student Traveller*, a free newspaper published by STA Travel and distributed on campuses.

Well worth trying is the Flight Centre (☎ (03) 670 0477) at 386 Little Bourke St, Melbourne. They also have branches under the name of the Flight Centre in Sydney (☎ (02) 235 0166) and Brisbane (☎ (07) 229 9211).

Some good deals are available from STA Travel and you don't have to be a student to use their services. They have offices in all the major Australian cities.

Departure tax from Australia is A$20 for passengers 12 years of age and over.

To/From New Zealand

Air New Zealand and Cathay Pacific fly Auckland to

Hong Kong from around NZ$1750 return, with restrictions. A flight to Beijing will cost from around NZ$1800 ($2550 return).

The departure tax from New Zealand is NZ$20. Children under the age of two are exempt.

To/From the UK

Air-ticket discounting is a long-running business in the UK. The various agents advertise their fares and there's nothing under-the-counter about it at all. To find out what's avaliable, there are a number of magazines in Britain which have good information about flights and agents. These include: *Trailfinder*, free from the Trailfinders Travel Centre in Earls Court; and *Time Out* and *City Limits*, the London weekly entertainment guides widely available in the UK.

Discount tickets are almost exclusively available in London. The danger with discounted tickets in Britain is that some of the bucket shops are unsound. Sometimes the backstairs over-the-shop travel agents fold up and disappear after you've handed over the money and before you've got the tickets, so make sure you get the tickets before you hand over your cash.

Two reliable London bucket shops are Trailfinders in Earls Court; and STA Travel with several offices.

A standard-price one-way ticket with CAAC from London to Beijing will cost £300 (£550 return). Flights to Hong Kong are almost the same price.

To/From Europe

Fares similar to those from London are available from other European cities.

The Netherlands, Belgium and Switzerland are good places for buying discount air tickets. In Antwerp, WATS has been recommended. In Zurich try SOF Travel and Sindbad. In Geneva try Stohl Travel. In the Netherlands, NBBS is a reputable agency.

CAAC has flights between Beijing and Belgrade, Bucharest, Frankfurt, London, Moscow, Paris, Athens and Zurich. Russia's Aeroflot and Romania's Tarom often have cheap air fares, but also a poor safety record and are known for losing checked luggage.

To/From the USA

There are some very good open tickets which remain valid for six months or one year (opt for the latter unless you're sure) without locking you into any fixed dates of departure. For example, there are cheap tickets between the US west coast and Hong Kong with stopovers in Japan, Korea and Taiwan for very little extra money – the departure dates can be changed and you have one year to complete the journey. However, be careful during the peak season (summer and Chinese New Year) because seats will be hard to come by unless reserved months in advance.

Usually, and not surprisingly, the cheapest fares to China are offered by ethnic Chinese. San Francisco is the bucket shop capital of America, though some good deals can be found in Los Angeles, New York and other cities. Bucket shops can be found through the Yellow Pages or the major daily newspapers. Those listed in both Roman and Chinese scripts are usually discounters. A more direct way is to wander around San Francisco's Chinatown where most of the shops are – especially in the Clay St and Waverly Place area. Many of these are staffed by recent arrivals from Hong Kong and Taiwan who speak little English. Inquiries are best made in person and be sure to compare prices, because cheating is not unknown.

It's not advisable to send money (even cheques) through the post unless the agent is very well-established. Some travellers have reported being ripped off by fly-by-night mail-order ticket agents.

Council Travel is the largest student travel organisation, and though you don't have to be a student to use it, it does have specially discounted student tickets. Council Travel has an extensive network in all major US cities and is listed in the telephone book.

One of the cheapest and most reliable travel agents on the west coast is Overseas Tours (☎ (800) 323 8777 in California, (800) 227 5988 elsewhere), 475 El Camino Real, Room 206, Millbrae, CA 94030. Another good agent is Gateway Travel (☎ (214) 960 2000, (800) 441 1183), 4201 Spring Valley Rd, Suite 104, Dallas, TX 75244; they seem to be reliable for mail-order tickets.

Northwest and United airlines both fly to Beijing, and Northwest offers the most generous frequent flyer programme. It's worth knowing that both airlines sell open return tickets that are valid for only six months rather than one year – no problem for most travellers, but be sure that suits your schedule.

One-way trips usually cost 35% less than a round trip. From Hong Kong, one-way fares to the American west coast start from about US$350 (with APEX restrictions). Return APEX tickets begin at US$640. APEX fares to New York start from US$460 one way, US$630 return.

For direct flights from the USA to China the general

route is from San Francisco (with connections from New York, Los Angeles and Vancouver in Canada) to Tokyo, then Beijing, Shanghai or several other cities in China. It's entirely possible to go through to Beijing and then pick up the return flight in Shanghai. Tickets from the USA directly to China will cost around US$200 to US$300 more than tickets to Hong Kong, even though the flying distance is actually shorter.

To/From Canada

Travel CUTS is Canada's national student travel agency and has offices in Vancouver, Victoria, Edmonton, Saskatoon, Toronto, Ottawa, Montreal and Halifax. You don't have to be a student to use their services.

Getting discount tickets in Canada is much the same as in the USA. Go to the travel agents and shop around until you find a good deal. In Vancouver try Kowloon Travel, Westcan Treks and Travel CUTS.

In general, air fares from Vancouver to Hong Kong or China will cost about 5% to 10% more than tickets from the US west coast.

In Canada, departure taxes are included in the original price of the ticket and there is no additional charge at the airport.

Besides numerous flights to Hong Kong, CAAC has two flights weekly which originate in Toronto, then fly onward to Vancouver, Shanghai and Beijing (in that order).

To/From Singapore

There are heaps of direct flights between Singapore and Hong Kong, but you'll have to change to a CAAC or Dragonair flight to Beijing. Good places for buying cheap air tickets in Singapore are Airmaster Travel Centre and STA Travel. Other agents advertise in the *Straits Times* classifieds.

To/From Thailand

Bangkok is one of Asia's hot spots when it comes to finding bargain basement prices on air tickets.

There is a twice-weekly flight from Beijing to Bangkok via Canton (you can pick up the flight in Canton too), but it's not cheap at 9100 Baht one way. There is also a very popular flight from Kunming to Bangkok via Chiang Mai on Thai Airways, and from there you can pick up a domestic flight to Beijing.

To/From Malaysia

Penang is one of the cheapest places in the world to purchase air tickets. CAAC has direct (but expensive!) flights from Penang to Canton, and you'd have to change flights for Beijing. You'll do better by flying to Hong Kong first.

To/From Pakistan

CAAC has direct flights from Beijing to Karachi three times weekly.

To/From Turkey

There is a once-weekly flight between Beijing and Istanbul, stopping at Ürümqi en route. This ticket is outrageously expensive if bought in China (over US$1000), but travel agents in Istanbul can give generous discounts.

To/From Myanmar (Burma)

There is a once-weekly flight from Beijing to Rangoon with a stopover in Kunming. You can pick up the flight in Kunming too, but must have a visa for Myanmar – available in Beijing, not Kunming. You can stay in Myanmar for only two weeks and usually have to have an air ticket out of the country before they'll issue a visa.

To/From Japan

CAAC has several flights a week from Beijing to Tokyo and Osaka, via Shanghai. Japan Airlines (JAL) flies from Beijing and Shanghai to Tokyo, Osaka and Nagasaki. There are flights between Dalian and Fukuoka/Tokyo on All Nippon Airways.

Chinese visas obtained in Japan are outrageously expensive – US$80 to US$120 depending on which agent you use.

To/From South Korea

There are as yet no flights directly between Beijing and Seoul, so you have to fly into Tianjin. Tickets are available on CAAC and Asiana Airlines. The one-way fare is about US$300 and the flight takes three hours because the plane must go via Shanghai. The reasons for the ridiculous route are political: CAAC has been trying to bully Korea for a monopoly on the lucrative Beijing to Seoul route but the Koreans aren't buying it.

Discounted air tickets are available in Seoul from Joy Travel on the 9th Floor of the building behind City Hall (adjacent to the building housing UTS).

The Chinese visa office in Seoul is *not* in the Chinese Embassy, but is on the third floor of a building on Mugyo-dong, also behind City Hall. The service is lousy; it takes a week to get a visa valid for only 20 days, and the cost is US$20.

In Beijing, there is a shuttle bus costing Y110 which connects the Asiana Airlines office in the Jianguo Hotel with the airport at Tianjin; book in advance.

To/From North Korea

If you can get a visa for North Korea (a big *if*), there is a weekly flight between Beijing and Pyongyang for US$110. Getting a seat should be no problem, since the planes are mostly empty.

To/From the Philippines

CAAC has a twice-weekly flight from Beijing to Manila.

To/From Russia

Any air ticket you buy in Russia is likely to be expensive. You're not paying for fine service, you're paying for the lack of competition. Aeroflot, the only Russian airline, is well-known for frequent cancellations, high prices, poor safety and lost or stolen luggage.

A direct Moscow to Beijing flight costs US$1200, and foreigners are required to pay in dollars even for domestic flights within Russia – forget any rumours you've heard about cheap rouble-denominated tickets. Nevertheless, there are a couple of tricks for reducing the cost significantly. One of the best ways is to take a domestic flight from Moscow to the Siberian city of Irkutsk, then fly internationally from Irkutsk to Shenyang in northeast China. The combined Moscow-Irkutsk-Shenyang ticket costs US$495. From Shenyang, you can take a domestic flight to Beijing on CAAC for Y220. Taking this route may be slower and less convenient, but the saving of over US$700 is a powerful incentive.

To/From Vietnam

The Beijing to Hanoi flight on China Southern Airlines now stops at Nanning (capital of China's Guangxi Province) en route, and you can board or exit the plane there. Unfortunately, this flight is a favourite with traders ('smugglers' as far as the authorities are concerned). This not only makes it difficult to get a ticket, but travellers arriving in Hanoi on this flight have reported vigorous baggage searches and numerous hassles with Customs.

Domestic Flights

Foreigners pay a surcharge of 75% on top of the fare charged to local Chinese people, but if you're a student or foreign expert with a legitimate residence permit, this can be waived. If you do somehow happen to score the Chinese price and it's discovered, your ticket will be confiscated and no refund given. Children over 12 years are charged the adult fare.

On domestic flights, if you cancel 24 hours before departure you lose 10% of the fare; if you cancel between two and 24 hours before the flight you lose 20%; and if you cancel less than two hours before the flight you lose 30%. If you don't show up for a domestic flight, you are entitled to a refund of 50%.

Service is generally mediocre on domestic flights, with the food being a frequent source of complaint. A typical meal consists of a little bag of sweets with a keyring thrown in as a souvenir, which almost justifies the 75% tourist surcharge. CAAC's safety record is also not a good one.

In theory, you can reserve seats without paying for them. In practice, this doesn't always work. The staff at some booking offices will hold a seat for more than a week, while other offices will only hold a seat for a few hours so you can run to the bank and change money. Until you've actually paid for and received your ticket, nothing can be guaranteed. On some routes, competition for seats is keen and people with connections can often jump the queue. Stand-by tickets do exist, a fact worth knowing about if you're desperate.

More and more booking offices have been computerised over recent years. These offices allow you to purchase a ticket to or from any other destination on the computer reservation system. If the city you want to fly from is not on the system, you'll have to go there first and buy the ticket in person.

Airline Offices

Dragonair
    1st Floor, L107, World Trade Tower, 1 Jianguomenwai (☎ 505 4343; fax 505 4347)
Aeroflot
    Hotel Beijing-Toronto, Jianguomenwai (☎ 500 2412)

Air France
    2716 China World Trade Centre, 1 Jianguomenwai
    (☎ 505 1818)
Alitalia
    Room 139, Jianguo Hotel, 5 Jianguomenwai (☎ 500 2233
    ext 139)
All Nippon Airways
    Room 1510, China World Trade Centre, 1 Jianguomenwai
    (☎ 505 3311)
Asiana Airlines
    Room 134, Jianguo Hotel, 5 Jianguomenwai (☎ 500 2233
    ext 134)
British Airways
    Room 210, 2nd Floor, SCITE Tower, 22 Jianguomenwai
    (☎ 512 4070)
Canadian Airlines
    Room 135, Jianguo Hotel, 5 Jianguomenwai (☎ 500 3 950)
Finnair
    SCITE Tower, 22 Jianguomenwai (☎ 512 7180)
Iran Air
    Room 701, CITIC Building, 19 Jianguomenwai
    (☎ 512 4940)
JAL Japan Airlines
    Ground Floor, Changfugong Office Building, Hotel New
    Otani, 26A Jianguomenwai (☎ 513 0888)
JAT Yugoslav Airlines
    Room 414, Kunlun Hotel, 2 Xinyuan Nanlu (☎ 500 3388
    ext 414)
LOT Polish Airlines
    Room 102, West Wing Office Block, China World Trade
    Centre, 1 Jianguomenwai (☎ 505 0136)
Lufthansa
    Lufthansa Centre, 50 Liangmaqiao Lu (☎ 465 4488)
MIAT Mongolian Airlines
    CITIC Building, 19 Jianguomenwai (☎ 500 2255)
Malaysian Airline System
    Lot 115A/B Level One, West Wing Office Block, China
    World Trade Centre, 1 Jianguomenwai (☎ 505 2681)
Northwest Airlines
    Room 104, China World Trade Centre, 1 Jianguomenwai
    (☎ 505 3505)
Pakistan International
    Room 106, China World Trade Centre, 1 Jianguomenwai
    (☎ 505 1681)
Philippine Airlines
    12-53 Jianguomenwai (☎ 532 3992)
Qantas
    5th Floor, Hotel Beijing-Toronto, 3 Jianguomenwai
    (☎ 500 2235)
Romanian Air Transport
    Room 109, Jianguo Hotel, 5 Jianguomenwai (☎ 500 2233
    ext 109)
SAS-Scandinavian Airlines
    18th Floor, SCITE Tower, 22 Jianguomenwai (☎ 512 0575)

Singapore Airlines
  Room 109, China World Trade Centre, 1 Jianguomenwai
  (☎ 505 2233)
Swissair
  Room 201, SCITE Tower, 22 Jianguomenwai (☎ 512 3555)
Thai International
  Room 207, SCITE Tower, 22 Jianguomenwai (☎ 512 3881)
United Airlines
  Room 204, SCITE Tower, 22 Jianguomenwai (☎ 512 8888)

Baggage Allowance
On both international and domestic flights in China the
free-baggage allowance for an adult passenger is 20 kg
in economy class and 30 kg in 1st class. You are also
allowed five kg of hand luggage, though this is rarely
weighed.

Departure Tax
If leaving China by air, the departure tax is Y60. Domestic departure tax is Y15. You must pay in FEC unless you
can produce a magic student card.

SEA
While Beijing is not on the ocean, there is a seaport 2½
hours away by train at Tanggu (adjacent to Tianjin).

To/From Japan
Passenger ships ply the route from Kobe to Tanggu.
Departures from Kobe are every Thursday at noon,
arriving in Tanggu the next day. Economy/1st class
tickets cost US$247/333. The food on this boat gets poor
reviews so bring a few emergency munchies. Tickets can
be bought in Tianjin from the shipping office (☎ 312243)
at 89 Munan Dao, Heping District. In Kobe, the office is
at the port (☎ 321 5791).

To/From Korea
There is also a twice-weekly boat running between the
South Korean port of Inchon and Tanggu. This costs
US$110 in economy class.
  The Inchon International Ferry Terminal is the next to
last stop on the Inchon to Seoul commuter train (red
subway line from downtown). The train journey takes
one hour and from the station it's either a long walk or
short taxi ride to the terminal. You must arrive at the
terminal at least one hour before departure or you won't

be allowed to board. The boat arrives in Tanggu at 7 pm, and given the high cost of accommodation in that city you'd be wise to hop on the first train to Beijing if you're on a budget.

In Seoul, tickets can be bought from the Universal Travel Service (UTS) behind City Hall, just near the Seoul City Tourist Information Centre.

LAND

Bus

There are no international buses serving Beijing, but there are plenty of long-distance domestic buses. The advantage buses have over the train (besides cost) is that it's easier to get a seat on buses. In general, arriving in Beijing by bus is easier than departing mainly because it's very confusing figuring out which bus station has the bus you need.

The basic rule is that long-distance bus stations are on the perimeter of the city in the direction you want to go. The four major ones are at Dongzhimen (north-east), Haihutun (south), Beijiao (north – also called Deshengmen) and Majuan (east). In addition, there is a tiny bus station in the car park in front of Beijing railway station, and this is where you catch buses to Tianjin and the Great Wall at Badaling. Another tiny bus station is in the car park of the Workers' Stadium; this is mainly geared towards buses for destinations within Beijing municipality (like Miyun Reservoir).

One of the more useful stations is Haihutun on the south side of Beijing (shown on Map No 1 on the inside front cover of this book). It's at the intersection of Nansanhuan Zhonglu (the southern part of the third ring road) and Nanyuan Lu (which is what Qianmen Dajie is called in the far south of town). Long-distance buses from here head to cities such as Qingdao and Shanghai.

Beijiao station, also shown on Map No 1, is on the north side of the city. It's one km north of the second ring road on Deshengmenwai Dajie, and is often referred to as 'Deshengmen station'. Some long-distance buses depart from here. Otherwise, you might need to take bus No 345 from Deshengmen to the terminus (Changping) from where you can get other long-distance buses.

International Train

The Trans-Siberian Railway connects Europe to Asia, and has proven to be a popular route.

There is some confusion of terms here – there are, in fact, three railways. The 'true' Trans-Siberian line runs from Moscow to the eastern Siberian port of Nakhodka, from where one can catch a boat to Japan. There is also the Trans-Manchurian line which crosses the Russia-China border at Zabaikalsk-Manzhouli, connecting Beijing and Moscow but bypassing Mongolia. The Trans-Mongolian line connects Beijing to Moscow, passing through the Mongolian capital city, Ulaan Baatar.

Most readers of this book are not interested in the first option since it excludes China, so your decision is between the Trans-Manchurian or Trans-Mongolian. The Trans-Mongolian is marginally faster but requires you to purchase an additional visa and endure another border crossing. You get to see the Mongolian country-side as compensation.

There are different classes but all are acceptably comfortable. In deluxe class there are two beds per cabin while economy class has four beds.

Which direction you go makes a difference in cost and travelling time. The trains from Beijing take 1½ days to reach Ulaan Baatar, and Ulaan Baatar to Moscow is another four days.

There are major delays (six to 10 hours) at both the China/Mongolia and Mongolia/Russia borders. The delays are due to rigorous Customs inspection of all the freight being carried by traders/smugglers. Those holding passports from Western countries typically sail right through Customs without their bags even being opened, which is one reason why people on the train will approach you and ask if you'll carry some of their luggage across the border. During this time, you can get off the train and wander around the station, which is just as well since the toilets on the train are locked during the whole inspection procedure. You will not have your passport at this time, because the authorities take it away for stamping. When it is returned, inspect it closely – sometimes they make errors, such as cancelling return visas for China.

On the Chinese side of the Russian or Mongolian border, about two hours are spent changing the bogies (undercarriage wheels). This is necessary because Russia, Mongolia and all former East Bloc countries use a wider rail gauge than China and the rest of the world. The reason has to do with security; it seems the Russians feared an invasion by train.

Ticketing Hassles The international trains are very popular, so popular that it's hard to book this trip anytime except during winter. Travel agents in Europe say that it's even difficult to get an October booking in April! It's best to plan ahead as far as possible if you want to take this train.

Tickets – From Europe
Travel Service Asia (☎ 07371-4963, fax 07371-4769), Kirchberg 15, 7948 Dürmentingen, Germany, is highly recommended for low prices and good service. These people have been on the train themselves and have travelled to Mongolia, so they know what they're talking about.

In the UK, one of the experts in budget train travel is Regent Holidays (UK) Ltd (☎ (0272) 211 711, telex 444606, fax (0272) 254 866), 15 John St, Bristol BS1 2HR. Another agency geared towards budget travellers is Progressive Tours (☎ (071) 262 1676), 12 Porchester Place, Connaught Square, London W2 2BS.

Several travellers have recommended Scandinavian Student Travel Service (SSTS), 117 Hauchsvej, 1825 Copenhagen V, Denmark. This organisation has branch offices in Europe and North America and provides a range of basic tours for student or budget travellers, mostly during summer.

Tickets – From China
In theory, the cheapest place to buy a ticket is at the office of China International Travel Service (CITS) in the Beijing International Hotel. The problem with this theory is that CITS doesn't make advance reservations by phone, fax or through their Hong Kong office. In other words, you first must go to Beijing and fight like everyone else for a ticket, with a good chance that the next seat available will be three months later. There are no queues at the CITS office, just an unruly mob. A Beijing to Moscow ticket (if you can get one) costs US$175. Contrary to what the CITS brochures say, Trans-Siberian tickets bought from Beijing CITS are basically non-refundable – after a vociferous argument, you might get back 20% of the purchase price if you're lucky.

Your other alternative is to buy from a private travel agent. This will always be more expensive than CITS because the agents must purchase their tickets from CITS too. However, it may well work out cheaper to go through a travel agent, since hanging around Beijing for three months just to buy a ticket will also cost money. Almost all of these agents are based in Hong Kong.

The best organised of the Trans-Siberian ticket vendors is Monkey Business, officially known as Moonsky Star (☎ 723 1376, fax 723 6653), 4th Floor, Block

E, Flat 6, Chungking Mansions, 30 Nathan Rd, Tsimshatsui, Kowloon. Monkey Business also maintains an information office in Beijing at the Qiaoyuan Hotel (new building), room 716 (☎ 301 2244 ext 716), but it's best to book through their Hong Kong office as far in advance as possible. A booking can be done by telephone or fax and a deposit can be wired to them. One advantage of booking through them is that they keep all their passengers in a group (for mutual protection against theft). Monkey Business can also arrange visas and stopover tours to Mongolia and Irkutsk (Siberia).

You can get a very similar deal from Phoenix Services (☎ 722 7378) in Room B, 6th Floor, Milton Mansion, 96 Nathan Rd, Tsimshatsui, Kowloon.

Another Hong Kong agent selling Trans-Mongolian tickets is Time Travel (☎ 366 6222, fax 739 5413), 16th Floor, Block A, Chungking Mansions, 30 Nathan Rd, Tsimshatsui, Kowloon. Their current cheapest price for a Beijing to Moscow ticket is US$245. Their price is competitive but they offer no services beyond the ticket and cannot organise visas.

You can organise tickets and visas through Wallem Travel (☎ 528 6514), 46th Floor, Hopewell Centre, 183 Queen's Rd East, Wanchai, Hong Kong. However, this place is more into booking pricey tours than selling train tickets.

Black-market Tickets Once upon a time, black-market tickets were so common that it seemed like everyone on the train had one. Indeed, you were almost a fool not to buy one. The way it worked was that people with connections would go to Budapest and buy Beijing to Moscow tickets in bulk for around US$50 a piece, then take the tickets to Beijing and sell them for about US$150. A nice little business, while it lasted.

Those days are gone. Eastern European countries no longer sell tickets for ridiculously cheap subsidised prices. Not that the black market has disappeared; the problem is that the black-market scene has turned ugly. Rather than being cheaper, black-market tickets are now more expensive than tickets you could buy yourself. It's simply the law of supply and demand. In Moscow and Beijing, local thugs buy up big blocks of tickets and sell them at whatever price the market will bear. In order for anyone to be able to buy up so many tickets, connections on the inside are needed, which requires the payment of considerable bribes.

If you attempt to buy a ticket from CITS, it's likely you'll be asked to 'come back tomorrow'. When you come back, you'll probably be told again to 'come back tomorrow'. This may continue for five days or so, at the end of which time you *might* get a ticket, but probably not. If you do, you'll be told that somebody 'cancelled' and that's why the ticket is suddenly available. This is nonsense – nobody cancels because CITS doesn't refund cancelled tickets. What happens is that CITS sells the tickets out the back door to black marketeers, and if any remain unsold, the black marketeers return them on the very last day and CITS tries to flog them off to the hopeful 'come back tomorrow' people.

There is also a problem with cheaper Russian tickets partially denominated in roubles, which are valid for Russian passport holders only. Black marketeers sell these Russian tickets to gullible foreigners who then find they can't use them. There has also been a problem with forged tickets. Once you try to get on the train and realise that your ticket is worthless, just try filing a complaint with your local black marketeer.

Black marketeers hang out around the CITS booking office in Beijing and will hustle any likely-looking customers. You'd be wise to ignore them.

Needs, Problems & Precautions Bring plenty of US dollars cash in small denominations for the journey, because only in China can you readily use the local currency. In China, food is plentiful and readily available from both the train's dining car and vendors in railway stations. In both Russia and Mongolia, food quality is poorer, but meals are available on the train. Once you get off the train it's a different story. Food can be extremely difficult to buy in both Russia and Mongolia so if you don't want to starve, bring plenty of munchies like biscuits, instant noodles, chocolate and fruit. No alcohol is sold on the Russian and Mongolian trains, but a limited selection of booze can be bought in the Chinese dining car. Except for beer, most Chinese alcohol tastes like low-grade jet fuel and you'd be wise to purchase your own stash before boarding the train.

Showers are only available in the deluxe carriages. In economy class, there is a washroom. You can manage a bath with a sponge but it's best to bring a large metal cup (available in most Chinese railway stations) and use it as a scoop to pour water over yourself from the washbasin. The metal cup is also ideal for making coffee, tea and instant soup. Hot water is available on the trains.

There is much theft on the train, so never leave your luggage unattended, even if the compartment is locked. Make sure at least one person stays in the compartment while the others go to the dining car. A lot of theft is being committed by Russian gangs who have master keys to the compartments, so don't assume that a 'foreign face' means honesty.

Mongolians, Russians and Polish passengers boarding the train will usually have mountains of luggage, which they will often try to put into your compartment. If there is even one Mongolian, Russian or Polish person staying in your compartment you're going to have a difficult time preventing this. If you're all foreigners, stand up for your rights aggressively, because if you don't you will truly be buried in bags. Many people riding the train are bringing back goods to sell, and they don't mind using your compartment as their cargo bin. If they get hassled by Customs at the border (very likely) they'll say the bags belong to you. These arguments over where would-be traders put their luggage is one of the worst aspects of making this journey.

The Chinese have now 'cracked down' and a luggage limit of 35 kg per passenger is being enforced. There are scales at the railway station and it's likely your luggage will be weighed. However, the new rules haven't done much to cut down on the cargo, because a few dollars in the right pocket can perform well-known miracles. The weight limits might better be thought of as 'guidelines'.

It's important to realise that food in the dining car is priced in local currency. This is true even in Mongolia or Russia. Many foreigners have the mistaken impression that they must pay in US dollars. The railway staff will gladly accept your dollars instead of roubles or togrogs at some ridiculous exchange rate, which means you'll be paying many times the real price. There are black-market moneychangers at border railway stations, but all the usual dangers of black-market exchanges apply.

Books A popular book about this journey is the *Trans-Siberian Handbook* (Trailblazer Publications) by Bryn Thomas, in paperback only and distributed through Roger Lascelles in the UK.

Russian Visa If you take the train through Russia, you have a choice between getting a transit visa or a tourist visa. There is a very big difference between the two. Transit visas are valid for a maximum of 10 days and tourist visas are required if the journey is broken. In practice, you can stay in Moscow for three days on a transit visa and apply for an extension when you arrive. This only really works if you're going from Beijing to Moscow rather than the other way; otherwise you'll miss your train to Beijing. Trying to extend a tourist visa is much more expensive. The hotel 'service bureau' will do it for you through Intourist, but only with expensive hotel bookings.

With a tourist visa, you can stay in Russia much longer, but you will pay heavily for the privilege. All hotels must be booked through Intourist in advance of arrival. The attitude of Intourist is to milk travellers for every cent they can get (who said they aren't capitalists?). For a two-star hotel, expect to pay around US$65 outside of Moscow, and US$135 a day in Moscow. The hotel bookings must be confirmed by telex (which you will also have to pay for) and the whole bureaucratic procedure takes about three weeks. On a transit visa, you can sleep in the station or in one of the rapidly proliferating cheap private hostels.

Before you can get a transit visa, you must have a ticket in hand or a ticket voucher. A transit visa can be issued the same day or take two to five days depending on how much you pay. There are two fees you must pay: a visa application fee and a bizarre 'consular fee' for certain nationalities. Visa application fees are US$18 for a visa issued in five days; US$27 if issued in three days; and US$55 if issued the same day. The consular fee varies according to which passport you hold; free for Aussies, Kiwis, Canadians, Brits and Americans, but Swiss citizens pay US$50, it's US$35 for the Dutch and Austrians have the honor of paying US$80. Three photos are required. The embassy does not keep your passport, so you are free to travel while your application is being processed. Someone can apply for the visa on your behalf and use a photocopy of your passport (all relevant pages must be included). If you want to change an already-issued transit visa, this will cost you US$18. Reasons for changing could be if you want go on a different date or change the final destination (Budapest instead of Berlin, for example). Russian embassies are closed during all Russian public holidays: New Year's Day (1 January), Women's Day (8 March), Labour Day (1 & 2 May), Victory Day (9 May), Constitution Day (7 October), and October Revolution (7 & 8 November).

In Beijing, the Russian Embassy (☎ 532 2051, 532 1267) is at Beizhongjie 4, just off Dongzhimen and west of the Sanlitun Embassy Compound. Hours are Monday to Friday from 9 am until noon. You can avoid the long queues at the Beijing Embassy if you apply at the Russian Consulate (☎ 324 2682) in Shanghai, 20 Huangpu Lu, opposite the Pujiang Hotel. However, their opening hours are brief: Tuesday and Thursday from 10 am until 12.30 pm.

Mongolian Visa The Mongolian Embassy in Beijing

is open all day, but the visa section keeps short hours –
only on Monday, Tuesday, Thursday and Friday from
8.30 am to 11.30 am. They close for all Mongolian holidays, and they shut down completely for the entire week
of National Day (Naadam), which officially falls on 11-13
July.

Visas cost US$22 (US$28 for UK citizens) if picked up
the next day, or US$26 (US$36 for UK citizens) for same-
day delivery; they will accept payment in FEC. Some
nationalities can get visas for free (India, Finland etc).
One photo is required for a tourist visa but none is
needed for a transit visa. In the UK, the Mongolian
Embassy (☎ (071) 937 0150, 937 5235) is at 7 Kensington
Court, London W85 DL.

It's easy enough to get a transit visa for Mongolia, but
obtaining a tourist visa requires the same bureaucratic
somersaults as are required for getting a Russian tourist
visa.

Polish Visa Most travellers between Western Europe
and Moscow go via Poland, though there are alternative
routes via Finland or Hungary. A Polish visa is not
needed by nationals of Austria, Belgium, Denmark,
Finland, France, Germany, the Netherlands, Italy, Lux-
embourg, Malta, Norway, Sweden, Switzerland and the
USA. Polish visas are required for Australians, British
and New Zealanders, and cost US$32. You get a discount
on these fees if you have a student (ISIC) card. These
prices are for transit visas; tourist visas cost even more.
Two photos are needed.

Domestic Train

China's extensive rail network covers every province
except Tibet, and service is generally efficient. The main
problem is ticketing hassles, particularly if you want
something more comfortable than the lowest class
known as 'hard-seat'.

Just about all railway stations have left-luggage
rooms (jìcún chù) where you can safely dump your bags
for a few RMB.

Hard-Seat Except on the trains which serve some of
the branch or more obscure lines, hard-seat is not in fact
hard but is padded. But it's hard on your sanity – it tends
to be spectacularly dirty, noisy and smokey, and you'll
get little sleep in the upright seats.

Since hard-seat is the only thing the locals can afford
it's packed to the gills. If you're lucky, you'll get a ticket
with an assigned seat number, but in many cases you'll

have no seat reservation and must battle for a seat or piece of floor space with 10,000 other hopefuls.

Hard-seat is survivable for a day trip; some foreigners can't take more than five hours of it, while others have a threshold of 12 hours or even longer. A few brave, penniless souls have even been known to travel *long-distance* this way – some roll out a mat on the floor under the seats and go to sleep on top of the peanut shells, chicken bones and spittle.

You may have to travel hard-seat even if you're willing to pay more for a higher class. The reason is that hard-seat tickets are relatively easy to obtain.

Hard-Sleeper These are very comfortable and only a fixed number of people are allowed in the sleeper carriage. The carriage is made up of doorless compartments with half a dozen bunks in three tiers, and sheets, pillows and blankets are provided. It does very nicely as an overnight hotel. The best bunk to get is a middle one since the lower one is invaded by all and sundry who use it as a seat during the day, while the top one has little headroom. The worst possible bunks are the top ones at either end of the carriage or right in the middle; they've right up against the speakers and you'll get a rude shock in the morning at about 6 am. Lights and speakers in hard-sleeper go out at around 9.30 to 10 pm.

Hard-sleeper tickets are the most difficult of all to buy; you almost always need to buy these far in advance.

Soft-Seat On shorter journeys (such as Beijing to Tianjin) some trains have soft-seat carriages. The seats are comfortable and overcrowding is not permitted. Smoking is prohibited, a significant advantage unless you enjoy asphyxiation. If you want to smoke in the soft-seat section, you can do so only by going out into the corridor between cars. Soft-seats cost about the same as hard-sleeper and are well worth it. Unfortunately, soft-seat cars are a rarity.

Soft-Sleeper Luxury. Softies get the works with four comfortable bunks in a closed compartment – complete with straps to stop the top fatso from falling off in the middle of the night, wood panelling, potted plants, lace curtains, teacup set, clean washrooms, carpets (so no spitting), and often air-conditioning. As for those speakers, not only do you have a volume control, you can turn the bloody things off! Soft-sleeper costs twice as much as hard-sleeper, and almost the same price as flying (on some routes even *more* than flying!). It's relatively easy to get soft-sleeper because few Chinese can afford it. However, improvements in living standards has made it more difficult to obtain soft-sleeper tickets at short notice.

Dining Car For the desperate, you may be allowed to sleep in the dining car after it closes for meals. There is usually a charge for this – Y15 is typical. It's not terribly comfortable but less horrible than hard-seat.

Platform Tickets An alternative to all the above is not to bother with a ticket at all and simply walk on to the train. To do this, you need to buy a platform ticket *(zhàntái piào)*. These are available from the station's information booth for a few jiao. You then buy your ticket on the train. This method is usually more hassle than it's worth, but may be necessary if you arrive at the station without enough time to get your ticket.

Black-market Tickets These certainly exist and many travellers have made use of them. The way it works is that some local Chinese buy up hard-sleepers on the most popular lines (which frequently sell out), then sell these tickets to travellers (both Chinese and foreigners) at a profit. The black marketeers usually stand outside the station hawking their tickets. This is supposedly illegal, but they often pay off the local police.

Since foreigners have to pay double anyway, black-market tickets can be a bargain even if they cost more than the usual Chinese price. However, be sure you know just what you're looking for as far as a legitimate ticket goes! Otherwise, you could be buying a worthless piece of cardboard, or a hard-seat when you expected a hard-sleeper. Ticket counterfeiting has become a new growth-industry in China.

Upgrading If you get on the train with an unreserved seating ticket, you can seek out the conductor and upgrade *(bǔpiào)* yourself to a hard-sleeper, soft-seat or soft-sleeper if there are any available. It is rare that you will be charged foreigners' prices or even asked to pay FEC for this service, and though there are risks involved (no sleepers left) it is sometimes the only way to get a sleeper or even a seat.

If the sleeper carriages are full then you may have to wait until someone gets off. That sleeper may only be available to you until the next major station which is allowed to issue sleepers, but you may be able to get several hours of sleep. The sleeper price will be calculated for the distance that you used it for.

Over 95% of foreigners arriving or departing by train do so at the Beijing main railway station *(běijīng huǒchē zhàn)*. There are also two other stations of significance in the city, Yongdingmen (the south railway station) and Xizhimen (the north railway station). There are plans on the drawing board to build an as-yet-unnamed west railway station.

There is a Foreigners' Ticketing Office at the main Beijing railway station. Refer to Central Beijing Map No 10 at the end of the book to find the location of the railway station. Enter the station and it's to the rear and left side; you'll see a small sign in English saying 'International Passenger Booking Office'. The ticketing office is inside the foreigners' waiting room. It's open daily, from 5.30 to 7.30 am, 8 am to 5.30 pm and 7 pm to 12.30 am. At least those are the official times, but foreigners have often found the staff unwilling to sell tickets in the early morning. Before you can buy a ticket, you must first fill out a reservation slip *(dēngjì dān)* which you get from the staff at window No 1. Return to window No 1 with the filled-in form, and if anything is available, you'll be given a confirmation slip which you take to window Nos 2 or 3 to pick up the ticket.

Whether or not you get a ticket here is potluck. Sometimes the staff are friendly and helpful, at other times downright hostile. Tickets can be booked several days in advance. Your chances of getting a sleeper (hard or soft) are good so long as you book ahead.

The Foreigners' Ticketing Office sometimes has English timetables for sale. There is a comfortable waiting lounge, and lockers are available here although these are often full, in which case you'll have to use the left-luggage rooms outside the station (head out of the station and car park, then to the right).

Getting a Chinese person to buy your ticket from the regular ticket windows involves major tactical difficulties, the main one being that the ticket windows, some two dozen of them, can't be seen half the time for the crowds!

Outside Beijing, obtaining tickets is not so straightforward. Shanghai and a few other cities also have booking offices for foreigners, but in many cases your only hope of obtaining a sleeper is to seek the assistance of a travel agent. Most hotels employ an in-house travel agent to book train tickets, so inquire at the reception desk. If the hotel won't do this, your alternatives are

CITS, CTS and CYTS. You must give your passport to the travel agents when they go to buy your ticket, but an old expired passport will do just fine. If none of the foregoing works, go to the railway station and fight it out yourself.

If you have a sleeper ticket the carriage attendant will take it from you and give you a metal or plastic chit, then when your destination is close he or she will swap it back and give you the original ticket. Keep your ticket until you get through the barriers at the other end, as you'll need to show it there.

Timetables There are paperback railway timetables in both Chinese and English. The English timetables are hard to find in Beijing, so try to get a copy in Hong Kong at Swindon's Bookstore or the Joint Publishing Company. The English name is simply *China Railway Timetable*.

No matter where you get them, the timetables are so excruciatingly detailed that it's a drag working your way through them. Even the Chinese complain about this. Thinner versions listing the major trains can sometimes be bought from hawkers outside the railway stations.

Costs The most important thing to remember is the double-pricing system on Chinese trains. Most foreigners are required to pay 100% more than PRC people for their train tickets. Foreign students and foreign experts can pay the Chinese price with the proper credentials. All train fares mentioned in this book are standard tourist price.

You can also get a local Chinese person to do it and give them a tip, but exercise caution, because they could get into trouble or they could pocket your money and run away. It's best to have them pay first with their own cash and then reimburse them, though many will not have the cash to do this.

Students are your best bet if you want someone to buy tickets for you. They appreciate any tip you give them and they are usually (but not always) honest.

Most railway workers don't care if you get a Chinese-priced ticket, but some do. If you get on the train with a Chinese-priced ticket the conductor can still charge you the full fare, or you could be stopped at the railway station exit gate at your destination, have your tickets checked and be charged the full fare. In practice, this seldom happens.

TOURS

Are tours worth it to you? Perhaps, but apart from the expense, they tend to screen you from some of the basic realities of China travel. Most people who come back with glowing reports of the PRC never had to travel proletariat class on the trains or battle their way on board a local bus in the whole three days of their stay.

Tours do make everything easy, but that assumes your tour operator gives a damn. There have been negative comments from travellers who have booked through CITS and CTS, but service is *slowly* improving.

A number of travel agents in the West do China tours, but most are forced into some sort of cooperative joint-venture with CITS or other government bodies, which means high prices.

LEAVING BEIJING

In general, there are few hassles on departure. Baggage may be x-rayed even at land crossings but the machines are supposedly 'film-safe'. Antiques or things which look antique could cause hassles with Customs, and it's illegal to carry RMB out of the country. Lest you need to be reminded, most of China's neighbours (including Hong Kong) take a *very* dim view of drugs.

Once you've checked in at Beijing Airport there is nowhere inside to eat anything, just a pathetic coffee bar serving overpriced drinks. If you're hungry, bring some food from outside or be satisfied pigging out on expensive chocolate-covered macadamia nuts from the duty-free shop.

Getting Around

TO/FROM THE AIRPORT

The airport is 25 km from the centre (Forbidden City area) but add another 10 km if you're going to the southern end of town.

For Y8 you can catch the airport shuttle bus from the Aviation Building *(mínháng dàshà)* on Xi Chang'an Jie, Xidan District – this is the location of Air China and China North-West Airlines, but *not* the same place as the CAAC office. Refer to our Central Beijing Map No 10 at the back of the book for its precise location. The bus departs on the opposite side of the street (south side of Xichang'an Jie), not from the car park of the Aviation Building.

At the airport, you catch this shuttle bus in front of the terminal building, and you have to buy the bus ticket from the counter inside the terminal building, not on the bus itself. The bus terminates at the Aviation Building in Xidan, but makes several stops en route. Get off at the second stop (Swissôtel-Hong Kong Macau Centre) if you want to take the subway.

A taxi from the airport to the Forbidden City area costs around Y70, or Y100 to the Qiaoyuan Hotel area in the south side of town.

BUS

Sharpen your elbows, chain your money to your underwear and muster all the patience you can because you'll need it. Overstuffed buses are in vogue in Beijing, and can be particularly nauseating at the height of summer when passengers drip with perspiration. They're cosy in winter if you haven't frozen to the bus stop by the time the trolley arrives, but difficult to exit from. Try the nearest window. Fares are typically two jiao depending on distance, but often it's free because you can't see (let alone reach) the conductor.

There are about 140 bus and trolley routes, which make navigation rather confusing, especially if you can't see out of the window in the first place. Bus maps save the day.

Buses run from around 5 am to 11 pm. One or two-digit bus numbers are city core, 100-series buses are trolleys, and 300-series are suburban lines.

Beijing trolley (RS)

SUBWAY (*dì xià tiě*)

The Underground Dragon is definitely the best way of travelling around. Unlike most other subways the crime rate is low (there is the odd pickpocket), graffiti is non-existent, and messy suicides are said to be rare. Trains can move at up to 70 km/hour, which is the speed of a jaguar compared to the lumbering buses. The subway is also less crowded per sq cm than the buses, and trains run at a frequency of one every few minutes during peak times. The carriages have seats for 60 and standing room for 200. Platform signs are in Chinese and pinyin. The fare is a flat five jiao regardless of distance; like other subways, it loses money. Trains run from 5 am to 11 pm. The subway map, Map No 24, on the inside back cover of this book is a handy guide to the routes and stations.

Circle Line

This 16-km line presently has 18 stations: Beijing Zhan (railway station), Jianguomen, Chaoyangmen, Dongsishitiao, Dongzhimen, Yonghegong, Andingmen, Gulou Dajie, Jishuitan, Xizhimen (the north railway station and zoo), Chegongzhuang, Fuchengmen, Fuxingmen, Changchun Jie, Xuanwumen, Heping Lu, Qianmen and Chongwenmen.

East-West Line

This line has 12 stops and runs from Xidan to Pingguoyuan which is – no, not the capital of North Korea – but a western suburb of Beijing whose name translates as 'Apple Orchard'. It takes 40 minutes to traverse the length of the line. The stops are Xidan, Nanlishilu, Muxudi, Junshibowuguan (Military Museum), Gongzhufen, Wanshoulu, Wukesong, Yuquanlu, Babaoshan, Bajiaocun, Guchenglu and Pingguoyuan. It's a five-minute walk between station B (Nanlishilu) on the East-West Line and station 13 on the Circle Line and there is no direct connection between them.

BICYCLE

The scale of Beijing is suddenly much reduced on a bike, which can also give you a great deal of freedom. Beijing's rush hour can be rather astounding, consisting of a

Bike rental entrepreneur (RS)

roving population of three million plus bicycles – a fact explained by the agony of bus rides.

Bicycles can be hired at the Qiaoyuan Hotel for about Y3 per day. Another good place is the bike shop near the Chongwenmen intersection, on the north side at No 94. The Rainbow Hotel has bikes in top-notch condition but wants a comparatively steep Y20 per day. The renter may demand you leave your passport, but a deposit of about Y100 will usually do.

If pedalling is your thing, you might like to go on the bicycle tour we've planned, which covers several of the main sites and areas of interest in Beijing. It is described in detail in the Things To See & Do chapter, and the route is traced out in Map No 11 which you'll find at the back of the book.

Several shopping areas are closed to cyclists from 6 am to 6 pm; Wangfujing is an important one. Bike parks are everywhere and cost peanuts – compulsory peanuts since your trusty steed can otherwise be towed away. Bike theft is a problem; a cable lock (available from department stores) increases security and is highly recommended.

It's not hard to find picture displays around Beijing exhibiting the gory remains of cyclists who didn't look where they were going and wound up looking like Y3 worth of fried noodles. These displays also give tips on how to avoid accidents and show 're-education classes' for offenders who have had several accidents. To avoid becoming a feature in the next billboard display, take care when you're riding.

Beijing in winter presents special problems, like slippery roads (black ice) and frostbite. The fierce winds during springtime present another challenge – not exactly optimum cycling conditions but if you follow the example of the locals, nothing will deter you.

Dogs – bane of cyclists the world over – are less of a problem in China than elsewhere. This is because Fido is more likely to be stir-fried than menacing cyclists on street corners.

Bringing your own bike to China is not particularly recommended, because local ones are cheap and good enough for all but very long-distance tours. If you plan a long-distance bike tour, this presents special problems, in particular those faceless, cold-hearted figures collectively known as 'the authorities'. Although no law actually prohibits foreigners from riding in the countryside, local PSB officials pretty much make up their own law because they can't stand to see foreigners getting away so cheaply. After all, 'respectable' foreigners only travel by tour bus, taxi or limousine.

CAR

Resident foreigners are allowed to drive their own cars in the capital, and to drive on the Beijing to Tianjin highway. Most are not permitted to drive more than 40 km from the capital without special permission. Chauffeur-driven cars and minibuses can be hired from some of the major hotels, but why not just rent a taxi by the day for less money?

It now seems that private car rental in the capital is going to be permitted. You are restricted on just how far you can drive, so find out the rules before you set out. Several companies are ready to dive into this business; one of the first is called First Car Rental Company (☎ 422 3950).

TAXI

In 1986 there were fewer than 1000 taxis available in the capital so if you wanted one, it had to be booked hours in advance. By 1993, the number of taxis exceeded 40,000 and is still increasing rapidly.

In other words, finding a cab is seldom a problem, though surging demand means that during rush hours you may have to battle it out with the other 10 million plus residents of Beijing. One government brochure claims that 80% of Beijing taxi drivers can speak English. Perhaps they meant 80 drivers, since out of the total 40,000 that would be just about the right percentage. If you don't speak Chinese, bring a map or have your destination written down in characters.

The vehicles usually have a sticker on the window indicating their per-km charge, which varies all the way from Y1 to Y2 with a Y10 minimum. If you don't get one with a meter, be sure to negotiate the fare in advance. When negotiating, you can usually get a cheaper rate if you say in advance, 'I don't need an official receipt' *(wǒ bùbì fāpiào)*. The small yellow micro-buses are usually cheapest. Taxis can be summoned to a location of your choosing or hailed in the streets. They're scarce at certain times, most notably in the rush hour or during the sacred lunch-time siesta.

PEDICAB

Three-wheeled bicycles can accommodate one or two passengers in the back plus the driver up front. These look like a charming and aesthetic way to enjoy travelling around Beijing, but sadly they are not. What ruins

Pedicab drivers (RS)

it is that the drivers are almost universally dishonest. Whatever fare you've agreed on in advance almost always gets multiplied by 10 when you arrive at your destination and the final price is usually several times what a taxi would cost. Unless you enjoy vociferous arguments and near-violent confrontations, this mode of transport is not recommended.

HITCHING

Many people have hitchhiked in China, and some have been amazingly successful. It's not officially sanctioned, so don't bother trying to get permission. The best place to get a lift is on the outskirts of Beijing; hitching can be virtually the only way to reach some of the further places of interest in Beijing municipality.

Hitching in China is rarely free – passengers are expected to offer at least a tip, and some drivers might even ask for an unreasonable amount of money. Try to establish a figure early on in the ride to avoid problems later, as communicating can be difficult if you don't speak Chinese. As far as we know, there is no Chinese signal for hitching, so just try waving down the vehicles. Unless you speak Chinese, you'll need to have where you want to go written down in Chinese characters.

While China is a relatively safe country in which to hitch, bear in mind that hitching invariably carries an element of risk. Exercise caution, and if you're in any doubt as to the intentions of your prospective driver, say no. A lone female would be wise to travel with a male companion.

TOURS

CITS operates a number of high-priced tours to destinations in and around Beijing (Great Wall and Ming Tombs, Y130, including guide and lunch). You can dispense with the guide and food and go for the Chinese tour-bus operators who offer the same tour for Y25.

Typical tours take in the Great Wall and Ming Tombs; Western Hills and Summer Palace; Old Summer Palace and Sleeping Buddha Temple; Tanzhe Temple; Yunshui Caves; Peking Man Site; and Zunhua (Eastern Qing Tombs). Tours further afield to Chengde (three days) and Beidaihe (five days) are possible.

Things to See & Do

HIGHLIGHTS

Beijing has so much worth seeing that it's difficult to know where to begin. Many start with Qianmen, Tiananmen Square and the Forbidden City, followed by a jaunt through nearby Jingshan and Beihai parks. Another busy day could be spent at the Summer Palace and Fragrant Hills. A major excursion out of town is the journey to the Great Wall and nearby Ming Tombs. Those with an extra day may wish to explore Tianjin.

Our maps of Beijing (Map No 1 on the inside front cover) and of Central Beijing and Wangfujing (Map Nos 10 and 12 respectively, at the end of the book) can help you to locate the places of special interest to you and from there plan an itinerary.

Strategies

Sunday and holidays are *not* good times to go sightseeing in Beijing. All places from the Great Wall to the shopping malls look like a phone booth stuffing contest. Crowds are thinner on Monday, but many museums are closed at that time.

Admission Fees

Beijing officials have antagonised foreigners with an avaricious policy regarding the admission fees charged for parks, scenic spots, etc. To understand the new policy, you need to realise that in many parks, museums and other tourist sites (the Forbidden City being a good example) there are numerous sites within the compound, and each one has its own admission gate charging separate fees. The locals have the option of buying a general admission ticket for the compound and then buying separate tickets for each pavilion, or just one high-priced all-inclusive ticket which grants admission to every pavilion. For foreigners, the first option is eliminated; the staff want you to buy the all-inclusive ticket, whether you want it or not. This usually works out to be much more expensive than buying separate tickets,

134

especially if you don't want to visit each and every building, pavilion and chamber.

Even more irritating is that even after you've bought the pricey ticket, a few things are not included so you have to pay even more.

At most (but not all) places it's optional; you can buy the general admission ticket rather than the expensive all-inclusive tourist ticket. This is true for Beihai Park, for example, but at the Summer Palace you don't have the option. At some parks where you have a choice of two tickets, making your wishes known to the staff can be a problem if you don't speak Chinese. Many foreigners become exceedingly upset when they realise they've overpaid by 10 times for a ticket when it wasn't necessary. The bitter arguments that sometimes ensue haven't helped Beijing's image.

It's useful to know the correct vocabulary. The all-inclusive tickets are *tàopiào* in Chinese. The general admission tickets are called 'door tickets' *(ménpiào)* or 'common tickets' *(pǔtōngpiào)*.

SQUARES, GATES & HALLS

Tiananmen Square
(tiān'ānmén guǎngchǎng) 天安门广场

Though it was a gathering place and the location of government offices in the imperial days, the square is Mao's creation, as is Chang'an Jie leading onto it. This is the heart of Beijing, a vast desert of paving and photo booths. Major rallies took place here during the Cultural Revolution when Mao, wearing a Red Guard armband, reviewed parades of up to a million people. In 1976 another million people jammed the square to pay their last respects. In 1989, army tanks and soldiers cut down pro-democracy demonstrators here. Today the square is a place for people to wander and fly decorated kites or balloons for the kiddies. Surrounding or studding the square are a strange mish-mash of monuments past and present: Tiananmen (Gate of Heavenly Peace), the History Museum & Museum of the Revolution, the Great Hall of the People, Qianmen (Front Gate), the Mao Mausoleum and the Monument to the People's Heroes.

If you get up early you can watch the flag-raising ceremony at sunrise, performed by a troop of PLA soldiers drilled to march at precisely 108 paces per minute, 75 cm per pace. The same ceremony in reverse gets performed at sunset, but you can hardly see the soldiers from the throngs gathered to watch.

Tiananmen Gate

(tiân'ânmén) 天安门

Tiananmen, or 'Gate of Heavenly Peace', is a national symbol which pops up on everything from airline tickets to policemen's caps. The gate was built in the 15th century and restored in the 17th. From imperial days it functioned as a rostrum for dealing with or proclaiming to the assembled masses. There are five doors to the gate, and in front of it are seven bridges spanning a stream. Each of these bridges was restricted in its use, and only

Top: Tiananmen (AS)
Bottom: Monument to the People's Heroes (RS)

the emperor could use the central door and bridge. The dominating feature is now the gigantic portrait of Mao, the required backdrop for any photo the Chinese take of themselves at the gate. To the left of the portrait is a slogan, 'Long Live the People's Republic of China' and to the right is another, 'Long Live the Unity of the Peoples of the World'.

You pass through Tiananmen Gate on your way into the Forbidden City (assuming you enter from the south side). There is no fee for walking through the gate, but to go upstairs and look down on the square costs a whopping Y30 for foreigners, Y10 for Chinese. It's hardly worth it, since you can get a similar view of the square from inside Qianmen Gate for a fraction of the price.

Qianmen
(qiánmén) 前门

Qianmen (Front Gate) sits on the south side of Tiananmen Square. Qianmen guarded the wall division between the ancient Inner City and the outer suburban zone, and dates back to the reign of Emperor Yong Le in the 15th century. With the disappearance of the city walls, the gate has had its context removed, but it's still an impressive sight.

Relaxing in a family group (CT)

There are actually two gates – the southern one is called Arrow Tower *(jiàn lóu)* and the rear one is Zhongyang Gate *(zhōngyángmén*, also called *chéng lóu)*. You can go upstairs into Zhongyang Gate, and it's certainly worth the Y2 admission price. There are plans to open the Arrow Tower to visitors, but at the time of writing this it still hadn't happened.

Great Hall of the People
(rénmín dàhuì táng) 人民大会堂

This is the venue of the rubber-stamp legislature, the National People's Congress. It's open to the public when the Congress is not sitting, and to earn some hard currency it's even rented out occasionally to foreigners for conventions! You tramp through the halls of power, many of them named after provinces and regions of China and decorated appropriately. You can see the 5000-seat banquet room and the 10,000-seat auditorium with the familiar red star embedded in a galaxy of lights in the ceiling. The hall was completed over a 10-month period, from 1958 to 1959.

The hall is on the west side of Tiananmen Square and admission costs a mind-boggling Y30.

MONUMENTS & MAUSOLEUMS

Monument to the People's Heroes
(rénmín yīngxióng jìniàn bēi)
人民英雄纪念碑

This monument on the southern end of Tiananmen Square was completed in 1958 and sits on the site of the old Outer Palace Gate. The 36-metre obelisk, made of Qingdao granite, bears bas-relief carvings of key revolutionary events (one relief shows the Chinese destroying opium in the 19th century) as well as appropriate calligraphy from Mao Zedong and Zhou Enlai.

Mao Zedong Mausoleum
(máo zhǔxí jìniàn táng) 毛主席纪念堂

Behind the Monument to the People's Heroes stands this giant mausoleum built to house the body of Chairman Mao. Mao died in September 1976, and the mausoleum was constructed over a period of 10 months from 1976 to 1977. It occupies a prominent position on the powerful north-south axis of the city, but against all laws of geomancy this marble structure faces north. At the end of 1983 the mausoleum was re-opened as a museum with exhibitions on the lives of Zhou Enlai, Zhu De, Mao and the man he persecuted, Liu Shaoqi. Mao's body still remains in its place.

Whatever history will make of Mao, his impact on its course will remain enormous. Easy as it now is to vilify his deeds and excesses, many Chinese show deep respect when confronted with the physical presence of the man. Shoving a couple of museums into the mausoleum was meant to knock Mao another rung down the divine ladder. Nevertheless the atmosphere in the inner sanctum is one of hushed reverence, with a thick red pile carpet muting any sound. Foreigners are advised to avoid loud talk, not to crack jokes ('Is he dead?') nor indulge in other behaviour that will get you arrested.

Photos are prohibited inside the mausoleum and your cameras and bags will be checked at the shed outside the entrance. The mausoleum is open daily from 8.30 to 11.30 am and occasionally from 1 pm until 3.30 pm. Join the enormous queue of Chinese sightseers, but don't expect more than a quick glimpse of the body as you file past the sarcophagus. Mao looks so well-preserved that some say the body on view is really a fake. Take a look and decide for yourself.

CITS guides freely quote the old 7:3 ratio on Mao that first surfaced in 1976. Mao was 70% right and 30% wrong (what, one wonders, are the figures for CITS itself?) and this is now the official Party line. His gross errors in the Cultural Revolution, it is said, are far outweighed by his contributions.

Whatever Mao might have done to the Chinese economy while he was alive, sales of Mao memorabilia are certainly giving the free market a boost these days. At the souvenir shacks outside the mausoleum you can pick up Chairman Mao keyrings, thermometers, face towels, handkerchiefs, sun visors, address books and cartons of cigarettes (a comment on his chain-smoking habit?).

PALACES

Being the capital of China for a number of centuries, Beijing has acquired a substantial number of upmarket residences for various emperors and empresses. In addition, the royal families required housing for their various servants, consorts, concubines, eunuchs and so on. It should not be forgotten that this is still the capital, and the construction of palaces is an ongoing process.

Forbidden City

(zǐjìn chéng) 紫禁城

The Forbidden City, so called because it was off limits for 500 years, is the largest and best-preserved cluster of ancient buildings in China – see Map No 20 at the back of the book for details. It was home to two dynasties of emperors, the Ming and the Qing, who didn't stray from this pleasuredome unless they absolutely had to.

The Forbidden City is open daily from 8.30 am to 5 pm, with last admission tickets being sold at 3.30 pm. Two hundred years ago the admission price would have been instant death, but this has dropped considerably to Y45 FEC for foreigners and Y10 RMB for Chinese. The Y45 ticket allows admission to all the special exhibition halls, but if you pay the Chinese price these cost extra, although it would still work out much cheaper if you could get the Chinese price. That appears to be damn near impossible at the Forbidden City unless you actually look Chinese, even if you possess legitimate student cards. By way of compensation, your Y45 includes rental of a cassette tape player and tape for a self-guided tour. The tape player requires a refundable Y100 deposit, but you can use your own personal stereo instead. For the tape to make sense you must enter the Forbidden City from the south gate and exit from the north. The tape is available in a number of languages, including English, German, Japanese, French, Spanish, Italian, Korean, Russian, Cantonese and, of course, Mandarin Chinese.

Many foreigners get Tiananmen Gate confused with the Forbidden City entrance because the two are physically attached and there are no signs in English. As a result, some people wind up purchasing the Tiananmen Gate admission ticket by mistake, not realising that this only gains you admission to the upstairs portion of the gate. To find the Forbidden City ticket booths, keep walking north until you can't walk any further without paying.

The basic layout was built between 1406 and 1420 by Emperor Yong Le, commanding battalions of labourers and craftspeople – some estimate up to a million of them. From this palace the emperors governed China, often rather erratically as they tended to become lost in this self-contained little world and allocate real power to the court eunuchs.

The buildings now seen are mostly post-18th century, as with a lot of restored or rebuilt structures around Beijing. The palace was constantly going up in flames – a lantern festival combined with a sudden gust of Gobi wind would easily do the trick, as would a fireworks

The Forbidden City:
   Top: Roof detail (JO)
   Middle: Bird's eye view (JO)
   Bottom: Entrance gate (RS)

display. There were also deliberate fires lit by court eunuchs and officials who could get rich off the repair bills. In 1664, the Manchus stormed in and burned the palace to the ground.

It was not just the buildings that went up in smoke, but rare books, paintings, calligraphy and anything else which was flammable. In this century there have been two major lootings of the palace: first by the Japanese forces, and second by the Kuomintang Party, who on the eve of the Communist takeover in 1949 removed thousands of crates of relics to Taiwan, where they are now on display in Taipei's National Palace Museum (worth seeing). Perhaps just as well, since the Cultural Revolution turned much of China's precious artwork into confetti. The gaps have been filled by bringing treasures, old and newly discovered, from other parts of China.

The palace is so large (720,000 sq metres, 800 buildings, 9000 rooms) that a permanent restoration squad moves around repainting and repairing. It's estimated to take about 10 years to do a full renovation, by which time the beginning is due for repairs again. The complex was opened to the public in 1949.

At the northern end of the Forbidden City is the Imperial Garden, a classical Chinese garden of 7000 sq metres of fine landscaping, with rockeries, walkways and pavilions. This is a good place to take a breather, with snack bars, WCs and souvenir shops. Two more gates lead out through the large Gate of Divine Military Genius (Shenwumen).

The western and eastern sides of the Forbidden City are the palatial former living quarters, once containing libraries, temples, theatres, gardens, even the tennis court of the last emperor. These buildings now function as museums requiring extra admission fees, but the foreigners' all-inclusive ticket covers them. Opening hours are irregular and no photos are allowed without prior permission. Special exhibits sometimes appear in the palace museum halls, so check the China Daily for details.

Zhongshan Park (zhōngshān gōngyuán), otherwise known as Sun Yatsen Park, is in the south-west of the Forbidden City and was laid out at the same time as the palace. Here you'll find the Altar of Land and Grain, which is divided into five sections, each filled with earth of a different colour (red, green, black, yellow and white) to symbolise all the earth belonging to the emperor. There is also a concert hall and a 'modernisation' playground in the park.

The Workers' Cultural Palace (láodòng rénmín wénhuà gōng) in the south-east sector of the Forbidden City is a

Behind the Wall

If ceremonial and administrative duties occupied most of the emperor's working hours, then behind the high walls of the Forbidden City it was the pursuit of pleasure which occupied much of his attention during the evenings. One of the imperial bedtime systems was to keep the names of royal wives, consorts and favourites on jade tablets near the emperor's chambers – sometimes as many as 50 of them.

By turning the tablet over the emperor made his request for the evening, and the eunuch on duty would rush off to find the lucky lady. Stripped naked and therefore weaponless, she was gift-wrapped in a yellow cloth, and the little bound-footed creature was piggy-backed over to the royal boudoir and dumped at the feet of the emperor; the eunuch recorded the date and time to verify legitimacy of a possible child.

Financing the affairs of state probably cost less than financing the affairs of the emperor; keeping the pleasuredome functioning drew heavily on the resources of the empire. During the Ming Dynasty there were an estimated 9000 maids of honour and 70,000 eunuchs serving the court. Apart from the servants and the prize concubines there were also the royal elephants to upkeep. These were gifts from Burma and were stabled south-west of the Forbidden City. Accorded rank by the emperor, when one died a period of mourning was declared. Periodically the elephant keepers embezzled the funds intended for elephant chow. When this occurred, the ravenous pachyderms went on a rampage.

While pocketing this cash was illegal, selling elephant dung for use as shampoo was not, and it was believed to give the hair that extra sheen. Back in the harem the cosmetic bills piled up to 400,000 taels of silver. Then, of course, the concubines who had grown old and gone out of active service were still supposed to be cared for. Rather than cut back on expenditure, the emperor sent out eunuchs to collect emergency taxes whenever money ran short.

As for the palace eunuchs, the royal chop was administered at the Eunuch Clinic near the Forbidden City, using a swift knife and a special chair with a hole in the seat. The candidates sought to better their lives in the service of the court but half of them died after the operation. Mutilation of any kind was considered grounds for exclusion from the next life, so many eunuchs carried their appendages around in pouches, believing that at the time of death the spirits might be deceived into thinking of them as whole. ∎

park with halls dating from 1462 which were used as ancestral temples under the Ming and Qing; they come complete with marble balustrades, terraces and detailed gargoyles. The park is now used for movies, temporary exhibits, cultural performances and the odd mass wedding.

The Forbidden City gets 10,000 visitors a day – visiting on a weekday during winter is your best bet.

Zhongnanhai
(zhōngnánhǎi) 中南海

Just west of the Forbidden City is China's new forbidden city, Zhongnanhai. The interior is off-limits to tourists, but you can gawk at the entrance. The name means 'the central and south seas', in this case called after the two large lakes in the compound. The southern entrance is via Xinhuamen (Gate of New China) which you'll see on Chang'an Jie; it's guarded by two PLA soldiers and fronted by a flagpole with the red flag flying. The gate was built in 1758 and was then known as the Tower of the Treasured Moon.

The compound was first built between the 10th and 13th centuries as a sort of playground for the emperors and their retinues. It was expanded during Ming times but most of the present buildings only date from the Qing Dynasty. After the overthrow of the imperial government and the establishment of the Republic it served as the site of the presidential palace.

Since the founding of the People's Republic in 1949, Zhongnanhai has been the site of the residence and offices of the highest-ranking members of the Communist Party.

Empress Dowager Cixi once lived here; after the failure of the 1898 reform movement she imprisoned Emperor Guangxu in the Hall of Impregnating Vitality where, ironically, he later died. Yuan Shikai used Zhongnanhai for ceremonial occasions during his brief presidency of the Chinese Republic; his vice-president moved into Guangxu's death-house.

Summer Palace
(yíhéyuán) 颐和园

One of Beijing's finest sights, the Summer Palace is an immense park containing some newish Qing architecture. The site had long been a royal garden and was considerably enlarged and embellished by Emperor Qianlong in the 18th century. He deepened and

Top: Summer Palace (RS)
Bottom: Roof detail in the Long Corridor (RI'A)

expanded Kunming Lake with the help of 100,000 labourers, and reputedly surveyed imperial navy drills from a hilltop perch.

Empress Dowager Cixi began rebuilding in 1888 using money that was supposedly reserved for the construction of a modern navy – but she did restore a marble boat that sits immobile at the edge of the lake.

In 1900 foreign troops, annoyed by the Boxer Rebellion, had another go at roasting the Summer Palace. Restorations took place a few years later and a major renovation occurred after 1949, by which time the palace had once more fallen into disrepair.

The original palace was used as a summer residence, as its name implies. The residents of the Forbidden City packed up and decamped here for their holidays, so the emphasis was on cool features – water, gardens, hills. It was divided into four sections: court reception, residences, temples and strolling or sightseeing areas.

Three-quarters of the park is occupied by Kunming Lake, and most items of structural interest are towards the east or north gates – see Map No 21 at the back of the book. The main building is the Hall of Benevolence & Longevity, just off the lake toward the east gate. It houses a hardwood throne and has a courtyard with bronze animals. In it the emperor-in-residence handled state affairs and received envoys.

Along the north shore of the lake is the Long Corridor, over 700 metres long, which is decorated with mythical scenes. If the paint looks new it's because a lot of pictures were whitewashed during the Cultural Revolution.

On artificial Longevity Hill are a number of temples. The Pavilion of Precious Clouds on the western slopes is one of the few structures to escape destruction by the Anglo-French forces. It contains some elaborate bronzes. At the top of the hill sits the Buddhist Temple of the Sea of Wisdom, made of glazed tiles; good views of the lake can be had from this spot.

Other sights are largely associated with Empress Cixi, like the place where she kept Emperor Guangxu under house arrest, the place where she celebrated her birthdays, and exhibitions of her furniture and memorabilia.

The Tingliguan Restaurant serves imperial banquet food – fish from Kunming Lake, velvet chicken, dumplings – on regal tableware lookalikes. It has a splendid alfresco location and exorbitant prices, and is housed in what was once an imperial theatre; nowadays there are attached souvenir shops.

Another noteworthy feature is the 17-arch bridge spanning 150 metres to South Lake Island; on the mainland side is a beautiful bronze ox. Also note the Jade Belt

Bridge on the mid-west side of the lake; and the Garden of Harmonious Interest at the north-east end which is a copy of a Wuxi garden.

You can get around the lake by rowing boat, or on a pair of ice skates in winter. As with the Forbidden City Moat, it used to be a common practice to cut slabs of ice from the lake in winter and store them for summer use.

The park is about 12 km north-west of the centre of Beijing. The easiest way to get there is to take the subway to Xizhimen (close to the zoo), then a minibus for Y3. Bus No 332 from the zoo is slower but will get you there eventually. There are lots of minibuses returning to the city centre from the Summer Palace, but get the price and destination settled before departure. You can also get there by bicycle; it takes about 1½ to two hours from downtown. Rather than taking the main roads, it's far more pleasant to bike along the road following the Beijing to Miyun Diversion Canal.

Foreigners are charged Y15, payable in RMB or FEC. This ticket does *not* get you into everything; there are some additional fees inside. Admission for Chinese costs Y2 – foreigners need to be resident in Beijing with valid ID to get this price.

Old Summer Palace
(yuánmíngyuán) 圆明园

The original Summer Palace was laid out in the 12th century. By the reign of Emperor Qianlong, it had developed into a set of interlocking gardens. Qianlong set the Jesuits to work as architects of European palaces for the gardens, adding elaborate fountains and baroque statuary.

In the second Opium War (1860), British and French troops destroyed the place and sent the booty abroad. Since the Chinese pavilions and temples were made of wood they did not survive fires, but a marble facade, some broken columns and traces of the fountains stick out of the rice-paddies.

The ruins have long been a favourite picnic spot for foreign residents and Chinese twosomes seeking a bit of privacy. More recently, the government has decided to slowly restore the gardens, moats and buildings. It's uncertain yet just how far the restoration will go. Will it be allowed to remain as ruins or will it become another Chinese tourist circus like the Ming Tombs? At present, it's still a very worthwhile place to visit but can be crowded on Sunday. Refer to Map No 22 for details of the layout of the Old Summer Palace.

The site is enormous – 2½ km from east to west – so

Lotus flower (JO)

be prepared to do some walking. There are three entrance gates to the compound, all on the south side. The western section is the main area, Yuanmingyuan. The south-east corner of the site is the Beautiful Spring Garden (Yichunyuan). The eastern section is the Eternal Spring Garden (Changchunyuan). It's here that you'll find the Great Fountain Ruins, considered the best preserved relic in the palace and featured prominently in the tourist brochures.

Minibuses connect the new Summer Palace with the old one, for about Y2. There are some slower but pleasant trips you can do around the area by public transport.

Take bus No 332 from the zoo to the Old Summer Palace and to the Summer Palace; change to bus No 333 for the Fragrant Hills; change to bus No 360 to go directly back to the zoo.

Another round-trip route is to take the subway to Pingguoyuan (the last stop in the west) and then take bus No 318 to the Fragrant Hills; change to No 333 for the Summer Palace, and then to No 332 for the zoo.

MUSEUMS

As far as foreigners are concerned, Beijing's museums are worthwhile but poorly presented. There are almost no English explanations, not even in pamphlet form.

History Museum & Museum of the Revolution

(zhōngguó gémìng lìshǐ bówùguǎn)
中国革命历史博物馆

Housed in a sombre building on the east side of Tiananmen Square, access to the museum was long thwarted by special permission requirements. From 1966 to 1978 the museum was closed so that history could be reassessed in the light of recent events.

The presentation of history poses quite a problem for the Chinese Communist Party. It has failed to publish anything of note on its own history since it gained power, before, during or since the Cultural Revolution. This would have required reams of carefully worded revision according to what tack politics (here synonymous with history) might take, so it was better left unwritten.

There are actually two museums here combined into one – the Museum of History and the Museum of the Revolution. Explanations throughout most of the museums are entirely in Chinese, so you won't get much out of this labyrinth unless you're particularly fluent or pick up an English-speaking student. An English text relating to the History Museum is available inside.

The History Museum contains artefacts and cultural relics (many of them copies) from year zero to 1919, subdivided into primitive communal groups, slavery, feudalism and capitalism/imperialism, laced with Marxist commentary. Without a guide you can discern ancient weapons, inventions and musical instruments.

The Museum of the Revolution is split into five sections: the founding of the Chinese Communist Party (1919-21), the first civil war (1924-27), the second civil

war (1927-37), resistance against Japan (1937-45) and the
third civil war (1945-49).

The admission fee is Y3.

Military Museum
(jūnshì bówùguǎn) 军事博物馆

Perhaps more to the point than the Museum of the
Revolution, this traces the genesis of the PLA from 1927
to the present and has some interesting exhibits: pictures
of Mao in the early days, mind-boggling Socialist Realist
artwork, captured American tanks from the Korean War
and other tools of destruction. Explanations are in
Chinese only. You must have your bags checked at the
door, presumably to prevent you from liberating a
Sherman tank or MIG aircraft.

The museum is on Fuxing Lu on the western side of
the city; to get there take the subway to Junshibowuguan. Admission costs Y2.

Natural History Museum
(zìrán bówùguǎn) 自然博物馆

The four main exhibition halls are devoted to flora,
fauna, ancient fauna and human evolution. One of the
more impressive features is a complete dinosaur skele-
ton. There is also plenty of pickled wildlife, though
nothing worse than what you see for sale in some of the
street markets. Some of the exhibits were donated by the
British Museum, American Museum of Natural History
and other foreign sources.

The Natural History Museum is in the Tianqiao area,
just west of Tiantan Park, just north of the park's west
gate entrance. Admission costs Y2. The museum is open
daily except Monday from 8.30 am until 4 pm.

Lu Xun Museum
(lǔ xùn bówùguǎn) 鲁迅博物馆

Dedicated to China's No 1 Thinking Person's Revolutionary, this museum contains manuscripts, diaries,
letters and inscriptions by the famous writer. To the west
of the museum is a small Chinese walled compound
where Lu Xun lived from 1924 to 1926. The museum is
off Fuchengmennei Dajie, west of the Xisi intersection
on the north-western side of the city.

China Art Gallery
(zhōngguó měishù guǎn) 中国美术馆

Back in Cultural Revolution days one of the safest hobbies for an artist was to retouch classical-style landscapes with red flags, belching factory chimneys or bright red tractors. You can get some idea of the state of the arts in China at this gallery. At times very good exhibitions of current work including photo displays are held in an adjacent gallery. Check the China Daily for listings. The arts & crafts shop inside has an excellent range of woodblock prints and papercuts. The gallery is west of the Dongsi intersection.

Xu Beihong Museum
(xú bēihóng jìniàn guǎn) 徐悲鸿纪念馆

Here you'll find traditional Chinese paintings, oils, gouaches, sketches and memorabilia of the famous artist Xu Beihong, noted for his galloping horse paintings. Painting albums are on sale, as well as reproductions and Chinese stationery. The museum is at 53 Xinjiekou Beidajie, Xicheng District.

Song Qingling Museum
(sòng qìnglíng gùjū) 宋庆龄故居

Madam Song was the wife of Sun Yatsen, founder of the Republic of China. After 1981 her large residence was transformed into a museum dedicated to her memory and to that of Sun Yatsen. On display are personal items and pictures of historical interest. The museum is on the north side of Shisha Houhai Lake.

LIBRARIES

National Library
(běijīng túshūguǎn – xīn guǎn)
北京图书馆（新馆）

This holds around five million books and four million periodicals and newspapers, over a third of which are in foreign languages. Access to books is limited and access to rare books is even more limited, though you might be shown a microfilm copy if you're lucky. The large collection of rare books includes surviving imperial works such as the *Yong Le Encyclopedia* and selections from the old Jesuit library. Of interest to Ming-Qing scholars is the special collection, the *Shanbenbu*. The library is near the zoo. The old Beijing Library is near Beihai Park on the south side; Beijing University Library also has a large collection of rare books but you aren't likely to get into this place.

Capital Museum & Library
(shǒudū túshūguǎn) 首都图书馆

Actually, it's part of the Confucius Temple complex. The museum houses steles, stone inscriptions, bronzes, vases and documents. This place is within walking distance of the Lama Temple. The easiest way to get there is by subway to the Yonghegong station.

PARKS

In imperial days the parks were laid out at the compass points: to the west of the Forbidden City lies Yuetan Park; to the north lies Ditan Park; to the south lies Taoranting Park and to the east is Ritan Park. To the south-east of the Forbidden City is the showpiece of them all, Tiantan Park.

All of these parks were venues for ritual sacrifices offered by the emperors. Not much remains of the shaman structures, bar those of the Temple of Heaven, but if you arrive early in the morning you can witness taiji, fencing exercises, or perhaps opera-singers and musicians practising. It's well worth experiencing the very different rhythms of the city at this time.

Temporary exhibitions take place in the parks, including horticultural and cultural ones, and there is even the odd bit of open-air theatre as well as some worthy eating establishments. If you take up residence in Beijing, the parks become very important for preserving sanity. They are open late too, typically until 8 pm.

Jingshan Park
(jǐngshān gōngyuán) 景山公园

North of the Forbidden City is Jingshan (Coal Hill), which contains an artificial mound made of earth excavated to create the palace moat. If you clamber to the top pavilions of this regal pleasure garden you get a magnificent panorama of the capital and a great overview of the russet roofing of the Forbidden City. On the east side of the park is a locust tree where the last of the Mings, Emperor Chongzhen, hanged himself (after slaying his family) rather than see the palace razed by the Manchus. The hill supposedly protects the palace from the evil spirits – or dust storms – from the north, but didn't quite work for Chongzhen.

Entrance to Jingshan Park is a modest Y0.30, or you can pay over 30 times as much for a souvenir 'tourist passport ticket'; the latter is optional.

Beihai Park

(běihǎi gōngyuán) 北海公园

Just north-west of the Forbidden City, Beihai Park is the former playground of the emperors. It's rumoured to have been the private pleasure domain of the great dragon lady/witch Jiang Qing, widow of Mao who, until her death in May 1991, was serving a life sentence as No 1 of the Gang of Four. Half of the park is a lake. The island in the lower middle is composed of the heaped earth dug to create the lake – some attribute this to the handiwork of Kublai Khan.

The site is associated with the Great Khan's palace, the navel of Beijing before the creation of the Forbidden City. All that remains of the Khan's court is a large jar made of green jade, in the Round City near the south entrance. A present given in 1265, and said to have contained the Khan's wine, it was later discovered in the hands of Taoist priests who used it to store pickles. In the Light Receiving Hall, the main structure nearby, is a 1½-metre-high white jade Buddha inlaid with jewels, a gift from Burma to Empress Dowager Cixi.

From the 12th century on, Beihai Park was landscaped with artificial hills, pavilions, halls, temples and covered walkways. In the present era the structures have been

Lotuses & White Dagoba in Beihai Park (JO)

MAP 2

北海公园
Beihai Park

0   100   200 m

1 Beihai Playground
2 Glazed Pavilion
3 Dacizhenru Hall
4 Tianwang Hall
5 Nine Dragon Screen
6 Jingxin House
7 Rowboat Dock
8 North Gate
9 Qincan Hall
10 Kindergarten
11 Wanfulou
12 Gardens
13 Miniature Western Paradise
14 Beihai Restaurant
15 Rowboat Dock
16 Five Dragon Pavilion
17 Boat House
18 Painted Boat Studio
19 Rowboat Dock
20 Fangshan Restaurant
21 Painted Gallery
22 White Dagoba
23 East Gate
24 Falun Hall
25 West Gate
26 Light Receiving Hall
27 South Gate

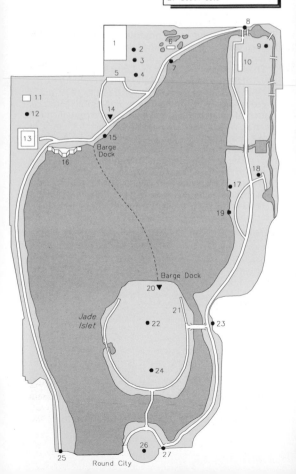

Barge Dock

Barge Dock

Jade
Islet

Round City

1	北海体育场	15	游船码头
2	琉璃阁	16	五龙亭
3	大慈真如殿	17	船坞
4	天王殿	18	画舫斋
5	九龙壁斋	19	游船码头
6	静心斋	20	仿膳饭庄
7	游船码头	21	团城
8	北门	22	白塔
9	亲蚕殿	23	东门
10	北海幼儿园	24	法轮殿
11	宝积楼	25	西门
12	植物园	26	承光殿
13	小西天	27	南门
14	北海餐厅夫		

massively restored and Beihai Park is now one of the best examples of a classical garden found in China. Dominating Jade Islet on the lake, the White Dagoba is a 36-metre-high pop-art 'Peppermint Bottle' originally dating from 1651. It was put up for a visit by the Dalai Lama and was rebuilt in 1741. It's believed that Lamaist scriptures, robes and other sacred objects are encased in this brick-and-stone landmark.

On the north-east shore of the islet is the handsome double-tiered Painted Gallery, with unusual architecture for a walkway. Near the boat-dock is the Fangshan Restaurant, dishing up recipes favoured by Empress Cixi. She liked 120-course dinners with about 30 kinds of desserts. The restaurant is expensive and high class, and reservations are necessary (but check out the decor!). Off to one side, however, is a snack bar that dispenses royal pastries much more cheaply.

From this point you can catch a barge to the north-west part of the park or, if energetic, double back and hire a rowing boat (there's another rowing-boat hire place on the north-west side). The attraction on the north side is the Nine Dragon Screen, five metres high and 27 metres long, made of coloured glazed tiles. The screen was to scare off evil spirits; it stands at the entrance to a temple which has disappeared. To the south-west of the boat dock on this side is the Five Dragon Pavilion dating from 1651, where the emperors liked to fish or camp out at night to watch the moon.

On the east side of the park are the 'gardens within gardens'. These waterside pavilions, winding corridors and rockeries were summer haunts of the imperial family, notably Emperor Qianlong and Empress Cixi.

View of White Dagoba, Beihai Park (RS)

They date back some 200 years, with structures like the Painted Boat Studio and the Studio of Mental Calmness. Until 1980 the villas were used as government offices.

Beihai Park is a relaxing place to stroll around, grab a snack, sip a beer, rent a rowing boat or, as the Chinese do, cuddle on a bench in the evening. It's crowded at weekends. Swimming in the lake is not permitted, but in winter there's skating. This is nothing new in China – skating apparently goes back to the 18th century when Emperor Qianlong reviewed the imperial skating parties here.

Tiantan Park
(tiāntán gōngyuán) 天坛公园

The perfection of Ming architecture, Tiantan (the Temple of Heaven) has come to symbolise Beijing. Its lines appear on countless pieces of tourist literature (including your five jiao tourist bill), and as a brand name for a wide range of products from tiger balm to plumbing fixtures. In the 1970s the complex got a face-lift and was freshly painted after pigment research. It is set in a 267-hectare park, with four gates at the compass points, and bounded by walls to the north and east. It originally functioned as a vast stage for solemn rites performed by the Son of Heaven who came here to pray for good harvests, seek divine clearance and atone for the sins of the people.

With this complicated mix in mind, the unique architectural features will delight numerologists, necromancers and the superstitious – not to mention acoustic engineers and carpenters. Shape, colour and sound take on symbolic significance. The temples, seen in aerial perspective, are round, and the bases are square, deriving from the ancient Chinese belief that heaven is

Tiantan (Temple of Heaven) Park (JO)

round, and the earth is square. Thus the north end of the park is semicircular and the south end is square (the Temple of Earth is on the northern compass point and the Temple of Heaven on the southern compass point).

Tiantan was considered highly sacred ground and it was here that the emperor performed the major ceremonial rites of the year. Just before the winter solstice, the emperor and his enormous entourage passed down Qianmen Dajie to the Imperial Vault of Heaven in total silence. Commoners were not permitted to view the ceremony and remained cloistered indoors. The procession included elephant chariots, horse chariots and long lines of lancers, nobles, officials and musicians, dressed in their finest, flags fluttering. The next day the emperor waited in a yellow silk tent at the south gate while officials moved the sacred tablets to the Round Altar, where the prayers and sacrificial rituals took place. The least hitch in any part of the proceedings was regarded as an ill omen, and it was thought that the nation's future was thus decided. This was the most important ceremony although other excursions to Ditan (Temple of Earth) also took place.

Round Altar The five-metre-high Round Altar was constructed in 1530 and rebuilt in 1740. It is composed of white marble arrayed in three tiers, and its geometry revolves around the imperial number nine. Odd numbers were considered heavenly, and nine is the largest single-digit odd number. The top tier, thought to symbolise heaven, has nine rings of stones, each ring composed of multiples of nine stones, so that the ninth ring has 81 stones. The middle tier – earth – has the 10th to 18th rings. The bottom tier – man – has the 19th to 27th rings, ending with a total of 243 stones in the largest ring, or 27 times nine. The number of stairs and balustrades are also multiples of nine. If you stand in the centre of the upper terrace and say something, the sound waves are bounced off the marble balustrades, making your voice appear louder (nine times?).

Echo Wall Just north of the altar, surrounding the entrance to the Imperial Vault of Heaven, is the Echo Wall, 65 metres in diameter. This enables a whisper to travel clearly from one end to your friend's ear at the other – that is, if there's not a group tour in the middle.

In the courtyard are the Triple Echo Stones. If you stand on the first one and clap or shout, the sound is echoed once, on the second stone twice, and on the third, three times. Should it return four times, you will almost

MAP 3

天坛公园

Tiantan Park
(Temple of Heaven)

0   250   500 m

Approximate Scale

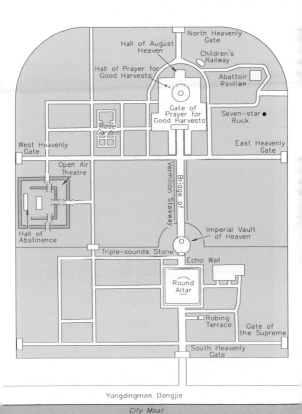

North Heavenly Gate

Hall of August Heaven

Children's Railway

Hall of Prayer for Good Harvests

Abattoir Pavilion

Gate of Prayer for Good Harvests

Seven-star Rock

Rose Garden

West Heavenly Gate

East Heavenly Gate

Open Air Theatre

Bridge of Vermilion Stairway

Hall of Abstinence

Imperial Vault of Heaven

Triple-sounds Stone

Echo Wall

Round Altar

Robing Terrace

Gate of the Supreme

South Heavenly Gate

Yongdingmen Dongjie

City Moat

certainly not get a train ticket that day, or any other day
that is a multiple of three.

Imperial Vault of Heaven This octagonal vault was
built at the same time as the Round Altar, and is struc-
tured along the lines of the older Hall of Prayer for Good
Harvests, though it is smaller. It used to contain tablets
of the emperor's ancestors, which were used in the
winter solstice ceremony. Proceeding up from the
Imperial Vault is a walkway: to the left is a molehill
composed of excess dirt dumped from digging air-raid
shelters and to the right is a rash of souvenir shops.

Hall of Prayer for Good Harvests The main
structure of the whole complex is the Hall of Prayer for
Good Harvests, which is a magnificent piece mounted
on a three-tiered marble terrace. Built in 1420, it was

Imperial Vault of Heaven (JO)

burnt to cinders in 1889 and heads rolled in apportioning blame. The cause seems to have been lightning. A faithful reproduction based on Ming architectural methods was erected the following year, using Oregon fir for the support pillars.

The four pillars at the centre represent the seasons, the 12 in the next ring denote the months of the year, and the 12 outer ones are symbolic of the day, broken into 12 'watches'. Embedded in the ceiling is a carved dragon, a symbol of royalty. The patterning, carving and gilt decoration of this ceiling and its swirl of colour is a dizzy sight, enough to carry you into the Seventh Heaven.

In fact it looks peculiarly modern, like a graphic from a sci-fi movie of a UFO about to blast into space. All this is made more amazing by the fact that the wooden pillars ingeniously support the ceiling without nails or cement. For a building 38 metres high and 30 metres in diameter, that's a stunning accomplishment of carpen-

Interior detail, Temple of Heaven (JO)

try. Capping the structure is a deep blue umbrella of tiles with a golden knob and two complementary eaves.

If you buy the general admission ticket for Tiantan Park (Y1), you need to pay extra to see the Hall of Prayer for Good Harvests. If you buy the overpriced tourist ticket (Y10), admission to everything is included.

Other Tiantan, it should not be forgotten, is also a park and a meeting place. Get there at 6.30 am to see taiji, dancing to Western music and some other games that people play. This is how Beijing awakes. It becomes just another Chinese parkland by 9 am as the tourists start to break the magic.

Ditan Park

(dìtán gōngyuán) 地坛公园

Although 'Ditan' sounds just like the Chinese word for 'carpet', in this case it means 'Temple of the Earth'. The park was built around 1530 as a place for the emperors to sacrifice lesser beings to keep on good terms with the Earth God. The park experienced many years of neglect, but re-opened in 1984 as a sort of activity centre for the elderly. The park is just north of the magnificent Lama Temple.

Ritan Park

(rìtán gōngyuán) 日坛公园

Ritan means 'Temple of the Sun' and it's one of Beijing's older parks, having been built in 1530. The park was built as an altar for ritual sacrifice to the Sun God. Situated practically right in the middle of Jianguomenwai embassyland, it's a big hit with diplomats, their families and other notables who like to rub elbows with important foreigners. The Ritan Restaurant is in the park and serves jiaozi in an older-style pavilion – this place is very popular with Westerners for snacks.

Yuetan Park

(yuètán gōngyuán) 月坛公园

The name means 'Temple of the Moon'. This is another one of Beijing's sacrificial parks, where the emperors reduced the surplus population to appease the Moon God. These days the Yuetan is notable for the Emei Restaurant on the north side of the park, which serves hot Sichuan food with no compromise for foreign palates. Sichuan food addicts prefer it to the Sichuan Restaurant itself.

Yuyuantan Park

(yùyuāntán gōngyuán) 玉渊潭公园

Off to the west of Yuetan Park is Yuyuantan (Jade Hole Pool). The park is notable for the palatial Diaoyutai State Guesthouse, the stomping ground of visiting diplomats and high-ranking cadres. Tourists wandering around the main gate will be politely told to get lost. Just to the south side of the park is the immense TV Tower, one of Beijing's most prominent landmarks. The park is just north of the Military Museum.

Taoranting Park

(táorántíng gōngyuán) 陶然亭公园

Taoranting (Happy Pavilion) Park is in the southern part of Beijing. The park dates back to at least the Qing Dynasty, when it gained fame chiefly because it was one of the very few accessible to the masses (most of the others were the private playgrounds of the emperors). In keeping with this tradition, the park is conveniently located just north of the Qiaoyuan Hotel, the centre of Beijing's budget traveller community. From the hotel, cross one of the pedestrian bridges over the sewage canal and you're practically there.

Zizhuyuan Park

(zǐzhúyuàn) 紫竹园

The park's name means 'Purple Bamboo', a reference to some of what has been planted here. This place doesn't have much history to distinguish it, being mainly former paddy fields, but during the Ming Dynasty there was a Temple of Longevity *(wànshòu sì)* at this site. The park is pleasant enough and there is a reasonably large lake which makes a good venue for ice skating in winter. Zizhuyuan is in a prestigious neighbourhood just west of the zoo.

Longtan Park

(lóngtán gōngyuán) 龙潭公园

Longtan (Dragon Pool) Park is of chief interest to budget travellers staying at the nearby Longtan Hotel in south-east Beijing; visit the park at dawn to see outstanding taiji performances.

The west side of Longtan Park has recently been converted into the Beijing Amusement Park, a world of balloons, cotton candy and nauseating rides (don't eat Sichuan food before getting on the 'Spider'). If this appeals to you, at least avoid it on weekends and holidays.

Grand View Garden
(dàguānyuán) 大观园

Off the south-west corner of town is Grand View Garden, also known as Daguanyuan Park. Unlike most of Beijing's parks which date back to imperial days, this one is new. Construction started in 1984 and was completed four years later. The park was built as a replica of the family gardens described in the Chinese novel *The Dream of the Red Chamber*, written by Cao Xueqin, which is a Chinese classic written in the late 18th century. While the park is not steeped in history, it could be of interest if you've read the novel. Otherwise, just relax and enjoy the birds and the trees.

Beijing Zoo
(běijīng dòngwùyuán) 北京动物园

For humans the zoo may be OK – an enormous park, pleasant lakes, good birds – but after you've been there you'll probably look as pissed-off as the animals. No attempt has been made to re-create their natural environments; they live in tiny cages with little shade or water. The Panda House, right by the gates, has four dirty specimens that would be better off dead, and you'll be happier looking at the stuffed toy pandas on sale in the zoo's souvenir shop. Parents can buy their children miniature plastic rifles with which they can practise shooting the animals. The children also enjoy throwing rocks at the monkeys and jabbing them with sticks. Some of the monkeys fight back by throwing their faeces.

Admission is a modest Y1, but there is a Y2 charge for the Panda House and other extra charges for special exhibits.

Getting to the zoo is easy enough; take the subway to the Xizhimen station. From there, it's a 15-minute walk to the west or a short ride on any of the trolley buses.

Near the zoo are the Beijing Planetarium and the bizarre Soviet-style Beijing Exhibition Hall (irregular industrial displays, theatre, Russian restaurant) which looks like some crazed architect's wedding-cake decoration.

TEMPLES

Lama Temple

(yōnghégōng) 雍和宫

This is by far the most colourful temple in Beijing, with its beautiful gardens, stunning frescoes and tapestries and incredible carpentry.

The Lama Temple was once modified to become the official residence of Count Yin Zhen. Nothing unusual in that, perhaps, but in 1723 he was promoted to emperor, and moved to the Forbidden City. His name was changed to Yong Zheng, and his former residence became Yonghe Palace. The green tiles were changed to yellow, the imperial colour, and – as was the custom –

Views of the Lama Temple (RS)

the place could not be used except as a temple. In 1744 it was converted into a lamasery, and became a residence for large numbers of monks from Mongolia and Tibet.

In 1792, Qianlong, having quelled an uprising in Tibet, instituted a new administrative system involving two gold vases. One was kept at the Jokhang Temple in Lhasa, where it was intended to be used for determining the reincarnation of the Dalai Lama (under the supervision of the Minister for Tibetan Affairs). The other was kept at the Lama Temple for the lottery for the Mongolian Grand Living Buddha. The Lama Temple thus assumed a new importance in ethnic minority control.

The lamasery has three richly-worked archways and five main halls strung in a line down the middle, each taller than the preceding one. Styles are mixed – Mongolian, Tibetan and Han – with courtyard enclosures and galleries.

The first hall, Lokapala, houses a statue of the Maitreya (future) Buddha, flanked by celestial guardians. The statue facing the back door is Weituo, guardian of Buddhism, made of white sandalwood. Beyond, in the courtyard, is a pond with a bronze mandala depicting Xumishan, the Buddhist paradise.

The second hall, Yonghedian, has three figures of Buddha – past, present and future.

The third hall, Yongyoudian, has statues of the Buddha of Longevity and the Buddha of Medicine (to the left). The courtyard following it has galleries with some nandikesvaras, or joyful buddhas, tangled up in multi-armed close encounters. These are coyly draped lest you be corrupted by the sight, and are to be found in other esoteric locations.

The Hall of the Wheel of Law, further north, contains a large bronze statue of Tsong Khapa (1357-1419), founder of the Gelukpa or Yellow Hat sect, and frescoes depicting his life. This Tibetan-style building is used for study and prayer.

The last hall, Wanfu Pavilion, has an 18-metre-high statue of the Maitreya Buddha in his Tibetan form, sculptured from a single piece of sandalwood and clothed in yellow satin. The smoke curling up from the yak-butter lamps transports you momentarily to Tibet, which is where the log for this statue came from.

In 1949 the Lama Temple was declared protected as a major historical relic. Miraculously it survived the Cultural Revolution without scars. In 1979 large amounts of money were spent on repairs and it was restocked with several dozen novices from Inner Mongolia, a token move on the part of the government to back up its claim that the Lama Temple is a 'symbol of religious freedom, national unity and stability in China'. The novices study Tibetan language and the secret practices of the Gelukpa (Yellow Hat) sect.

The temple is active again, though some question whether or not the monks in tennis shoes are really monks or PSB. Prayers take place early in the morning, not for public viewing, but if you inquire discreetly of the head lama you might be allowed to return the following morning. No photography is permitted inside the temple buildings, but the postcard industry thrives. The temple is open daily, except Monday, from 9 am to 4 pm. You can get there by subway to the Yonghegong station.

Confucius Temple & Imperial College
(kǒng miào) 孔庙

Just down the hutong opposite the gates of the Lama Temple is the former Confucius Temple and Imperial College (guózijiān). The Confucius Temple is the largest in the land after the one at Qufu. The temple was re-opened in 1981 after some mysterious use as a high-official residence and is now used as a museum, in sharp contrast to the Lama Temple.

The steles in the temple courtyard record the names of those successful in the civil service examinations (possibly the world's first) of the imperial court. To see his name engraved here was the ambition of every scholar, but it wasn't made easy. Candidates were locked in cubicles (about 8000 of them) measuring roughly 1½ by 1½ metres for a period of three days. Many died or went insane during their incarceration. Imagine that.

The Imperial College was the place where the emperor expounded the Confucian classics to an audience of thousands of kneeling students, professors and court officials; this was an annual rite. Built by the grandson of Kublai Khan in 1306, the former college was the only institution of its kind in China. It's now the Capital Library. Part of the 'collection' are the stone tablets commissioned by Emperor Qianlong. These are engraved with 13 Confucian classics – 800,000 characters or 12 years' work for the scholar who did it. There is an ancient 'Scholar-Tree' in the courtyard.

Great Bell Temple
(dàzhōng sì) 大钟寺

The biggest bell in China, this one weighs a hefty 46½ tonnes and is 6¾ metres tall. The bell is inscribed with

Buddhist sutras, a total of over 227,000 Chinese characters.

The bell was cast during the reign of Ming Emperor Yong Le in 1406 and the tower was built in 1733. Getting the bell from the foundry to the temple proved problematic, since back in those days it wasn't possible to contract the job out to a Hong Kong company. A shallow canal had to be built which froze over in winter, and the bell was moved across the ice by sled.

Within the grounds of the monastery at this site are several other buildings (besides the Bell Tower itself). They include the Guanyin Hall, Sutra-keeping Tower, Main Buddha Hall and Four Devas Hall. This monastery is one of the most popular in Beijing and was re-opened in 1980.

The Great Bell Temple is almost two km due east of the Friendship Hotel on Beisanhuan Xilu.

Wuta Temple

(wǔtǎ sì) 五塔寺

This is an Indian-style temple with five pagodas, first constructed in 1473 from a model presented to the court. The temple had a major renovation in 1761, was burned to the ground by uppity foreign troops in 1900, partially rebuilt, then closed during the Cultural Revolution. It has once again been restored and re-opened.

The temple is north-west of the zoo and somewhat difficult to find. Take Baishiqiao Lu north from the zoo for almost one km to a bridge, and turn east to the temple, which lies in the middle of a field.

White Dagoba Temple

(báitǎ sì) 白塔寺

The dagoba can be spotted from the top of Jingshan, and is similar (and close) to the one in Beihai Park. It was used as a factory during the Cultural Revolution but re-opened after restoration in 1980. The dagoba dates back to Kublai Khan's days and was completed with the help of a Nepalese architect, though the halls date only from the Qing Dynasty. It lies off Fuchengmennei Dajie.

Guangji Temple

(guǎngjì sì) 广济寺

The Guangji (Universal Rescue) Temple is on the north-west side of Xisi intersection, and east of the White

Dagoba Temple. It's the headquarters of the Chinese Buddhist Association.

Niujie Mosque
(*niújiē lǐbài sì*) 牛街礼拜寺

In the south west sector of Beijing, south of Guang'anmennei Dajie, is a Muslim residential area with a handsome mosque facing Mecca. Niu Jie (Ox St) is an area worth checking out with a feel all its own. In a lane further east of the mosque is the Fayuan (Source of Law) Temple. The temple was originally constructed in the 7th century and is still going strong – it's now a Buddhist college, open to visitors.

White Cloud Temple
(*báiyúnguān*) 白云观

This is in a district directly south of Yanjing Hotel and west of the moat. Once the Taoist centre of North China and the site of temple fairs, inside you'll find several courtyards containing a pool, bridge, several halls of worship and Taoist motifs. Check a map for directions. Walk south on Baiyun Lu and cross the moat; continue south along Baiyun Lu, turn into a curving street on the left and follow it for 250 metres to the temple entrance.

Black Temple
(*zhìhuà sì*) 智化寺

So nicknamed because of its deep blue tiling, this is a pretty example of Ming architecture (dating from 1443) but there's nothing else of note. If you strain over the bus map, looking north of the main railway station, you will find a hutong called Lumicang, which runs east off Chaoyangmen Nanxiaojie (about 1½ km north of the station). The temple is at the east end of Lumicang. The coffered ceiling of the third hall of the Growth of Intellect Temple is not at the east end of Lumicang – it's in the USA. Lumicang hutong had rice granaries in the Qing Dynasty.

CATHEDRALS

East Cathedral
(*dōngtáng*) 东堂

This building, at 74 Wangfujing, was built on the site of the house of the Jesuit priest Adam Schall. It was founded in 1666 and was later used by the Portuguese Lazarists. It has been rebuilt several times and is now used as a primary school during the week; Catholic services are held early on Sunday mornings.

South Cathedral
(nántáng) 南堂

On Qianmen Dajie at the Xuanwumen intersection (north-east side) above the subway station, the South Cathedral is built on the site of Matteo Ricci's house (first built 1703 and destroyed three times since then).

North Cathedral
(běitáng) 北堂

Also called the Cathedral of Our Saviour, it was built in 1887, but was badly damaged during the Cultural Revolution and converted to a factory warehouse. It was re-opened at the end of 1985 after restoration work was completed. The cathedral is at Xishiku, in Xicheng (West District).

MISCELLANEA

Underground City
(dì xià chéng) 地下城

With a Soviet invasion supposedly hanging over them in the late '60s, the Chinese built huge civil defence systems, especially in northern China. This hobby started before 1949 when the PLA used the tunnelling technique to surprise the enemy. Pressed for space, and trying to maximise the peacetime possibilities of the air-raid shelters (aside from the fact that the shelters are useless in the event of nuclear attack) Beijing has put them to use as warehouses, factories, shops, restaurants, hotels, rollerskating rinks, theatres and clinics.

It's not one of the most inspiring sights in Beijing, but CITS has tours to the Underground City for Y10, often combined with a visit to the Mao Mausoleum. The section you see on the brief tour is about 270 metres long with tunnels at the four, eight and 15-metre levels. It was constructed by volunteers and shop assistants living in the Qianmen area – about 2000 people and 10 years of spare-time work with simple tools – though the shelters were planned and construction was supervised by the army. The people reap a few benefits now such as preferential treatment for relatives and friends who can stay in a 100-bed hotel, use of the warehouse space, and there's a few bucks to be made from tourists. Some features of the system you can see are the telecommunications and first-aid rooms and ventilation system.

There are roughly 90 entrances to this particular complex. The guide claims that 10,000 shoppers in the Dazhalan area can be evacuated to the suburbs in five minutes (what about the other 70,000?!) in the event of an attack. Entrances are hidden in shops. The one you descend by is an ordinary-looking garment shop.

Ancient Observatory
(gǔguān xiàngtái) 古观象台

One interesting perspective on Beijing is the observatory mounted on the battlements of a watchtower, once part of the city walls. Dwarfed by embassy housing blocks, it's surrounded by traffic loops and highways just west of the Friendship Store, on the south-west corner of Jianguomennei Dajie and the second ring road. The views themselves are worth the visit. There are some English explanations. The observatory dates back to Kublai Khan's days when it was north of the present site. The Great Khan, as well as later Ming and Qing emperors, relied heavily on astrologers before making a move.

The present Beijing Observatory was built from 1437 to 1446, not only to facilitate astrological predictions but to aid seafaring navigators. Downstairs are displays of navigational equipment used by Chinese shipping. On the 1st floor are replicas of five 5000-year-old pottery jars, unearthed from Henan Province in 1972 and showing painted patterns of the sun. There are also four replicas of Han Dynasty eave tiles representing east, west, north and south. There is a map drawn on a wooden octagonal board with 1420 stars marked in gold foil or powder; it's a reproduction of the original, which is said to be Ming Dynasty but is based on an older Tang map. Busts of six prominent astronomers are also displayed.

On the roof is a variety of astronomical instruments designed by the Jesuits. The Jesuits, scholars as well as proselytisers, found their way into the capital in 1601 when Matteo Ricci and company were permitted to work with Chinese scientists. The emperor was keen to find out about European firearms and cannons from them.

The Jesuits outdid the resident Muslim calendar-setters and were given control of the observatory, becoming the Chinese court's advisors. Of the eight bronze instruments on display (including an equatorial armilla, celestial globe and altazimuth), six were designed and constructed under the supervision of the Belgian priest Ferdinand Verbiest, who came to China in 1659 to work at the Qing court. The instruments were built between 1669 and 1673, and are embellished with sculptured bronze dragons and other Chinese craftwork, a unique mix of east and west. The azimuth theodolite was supervised by Bernard Stumpf, also a missionary. The eighth instrument, the new armilla, was completed in 1754. It's not clear which instruments on display are the originals.

During the Boxer Rebellion, the instruments disappeared into the hands of the French and the Germans. Some were returned in 1902, while others came back under the provisions of the Treaty of Versailles (1919).

More recently, government officials were caught off guard when local and foreign rock bands got together and staged a dance party in the ancient tower. The observatory is open daily, except Monday, from 9 to 11 am and 1 to 4 pm.

Beijing University
(běidà) 北京大学

Beijing University and Qinghua University *(qīnghuá dàxué)* are the most prestigious institutes in China. Beida was founded at the turn of the century; it was then called Yanjing University and was administered by the Americans. Its students figured prominently in the 4 May 1919 demonstrations and the later resistance to the Japanese. In 1953 the university moved from Jingshan to its present location. In the 1960s the Red Guards first appeared here and the place witnessed some scenes of utter mayhem as the battles of the Cultural Revolution took place.

Beijing University has a beautiful campus, so it's a pity that you can't visit it. At one time it was open to foreigners, but students from this school were leaders in the democracy protests of 1989. Since then, the students have been kept on a tight leash and foreign influences are being kept out. The policy could change at any time, but at the time of writing this, foreigners require special permission to visit the campus and such permission is difficult to obtain.

Beijing has about 50 colleges and universities. An intriguing one is the Central College of Nationalities *(mínzú xuéyuàn)*, just north of the zoo. This college trains cadres for the regions where ethnic minorities live. Beijing University is on the bus No 332 route from the zoo, or about a 45-minute cycle ride from the city centre.

WALKING TOURS

Walking tours are close to impossible in sprawling Beijing. You can walk a bit in certain neighbourhoods like Wangfujing, Dazhalan and Jianguomenwai, but the city is so spread out that the obvious way to go is by bicycle.

BLOCKBUSTER BICYCLE TOUR

Tiantan Park (west side) – Natural History Museum – Dazhalan – Qianmen – Tiananmen Square – History Museum & Museum of the Revolution – Great Hall of the People – Tiananmen Gate – Forbidden City – Beihai Park – Jingshan Park – Song Qingling Museum – Drum Tower – Bell Tower – Confucius Temple – Lama Temple – China Art Gallery – Kentucky Fried Chicken or McDonald's – Wangfujing – Tiantan Park (east side) – Home?

Obviously this is far too much to attempt in one day; indeed, you could spend a full day in just the Forbidden City itself. But if you start out early (such as at dawn) you can see a good chunk of town and take in some of Beijing's many moods, and you can always continue the tour the next day if your schedule permits.

For the following tour, nonstop cycling time is about two hours – Chinese bike, Western legs, average pace. The starting point is the west side of Tiantan Park, and the finishing point is the east side of the same park. Refer to Map No 11 at the end of this book, in which the route is traced out.

The southern end of Qianmen Dajie is called Yongdingmen Dajie; it's here that you'll find the west entrance of Tiantan Park. The park is certainly worth exploring, but you can do that on the way back. Right now, our goal is just a little to the north, the Natural History Museum on the east side of Yongdingmen Dajie.

After you've had your dose of natural history, continue north to where Yongdingmen Dajie becomes Qianmen Dajie. Coming up on your left is Dazhalan, one of Beijing's most intriguing hutongs. Bikes cannot be ridden into this particular hutong, though you can explore most others on two wheels.

Slightly more than a stone's throw to the north is Qianmen, the front gate to the vast expanse of Tiananmen Square. Traffic is one way for north-south avenues on either side of the square. If you want to go to Tiananmen, dismount after the archway and wheel the bike to the parking areas along the sidewalk. Bicycles cannot be ridden across Tiananmen Square (apparently tanks are

OK), but you can walk the bike. Nearby are the History Museum, Museum of the Revolution, Great Hall of the People, Mao's Mausoleum, Tiananmen Gate and the Forbidden City itself.

Over to the west side of the Forbidden City you're heading into the most sensitive part of the capital, the Zhongnanhai Compound. On the right, going up Beichang Jie, you pass some older housing that lines the moat. On the left is a high wall which shields from view the area where top Party members live and work (it was decided not to rip down this section of the old walls). In 1973, when the new wing of the Beijing Hotel shot up, the PSB suddenly realised that guests with binoculars could observe activity in Zhongnanhai, so a fake building was erected along the western wall of the Forbidden City to short-circuit that possibility. Mysterious buildings, indeed, abound in this locale (also on the strip back at the traffic lights along the way to Jingshan Park), including private theatres for viewing foreign films.

Then it's Beihai Park, which by this time of day should be bustling with activity. You can exercise your arms as well as your legs by hiring a rowing boat. There's a café near the south gate overlooking Beihai Lake, where you can get beer, coffee, tea or cold drinks.

Back on the bike and you'll soon bump into Jingshan Park. There's bicycle parking by the entrance. Jingshan Park is a splendid place to survey the smog of Beijing, get your bearings with 360° views, and enjoy a good overview of the russet roofing of the Forbidden City opposite. There are snack bars both in the park and at the north end of the Forbidden City.

North of Jingshan Park it gets a bit tricky. You want to get off the main road into the small alleys running around the Shisha Hai Lakes. Worth checking out is **Prince Gong's Residence** (*gōngwángfǔ*), which lies more or less at the centre of the arc created by the lakes running from north to south. It's reputed to be the model mansion for Cao Xueqin's 18th-century classic, *A Dream of Red Mansions* (translated as the *The Story of the Stone* by David Hawkes, Penguin, 1980). It's one of the largest private residential compounds in Beijing, with a nine-courtyard layout, high walls and elaborate gardens. Prince Gong was the son of a Qing emperor.

The lake district is steeped in history; if you consult a Beijing map you will see that the set of lakes connects from north to south. In the Yuan Dynasty, barges would come through various canals to the top lake (Jishuitan), a sort of harbour for Beijing. Later the lakes were used for pleasure-boating, and were bordered by the residences of high officials.

The larger lake to the north-west is the **Shisha Houhai** (Lake of the Ten Back Monasteries). Below that is the **Shisha Qianhai** (Lake of the Ten Front Monasteries).

Also around the lakes you'll find the Song Qingling Museum, the retirement residence of Sun Yatsen's respected *taitai* (wife).

Make a small detour here. If you go north-east through the hutongs you will arrive at the Bamboo Garden Hotel *(zhúyuán bīnguǎn)*, which is a wonderful illustration of the surprises that hutongs hold. This was originally the personal garden of Sheng Xuanhai, an important Qing official. There are exquisite gardens and courtyards, renovated compound architecture, and an

---

Hutong Hopping

A completely different side of Beijing emerges in the hutongs or back lanes. The original plan of the city allowed for enclosed courtyards buried down alleys, and though the politics have changed many of the courtyards remain. Given the choice between a high-rise block and a traditional compound, most residents of Beijing would opt for the latter. The compounds have loads more character – and offer courtyards to grow vegetables in.

There are over 3000 hutongs in Beijing, so there's a lot out there to discover. The word derives from Mongolian and means a passageway between tents or yurts. Many of the hutongs are named after markets (fish, pig, rice, sheep) or trades (hats, bowstrings, trousers) once conducted along them. Others took their names as the seats of government offices, or specialised suppliers to the palace (granaries, red lacquer, armour). Yet others were named after dukes and officers.

Around the Forbidden City of yore there were some very odd industries. Wet-Nurse Lane was full of young mothers who breastfed the imperial offspring. They were selected from around China on scouting trips four times a year. Clothes-Washing Lane was where the women who did the imperial laundry lived. The maids, grown old in the service of the court, were packed off to far-away places for a few years so that their intimate knowledge of the royal undergarments would be out of date by the time they got round to gossiping.

Walking along the hutongs kind of destroys the advantage of a lightning visit, and may well lead to you acquiring a Chinese entourage. Charging off on a bicycle is the best way to go. If you see an interesting compound you can stop and peer in, maybe even be invited in; the duller bits you can cruise by. ■

Top: Bike parking zone (RS)
Bottom: Street scene, Liulichang (RS)

expensive restaurant (English menu, alfresco in summer). It's a quiet place to sip a drink.

Another small detour brings you to the Kaorouji Restaurant – not necessarily the cheapest place to get your roast chicken, but the balcony dining in summer is pleasant enough.

Back on the main drag and you come to the **Drum Tower** (*gǔlóu*). It was built in 1420 and has several drums which were beaten to mark the hours of the day, in effect the Big Ben of Beijing. Time was kept with a water clock. It's in pretty sad shape, but an impressive structure nonetheless with a solid brick base. Occasional exhibitions take place here since the tower is connected with local artisans.

Behind the Drum Tower, down an alley directly north, is the **Bell Tower** (*zhōnglóu*), which was originally built at the same time as the Drum Tower, but burnt down. The present structure is 18th-century, and the gigantic bell which used to hang there has been moved to the Drum Tower. Legend has it that the bellmaker's daughter plunged into the molten iron before the bell was cast. Her father only managed to grab her shoe as she did so, and the bell's soft sound resembled that of the Chinese for 'shoe' (*xié*). The same story is told about a couple of other bells in China.

Back on the road you'll reach the former Confucius Temple & Imperial College, now a museum/library complex. Unless you can read stele-calligraphy, you probably won't spend much time here. A stele standing in the hutong ordered officials to dismount at this point but you can ignore that.

By contrast, just down the road is the Lama Temple, one of Beijing's finest. Along the way to the Lama Temple you might pass through several decorated lintels; these graceful archways (*páilóu*), which commemorate mandarin officials or chaste widows, were ripped out of the thoroughfares of Beijing in the 1950s. The reason given was the facilitation of traffic movement. Some have been relocated in parks. The ones you see in this hutong are rarities.

This is the northernmost point of today's journey (you're still with us, aren't you?). Head south, and if you're ready for yet another museum there's the China Art Gallery, a slight detour to the west at the northern end of Wangfujing. Unfortunately, Wangfujing itself is closed to cyclists, so head back to the east on Dongsi Xidajie and you'll find Kentucky Fried Chicken. If the Colonel's fried chicken delights aren't what you had in mind, you could try McDonald's, at the southern end of Wangfujing. No matter what you think of the food, these restaurants are at least as popular as the Forbidden City – and just remember that none of China's emperors ever had the chance to taste a Big Mac, Thickshake or Egg McMuffin.

Launch yourself into the sea of cyclists, throw your legs into cruising speed, and cycle the length of Dongdan south to the east entrance of Tiantan Park. If this is still Day One of your bike tour, you're probably too exhausted to walk inside to see the Temple of Heaven – well, there's always tomorrow. From this point, you're well-positioned to head home (wherever that is).

Places to Stay

In China, you can't simply stay in any hotel which has a vacancy – the hotel must be designated a 'tourism hotel'. It's no use trying to force your way into a Chinese-only hotel; even if the staff would love you to stay, they dare not break the rules, which are enforced by the PSB.

There is more latitude when it comes to price. Foreigners are usually charged twice as much as Chinese for the exact same room, and foreigners are expected to pay in FEC whereas Chinese can pay with RMB. However, these rules are house rules, and the management can offer discounts if so inclined. If you have a residence permit to live or work in China, you can usually pay the Chinese price in RMB. During the off-season (winter, except Chinese New Year) discounting is common, and you may be able to negotiate a better rate for a longer stay, especially at better hotels. There's not much discounting at the budget backpackers' dormitories; prices are low but firmly fixed, though you may be able to pay in RMB with some gentle persuasion and a student ID card.

The majority of accommodation places mentioned here are shown on Map No 1 of Beijing (inside front cover) and on Map Nos 10 and 12 of Central Beijing and the Wangfujing Area (at the back of the book).

PLACES TO STAY – BOTTOM END

Hotels offering budget accommodation are almost entirely concentrated in the south side of the city. While a bit far from the centre of things, transport along the second and third ring roads makes it reasonably fast to get there, at least by taxi. Buses and minibuses from the Beijing railway station are also frequent.

Beijing's most well-known backpackers' hostel is the *Qiaoyuan Hotel (qiáoyuán fàndiàn)* on Dongbinhe Lu in the south of the city near the Yongdingmen railway station. There are different phone numbers for the front building (☎ 303 8861) and rear building (☎ 301 2244). Dorm beds are Y25, double rooms cost from Y60 to Y80 with shower. The rear building is more luxurious but it must be made out of cornflakes because it's falling apart even though it's brand new. The problem with this place is incompetent management – broken plumbing, sneering employees, 'no beds available' in the dorms when the dorms are empty, no one on duty when you want to check out, etc. There have been frequent reports that the foreign-exchange counter in the lobby rips off travellers by sticking a few RMB notes into the pile of FEC when you cash a travellers' cheque. On the other hand, we need to add that many travellers have provoked the staff and contributed to the ill will, so keep your temper in check. This will make it easier for yourself and those who come after you. By way of compensation, there are numerous privately-run services for travellers just outside the hotel such as cheap restaurants, bike hire, laundry service, etc. In summer, the area becomes a true travellers' hang-out right down to the banana muesli pancakes and thieving black-market moneychangers. To get there, take bus No 20 or 54 from the main Beijing railway station to the terminal (Yongdingmen). Or from

Roofscapes in traditional style (RS)

just north of the Chongwenmen Hotel take trolley bus No 106 to the terminal. From the Yongdingmen terminal, walk for about five minutes to the west following the big highway next to the canal. There are also minibuses for Yongdingmen which leave from opposite the main railway station; these cost Y5 and depart when full. From the airport, the cheapest route is to take the airport bus to the second stop (Swissôtel, next to a subway station), then take the subway to Beijing railway station and finally bus Nos 20 or 54 to Yongdingmen.

A lot of people dislike the Qiaoyuan, but there are alternatives. One is the *Jingtai Hotel* (☎ 721 2476, 722 4675) (*jǐngtài bīnguǎn*) at 65 Yongwai Jingtaixi, a small alley running off Anlelin Lu in the south of the city. Dorm beds cost Y20; doubles/triples without bathroom Y50/60; doubles with bathroom Y70, Y90 and Y120. The hotel is clean and pleasant, has hot water all day, and a bar that serves cold beer. The Jingtai will (reluctantly) accept payment in RMB. From the railway station take bus No 39 to the first stop after it crosses the canal; the name of the bus stop is Puhuangyu. From there, you've got a 10-minute walk west on Anlelin Lu. Alternatively, bus No 45 will drop you off at the intersection of Yongdingmennei Jie and Anlelin Lu, also a 10-minute walk from the hotel. Bus No 25 goes right down Anlelin Lu and will drop you off near the hotel; this bus both starts and terminates at the Anlelin Lu's east end.

Just a two-minute walk from the Jingtai Hotel is the *Yongdingmen Hotel* (☎ 721 2125, 721 3344) (*yǒngdìngmén fàndiàn*) at 77 Anlelin Lu. This place is not as good as the Jingtai, but if you arrive during the busy season and the Jingtai is packed out, it beats sleeping on the streets. Doubles/triples are Y58/75 – payment in RMB is acceptable here, but taken with reluctance. Take bus No 39 from the railway station, or follow one of the other routes described above.

The *Jinghua Hotel* (☎ 722 2211) (*jīnghuá fàndiàn*) is on Nansanhuan Xilu, the southern part of the third ring road around Beijing. It's an adequate and friendly place to stay, but the neighbourhood may leave you cold with its ugly apartment blocks. Doubles with private bathroom cost Y50 and Y65. Bus Nos 2 and 17 from Qianmen drop you off nearby. This place is also very convenient for the Haihutun long-distance bus station (buses to cities south of Beijing).

Within walking distance of the Jinghua is the *Lihua Hotel* (☎ 721 1144) (*lìhuá fàndiàn*), 71 Yangqiao, Yongdingmenwai. Dorms cost Y25 and doubles are Y90. Bus No 343 brings you the closest to the Lihua, but No 14 will also do.

The *Longtan Hotel* (☎ 771 1602; fax 771 4028) (*lóngtán fàndiàn*), 15 Panjiayuan Nanli, Chaoyang District, is an excellent alternative to all of the preceding and many budget travellers now stay here. The staff are friendly and there is a good (but not cheap) restaurant. Beds go for Y30 in three-bed rooms or Y20 in a five-bed room and paying in RMB is possible. The communal bathrooms deserve honorable mention for being in extraordinarily good condition. Doubles cost Y80. The hotel is opposite Longtan Park in the south of the city, close to a hospital. Bus No 51 (to the last stop) lets you out near the hotel, but bus No 63 from the railway station is somewhat more frequent. Beware of the rip-off moneychangers hanging around the car park; they are thieves.

The *Traffic Hotel* (☎ 701 1114) (*jiāotōng fàndiàn*), 35 Dongsi Kuaiyu Nanjie, has 82 comfortable rooms but no dorms. Doubles with shared bathroom are Y60; with private bathroom the charge is Y96. The hotel is in a narrow alley running south from Tiyuguan Lu, and signs in English point the way. Bus No 41 runs along Tiyuguan Lu and drops you off at the alley's entrance.

University Dormitories

Typical prices are Y30 for dormitories, Y60 for double rooms. Most of these places have no beds – just Japanese-style tatami mats – but they're reasonably comfortable. There are some problems with staying in these places, however; they aren't hotels, so staff are only on duty from around 8 am to 5 pm with the usual two-hour lunch break. Few staff speak English, and if you start arguing with them about FEC and dirty toilets, you'll be asked to leave. They really don't have to take foreigners, so be on your best behaviour here or risk getting kicked out. They provide no special amenities like laundry service or bike rentals but they often have cheap student cafeterias, although these are only open for short hours such as 5 to 6 pm. Overall, it's usually better to stay in the budget hotels, but the university hostels offer an alternative if the hotels are packed out. And finally, we've had complaints from travellers that some of their small items have been nicked from their rooms, apparently by the staff working in some of these places.

One possible place to stay with a very central location is the *Central Institute of Fine Arts* (☎ 55 4731) (*zhōngyāng měishù xuéyuàn*), at 5 Xiaowei Hutong in an alley off Wangfujing near the Beijing Hotel. The main problem with this place is that it's too popular and beds are hard to get, so give them a call first. This school built the now famous 'Goddess of Democracy' which came to symbolise the democracy movement during the Tiananmen protests in 1989. From the railway station take bus 103 to Wangfujing. After you enter the gate of the campus, go to the eighth floor of the building on your left.

One other university that accepts foreigners is the *Beijing Language Institute* (☎ 201 7798) *(běijīng yǔyán xuéyuàn)*, 15 Xueyuan Lu, Haidian District. Many foreigners come here to study Chinese. Bus No 331 stops in front of the school.

Other possibilities include the *Beijing Teachers' College (běishīdà)*, *People's University (rénmín dàxué)* and *Qinghua University (qīnghuá dàxué)*, all in the northern part of the city.

PLACES TO STAY – MIDDLE

Oddly enough, bargaining for a room is usually more successful in the mid-range hotels than in the budget places. Many travellers report getting discounts of 30% or more (during off-season at least) if paying several days rent in advance

The *Tiantan Sports Hotel* (☎ 701 3388; fax 701 5388) *(tiāntán tǐyù bīnguǎn)* is at 10 Tiyuguan Lu, Chongwen District. The hotel derives its name from its position between Tiantan Park and the gymnasium. It hosts sports-minded group tours but will take whoever else turns up. The hotel has a YMCA tinge to it but is a bright, airy place in a good location with friendly staff. It even boasts the *Shanghai Jakarta Restaurant*, which dishes up decent Indonesian-style food. To get there take the subway one stop from the main railway station to Chongwenmen, then bus Nos 39, 41 or 43. Doubles are Y130.

Also in the south-east of Beijing, east of Longtan Park, is *Leyou Hotel* (☎ 771 2266; fax 771 1636) *lèyóu fàndiàn* at 13 Dongsanhuan Nanlu, Chaoyang District. This decent mid-range hotel has 171 rooms with doubles for Y130, Y150, Y180 and Y280. Take bus Nos 28 or 52 to the terminus.

Beiwei Hotel (☎ 301 2266; fax 301 1366) *(běiwěi fàndiàn)* at 13 Xijing Lu, Xuanwu District is on the west side of Tiantan Park. Take the subway to Qianmen, then bus No 5 south; or you can take bus No 20 direct from the main railway station. Standard rooms are Y130, superior Y150 and suites Y200. This place belongs to the neighbouring Rainbow Hotel but is cheaper.

The *Far East Hotel* (☎ 301 8811; fax 301 8233) *(yuǎndōng fàndiàn)*, at 90 Tieshuxie Jie, Qianmenwai, Xuanwu District, is actually on the west end of Dazhalan (south-west of Qianmen). It's an excellent location. With double rooms costing Y75 to Y140, this place would qualify as budget accommodation except that the cheap rooms are almost always full. The pricier rooms still aren't a bad deal and this place is worth checking out.

Not far away is the *Dongfang Hotel* (☎ 301 4466; fax 304 4801) (*dōngfāng fàndiàn*), at 11 Wanming Lu (south of Qianmen). Standard doubles are Y198, superior rooms cost Y258. It's good value for the high standards and central location.

Lüsongyuan Hotel (☎ 401 1116; 403 0416) (*lǚsōngyuán bīnguǎn*) is at 22 Banchang Hutong, Dongcheng District. Doubles cost Y160, the staff are very friendly and the place is highly recommended. The problem is that it's difficult to find. When you approach the hutong from either end, it doesn't seem that there could be a building of such high standard halfway down; but rest assured, the hotel does exist. The hutong is one way and many taxi drivers are reluctant to drive down it in the wrong direction, but others are perfectly willing to do so. To get there, head north up Wangfujing, following the road in a sharp left and then right turn round the back of the China Art Gallery. Continue as far as the second hutong north of Di'anmen, then turn left. Bus No 104 from Beijing railway station comes close. *Chongwenmen Hotel* (☎ 512 2211; fax 512 2122) (*chóngwénmén fàndiàn*) at 2 Chongwenmen Xi Dajie is a good, mid-range place with a very central location that makes the five-star hotels jealous. Standard rooms are Y190, suites cost Y260 to Y300.

The *Yuexiu Hotel* (☎ 301 4499; fax 301 4609) (*yuèxiù dàfàndiàn*), at 24 Xuanwumen Dong Dajie, is a few blocks south of the Xidan shopping district and CAAC. Economy doubles are Y130, standard Y150, superior Y160, deluxe Y180 and suites Y240 to Y370. It's a bargain for such a well-located hotel of this standard.

Huabei Hotel (☎ 202 2266) (*huáběi dàjiǔdiàn*), at 3 Gulouwai Huangsi Dajie, is in north-central Beijing (north of Ditan Park). Singles are Y160, doubles Y200 to Y320, triples Y240. This place is popular with Taiwanese, which means they crank up the karaoke at night.

The *Sihai Hotel* (☎ 500 6699) (*sìhǎi bīnguǎn*), at Liugongfen, Dongzhimenwai, is close to the Holiday Inn Lido and the airport. Despite this, doubles are only Y120, making it the best deal in this neighbourhood. The desk staff seem friendly enough.

The *Guanghua Hotel* (☎ 501 8866; fax 501 6516) (*guānghuá fàndiàn*), at 38 Donghuan Beilu, Chaoyang District, is just down the road from the China World Trade Centre on Jianguomenwai. At Y170 for a double, it's dirt cheap for this neighbourhood, but it's also a possible target for renovation and future high prices.

The *Shangyuan Hotel* (☎ 831 1122) *(shàngyuán fàndiàn)*, at Xie Jie, Xizhemenwai, Haidian District, is near the Xizhimen (north) railway station. Doubles are only Y120, which explains why it's usually full.

The *Xizhimen Hotel* (☎ 832 7755) *(xizhimèn fàndiàn)*, at 42 Xie Jie, is also next to the Xizhimen railway station. Doubles are Y108 which is excellent value, but like its neighbour this hotel is almost perpetually full.

PLACES TO STAY – TOP END

Keeping up with the top-end hotels in Beijing is like skiing uphill. No sooner does one extravaganza open its doors than the ground-breaking ceremony is held for an even more luxurious pleasure palace.

Foreign experts and students should be delighted to know that the Holiday Inn Lido Hotel offers rooms for US$20 per night (green card specials) if you have the right credentials. Ditto for many Swiss-owned hotels – give *Swissôtel* a try.

The *Beijing Hotel* (☎ 513 7766; fax 513 7307), *(běijīng fàndiàn)* at 33 Dong Chang'an Jie is the most central hotel in the capital and is therefore highly prized by visitors and dignitaries. Standard rooms cost Y460, superior ones Y920 and suites Y1610. Even at those rates, it's still significantly cheaper than renting an apartment or office in pricey Beijing and rooms are often leased out on a long-term basis. The roof of the west wing commands a great view of Tiananmen Square and the Forbidden City.

The *China World Hotel* (☎ 505 2266; fax 505 3167) *(zhōngguó dàfàndiàn)* is at 1 Jianguomenwai Dajie, east of the Friendship Store. Also known as the World Trade Centre, this is one of the finest places in Beijing. And it should be, with standard rooms at Y1035 and suites for Y1408. Despite the price, it's often full.

The *Jianguo Hotel* (☎ 500 2233; fax 500 2871) *(jiànguó fàndiàn)* is on the same street, at 5 Jianguomenwai Dajie. Opened in 1982, this was China's first joint-venture hotel. The Chinese staff of about 600 have no spittoons and are not allowed newspapers, cigarettes, naps or even chairs, but can rake in as much as three times an ordinary Beijinger's salary. Superior rooms are Y540, deluxe Y570, suites Y747 to Y920.

An unusual place to stay is the *Hua Thai Apartment Hotel* (☎ 771 6688; fax 771 5266) *(huátài fàndiàn)*, Jinsong Dongkou (south-east Beijing). It's unusual because you actually get an apartment with kitchen and other home-like facilities. This place might be worth considering if you're planning a long stay and have a sufficient budget. Twin rooms are Y300; a room with four beds costs Y400.

The *Friendship Hotel* (☎ 849 8888; fax 849 8866) *(yǒuyí bīnguǎn)*, at 3 Baishiqiao Lu, is halfway between the Beijing Zoo and the Summer Palace. Originally built in 1954 for Soviet advisors, the place has been upgraded substantially. Facilities are legendary, including the Olympic-size swimming pool (open to all), theatre, tennis courts and 1900 rooms. You practically need a map to find your way around. Standard rooms cost Y517, superior rooms Y748 and suites are Y1265-6210.

There are plenty of other upmarket places to stay in the capital. The following hotels are presented in alphabetical order:

Beijing Asia Hotel (☎ 500 7788; fax 500 8091) *(yàzhōu dàjiŭdiàn)*, 8 Xinzhong Xijie, Gongren Tiyuchang Beilu. Convenient for disembarking airport bus, and near to Dongsishitiao subway station. Standard Y345, deluxe Y374, suites Y690 to Y3450.

Beijing Grand Hotel (☎ 201 0033; fax 202 9893) *(yuánshān dàjiŭdiàn)*, 20 Yumin Dongli, Deshengmenwai, Xicheng District (north-central Beijing near Ditan Park). Taiwanese management; 187 rooms; standard Y288, superior Y316 and deluxe Y403.

Capital Hotel (☎ 512 9988; fax 512 0323) *(shŏudū bīnguǎn)*, 3 Qianmen Donglu (east of Qianmen – convenient location). Standard Y345, superior Y1035, deluxe Y1495, suites Y2472 to Y11, 500, plus 10% service charge.

Chains City Hotel (☎ 500 7799; fax 500 7668) *(chéngshì bīnguǎn)*, 4 Gongren Tiyuchang Donglu, Chaoyang District (east-central Beijing). Standard Y288, superior Y402.

Continental Grand Hotel (☎ 491 5588; fax 491 0106) *(wŭzhōu dàjiŭdiàn)*, 8 Beichen Donglu, Beisihuan Lu, Andingmenwai (in the Asian Games Village). Opened in 1990, this amazing place has 1259 rooms and resembles a city in itself. Standard rooms are Y348, superior Y406 and suites Y870 to Y1740.

CVIK Hotel (☎ 512 3388; fax 512 3542) *(sàitè fàndiàn)*, 22 Jianguomenwai Dajie (across from the Friendship Store), 341 rooms. Standard Y345 plus 10% service charge.

Gloria Plaza Hotel (☎ 515 8855; fax 515 8533) *(kǎilái dàjiŭdiàn)*, 2 Jianguomennan Dajie (short distance south-west of the Friendship Store). Standard Y375, superior Y690, deluxe Y920, plus 10% service charge.

Grace Hotel (☎ 436 2288; fax 436 1818), *(xīn wànshòu bīnguǎn)*, 8 Jiangtai Xilu, Chaoyang District, on the road to the airport in north-east Beijing. Standard singles/doubles Y490/546, superior Y690, deluxe Y863, suites Y1438 to Y2013.

Great Wall Sheraton (☎ 500 5566; fax 500 3398) *(chángchéng fàndiàn)*, Dongsanhuan Beilu (north-east Beijing). Deluxe doubles are Y512; five stars.

Holiday Inn Crowne Plaza (☎ 513 3388; fax 513 2513) (*guójì yìyuàn huángguān jiàrì fàndiàn*), 48 Wangfujing Dajie, Dengshixikou. Standard Y690, superior Y748, suites Y834 to Y2012, plus 15% service charge.

Holiday Inn Downtown (☎ 832 2288; fax 832 0696) (*jīndū jiàrì fàndiàn*), 98 Beilishi Lu, Xicheng District. Actually not right downtown, but on the west side of the second ring road near the Fuchengmen subway station. Standard singles/twins Y270/305; three stars.

Holiday Inn Lido (☎ 500 6688; fax 500 6237), (*lìdū jiàrì fàndiàn*), Jichang Lu, Jiangtai Lu, on the road to the airport in north-east Beijing. Outstanding facilities include one of the best delicatessens and bakeries in Beijing – if you don't stay here, at least eat here. Standard Y260, superior Y316, suite Y1495, plus 15% surcharge.

Hotel Beijing-Toronto (☎ 500 2266; fax 500 2022) (*jīnglún fàndiàn*), 3 Jianguomenwai Dajie (east of the Friendship Store). Standard Y375, deluxe Y431, plus 15% surcharge. Great buffets!

Hotel New Otani (☎ 512 5555; fax 512 5346) (*chángfù gōng*), 26 Jianguomenwai Dajie (directly opposite the International Club), 512 rooms. Standard singles/doubles Y690/805, deluxe Y805/920, suites Y1320 to Y2590.

Huadu Hotel (☎ 500 1166; fax 500 1615) (*huádū fàndiàn*), 8 Xinyuan Nanlu, north-east Beijing. Nice but somewhat overpriced. Standard Y260, superior Y300, suites Y400, plus 10% surcharge.

International Hotel (☎ 512 6688; fax 512 9972) (*guójì fàndiàn*), 9 Jianguomennei Dajie. Home to the CITS ticket office and very convenient for Beijing main railway station. Standard singles/doubles Y345/431, suites Y546 to Y3450.

Jingguang New World Hotel (☎ 501 8888; fax 501 3333) (*jīngguǎng xīn shìjiè fàndiàn*), Jingguang Zhongxin, Hujialou, Chaoyang District (east Beijing). An incredible five-star glass tower with indoor pool. Standard Y805, superior Y920, deluxe Y1092, suites Y2185 to Y5750.

Jinlang Hotel (☎ 513 2288; fax 512 5839) (*jīnlǎng dàjiǔdiàn*), 75 Chongnei Dajie, Dongcheng District (one block west of Beijing main railway station). Singles/doubles Y357/391 – overpriced, but you're paying for the convenient location.

Kunlun Hotel (☎ 500 3388; fax 500 3228) (*kūnlún fàndiàn*), 2 Xinyuan Nanlu, Chaoyang District (north-east Beijing). Standard rooms cost Y380 plus 15% service charge.

Mandarin Hotel (☎ 831 9988; fax 831 2136) (*xīndàdū fàndiàn*), 21 Chegongzhuang Lu, south of the Beijing Zoo; 354 rooms; economy rooms Y316, standard Y437, superior Y506, deluxe Y794, suite Y1080; four stars.

Minzu Hotel (☎ 601 4466; fax 601 4849) (*mínzú fàndiàn*), 51 Fuxingmennei Dajie (west of CAAC and Xidan). Standard Y276, superior Y316. Don't confuse this place with the palatial Minzu Cultural Palace just next door, an exclusive cadre hang-out off-limits to foreigners.

New Century Hotel (☎ 849 2001; fax 831 9183), *(xīn shìjì fàndiàn)*, 6 Shoudu Tiyuguan Nanlu, south-west of Beijing Zoo. Standard Y690, superior Y748, deluxe Y776, suites Y1208 to Y8050. Taiwanese, Japanese & French restaurants, a gleaming white high-rise.

Novotel (☎ 513 8822; fax 513 9088) *(sōnghè dàjiǔdiàn)*, 88 Dengshikou, Dongcheng District (north part of Wangfujing). Superior Y518, deluxe Y633, suites Y805.

Olympic Hotel (☎ 831 6688; fax 831 8390) *(àolínpǐkè fàndiàn)*, 52 Baishiqiao Lu, Haidian District, just north-west of the Beijing Zoo. Standard Y345, superior Y690, deluxe Y1380. Cold architecture, making it look like a giant CD player.

Palace Hotel (☎ 512 8899; fax 512 9050) *(wángfǔ fàndiàn)*, 8 Jinyu Hutong, Wangfujing. A five-star hotel notable for the Watson's pharmacy (drugstore) in the basement. Standard rooms are Y920.

Park Hotel (☎ 721 2233; fax 721 1615) *(bǎilè jiǔdiàn)*, 36 Puhuangyu Lu in the far south of Beijing. The hotel itself is in an incredibly dumpy neighbourhood and is definitely not worth the price. Doubles cost Y256.

Parkview Tiantan Hotel (☎ 701 2277; fax 701 6833) *(tiāntán fàndiàn)*, 1 Tiyuguan Lu, Chongwen District (east of Tiantan Park). Standard Y310, superior Y345, suite Y690, plus 10% service charge.

Peace Hotel (☎ 512 8833; fax 512 6863) *(hépíng bīnguǎn)*, 3 Jinyu Hutong, Wangfujing. Standard Y431, superior Y460, deluxe Y805, suites Y4600.

Qianmen Hotel (☎ 301 6688; fax 301 3883) *(qiánmén fàndiàn)*, 175 Yong'an Lu (south-west of Qianmen). Standard Y260, suites Y400 to Y800. Has bicycle rentals. A relative bargain and good place to stay.

Rainbow Hotel (☎ 301 2266; fax 301 1366) *(tiānqiáo bīnguǎn)*, Xijing Lu, Xuanwu District (south-west of Qianmen). Standard Y231, superior Y330 – a popular place to stay.

Sara Hotel (☎ 513 6666; fax 513 4248) *(huáqiáo dàshà)*, 2 Wangfujing Dajie. Superior Y805, deluxe Y920, suites Y1035 to Y4600. Raging disco and Mexican restaurant.

Shangri-La Hotel (☎ 841 2211; fax 841 8002) *(xiānggélǐlā fàndiàn)*, 29 Zhizhuyuan Lu, Haidian District (west of Zizhuyuan Park). Superior Y718, deluxe Y977, suites Y1150 to 2012, plus 15% service charge.

Swissôtel (☎ 501 2288; fax 501 2501) *(běijīng gǎng'aò zhōngxīn)* is on the corner of Gongren Tiyuchang Beilu & Chaoyangmen Bei Dajie. Convenient for disembarking airport bus, and near Dongsishitiao subway station; 454 rooms; superior Y520, deluxe Y575, suites Y690 to Y2875, all plus 15% surcharge.

Taiwan Hotel (☎ 513 6688; fax 513 6896) *(táiwān fàndiàn)*, 5 Jinyu Hutong, Wangfujing. Economy Y260, standard Y288, deluxe Y345, suites Y632 to Y747. Top-notch location.

Tianlun Dynasty Hotel (☎ 513 8888; fax 513 7866) *(tiānlún wángcháo fàndiàn)*, 50 Wangfujing Dajie. Standard Y357 plus 10% service charge. The 'aircraft-hanger' interior is positively weird; the front desk is on the third floor.

Xiyuan Hotel (☎ 831 3388; fax 831 4577), *(xīyuàn fàndiàn)*, 1 Sanlihe Lu, immediately south of the Beijing Zoo. The hotel has 709 rooms; singles/doubles Y400/575; four stars.

Yanjing Hotel (☎ 832 6611; fax 832 6130) *(yānjīng fàndiàn)*, 19 Fuxingmenwai Dajie (west Beijing). Standard Y220, superior Y242, deluxe Y330.

Yanshan Hotel (☎ 256 3388; fax 256 8640) *(yānshān dàjiǔdiàn)* is at 138A Haidian Lu, near the Friendship Hotel in far north-west Beijing. Twin rooms cost Y380 plus 15% service charge.

Yanxiang Hotel (☎ 437 6666; fax 437 6231), *(yānxiáng fàndiàn)*, 2A Jiangtai Lu, Dongzhimenwai, on the road to the airport in north-east Beijing. Doubles cost Y260. Three stars. This is a cadre hang-out – lots of guards and guns, but no doubt about the security! This hotel tends to be almost always full.

Yuyang Hotel (☎ 466 9988; fax 466 6638) *(yúyáng fàndiàn)*, Xinyuan Xili, Chaoyang District (north-east Beijing). Standard singles/doubles Y430/490, superior Y518/575, deluxe Y575/633, suites Y1150 to Y2300.

Zhaolong Hotel (☎ 500 2299; fax 500 3319) *(zhàolóng bīnguǎn)* is on the corner of Dongsanhuan Beilu & Gongren Tiyuchang Beilu (east Beijing on the third ring road). Standard Y316, deluxe Y661, suites Y3450 to Y5750, all plus 10% surcharge.

Zhongyuan Hotel (☎ 831 8888; fax 831 9887) *(zhōngyuàn bīnguǎn)*, 18 Xie Jie, Gaoliangqiao, Xizhimenwai. It's north-west of the Xizhimen (north) railway station in a somewhat isolated spot. The hotel has 414 rooms; superior Y430, deluxe Y488, villas Y546, suites Y805 to Y2243. Some nice villas around a swimming pool in addition to the main high-rise rooms.

LONG TERM

For those planning to live, work or study long-term in Beijing, the good news is that the standard of accommodation has been steadily improving. Years ago, foreigners had little choice but to live in luxury hotels. The bad news is that China's housing market is anything but free. Lots of regulations govern just where, when and how a foreigner can live.

The two basic rules are this: government policy is to keep Chinese and foreigners separated, and foreigners are expected to pay the earth for apartments. If you harbour dreams of living with a Chinese family as a paying guest in their dirt-cheap flat, you can stop dreaming, because it's nearly impossible. The PSB will eventually find out, you'll be kicked out and your host family will face the consequences.

If you are coming to study, your school will almost certainly have some sort of dormitory. If you teach or work for the government, your housing will probably be provided for free or at the Chinese price (next to nothing).

Housing costs really begin to escalate when you go to work for a foreign company or embassy, or if you want to set up your own office. In fact, it's not unusual for foreigners to live in their offices because maintaining two addresses is prohibitively expensive. Chinese apartment blocks are almost entirely government-owned, and the lack of a free market means you don't just browse through the newspapers looking at the classified ads because there aren't any. You will find some occasional half-page ads in the China Daily for luxury flats. Most of these are in big residential and office towers along Jianguomenwai and the Sanlitun area in northeast Beijing. Examples would include the Capital Mansion, the Landmark Towers or the China World Trade Centre. In these places, reckon on something like US$5000 per month for an apartment. Despite the ridiculous prices, there are waiting lists to get in!

One other possible option is to rent an old villa belonging to various government organisations and work units that need the money. Some foreigners have done this and succeeded in finding 'bargains' for US$2000 or so, but it's not easy to come across these places.

Places to Eat

Most eating houses named in this chapter are also located on our maps of Beijing. See Map No 1 on the inside front cover, and Map Nos 10 and 12 at the back of the book.

CHEAP EATS

Snacks can be found at roadside stalls, especially around breakfast time. Also try the market areas, and the ground floor of restaurants (the masses' section). Small vendors are making a comeback, ever since the return of the ice cream soda in 1980 after an absence of 14 years. In fact a health problem exists as a result of the unsupervised production of popsicles by home-based entrepreneurs.

Travellers residing in the Qiaoyuan Hotel or thereabouts can choose from a wide selection of cheapie restaurants which have sprung up to milk the backpacker market. English menus are a nice feature in this neighbourhood; the locals have learned to make decidedly un-Chinese specialities such as banana muesli. There are so many restaurants clustered in the alleys around the hotel that it's hard to know where to start, but all are good. Some popular ones include the *Candlelight*, *Monkey* and *Pink House*.

In bygone days, the Qianmen area of Beijing had the largest concentration of snack bars, and still is a good place to go hunting. Down Qianmen Dajie is the *Zhengmingzhai Cakeshop*. The *Jinfeng* at 157 Qianmenwai sells Beijing-style *baozi* (steamed buns).

Off the beginning of Dazhalan on Liangshidian hutong is *Zhimielou*, which sells dragon-whisker noodles – strands as fine as silk, an old Qing recipe.

The *Duyichu* at No 36 Qianmen and close to Dazhalan is an ancient restaurant serving shaomai (little steamed dumplings).

For baozi (steamed buns) and *jiaozi* (dumplings), try the *Hongxinglou* at 1 Beiwei Lu on the west side of the Temple of Heaven. It also serves shaomai and noodles. Twenty different kinds of jiaozi (in season) can be ordered and there's even frozen take-away. The crowded ground floor has two kinds of jiaozi, plus beer and cold cuts. The next floor has jiaozi and Shandong-style seafood and pork dishes. The seafood is not cheap, but if you stick to jiaozi this can be a very inexpensive place to eat.

Spices and beans (CT)

The *Ritan Park Restaurant* to the north of the Friendship Store has classy jiaozi and Western snacks. It's patronised by Westerners and housed in a classical-style building.

CHINESE FOOD

Beijing Duck

Otherwise known as the 'Big Duck', the *Qianmen Quanjude Roast Duck Restaurant* (☎ 701 1379) *(qiánmén quànjùdé kǎoyādiàn)* is at 32 Qianmen Dajie, on the east side, near Qianmen subway. This is one of the oldest restaurants in the capital, dating back to 1864. Prices are moderate, and there's a cheaper section through the right-hand doorway. Same duck, same kitchen. The cheap section is very crowded so if you don't get there by 6 pm, forget it. Beer is brewed on the premises. The duck is served in stages: first come boneless meat and crispy skin with a side dish of shallots, plum sauce and crêpes, followed by duck soup made of bones and all the other parts except the quack. Language is not really a problem; you just have to negotiate half or whole ducks.

The *Beijing Hotel* has a number of top-class restaurants. Of interest is the genial west-wing dining room on the seventh floor, where you can get painless Beijing Duck – easy to order, menus in English and no queues (but not cheap). Some think the food's not up to scratch, but perhaps their taste buds are more finely tuned than most. Other gourmet novelties like bear paws are served if you've got the bucks.

The *Bianyifang Duck Restaurant* (☎ 701 2244) (*biànyífāng kǎoyādiàn*) is at 2 Chongwenmenwai Dajie. This place uses a slightly different method of preparation – a closed oven.

Restaurant exterior (RS)

Sichuan

The place to go is the *Sichuan* (☎ 33 6356) *(sìchuān fàndiàn)* at No 51 Rongxian Hutong. To get there go south from Xidan intersection (where Xidan meets Chang'an), turn left into a hutong marked by traffic lights and a police-box, and continue along the hutong till you find the grey wall entrance. In contrast to the bland interiors and peeling paint of most of the capital's restaurants, this one is housed in the sumptuous former residence of Yuan Shikai (the general who tried to set himself up as an emperor in 1914). The compound decor is spectacular, and the several dining rooms will clean out your wallet very fast. For cheaper food continue to the back of the courtyard, veer right, and there's a dining room with good meals for a few yuan per head if you're sharing dishes. You'll need some drinks for this one! It's a good idea to bring your own in case they've run out (or better still, a flask of yoghurt to cool the flames). The food is out of this world: fiery pork, explosive prawns, bamboo shoots, bean curd (tofu), beef dishes, some seafood, and side dishes of cucumber. In the more expensive parts of the restaurant variety is greater, but the back dining room will sate the appetite.

Another favourite haunt is the *Emei Restaurant* (☎ 86 3068) *(éméi fàndiàn)* on Yuetan Beijie. This restaurant, on the north side of Yuetan Park about three km west of the Forbidden City, serves very cheap, hot Sichuan food and has friendly staff.

Next to the *Qianmen Roast Duck Restaurant* you'll find the *Lili* (☎ 75 1242) *(lìlì cāntīng)* at 30 Qianmen. The Sichuan-style spicy chicken and hot noodles with peanuts and chillies are very good. They serve some of the best dumplings in Beijing too.

Also try the *Shuxiang* (☎ 54 5176) *(shǔxiāng cānguǎn)* at 40 Chongwenmennei just across the street from the Chongwenmen Hotel.

Hunanese

The *Quyuan* (☎ 66 2196) *(qǔyuán jiǔlóu)* is at 133 Xidan Beidajie north of Chang'an, west side, in a red-fronted building by an overhead bridge. The Hunan food served here is hot and spicy like Sichuan cuisine. On the menu is onion dog, dog soup (reputed to be an aphrodisiac) and dog stew. For those with canine sensibilities, perhaps try the Hunan-style duck spiced with hot pepper, or some seafood, and several styles of noodles. The desserts with lychees are good; they can be varied or custom-made if you phone in advance. The food is cheap and the management nice.

The *Xiangshu* (☎ 55 8351) *(xiāngshǔ cāntīng)* is on the Wangfujing side of Dongfeng Market. The food is a combination of Sichuan and Hunan, highly recommended. Try the Xiangshu for the 'silver-thread rolls' which are Beijing's best pastry.

Mongolian Hotpot & Muslim Barbecue

Kaorouwan (☎ 65 7707) *(kǎoròuwǎn fànzhuāng)* at 102 Xuanwumennei, south of the Xidan intersection and on the east side of the street, serves Muslim barbecues. You can do your own skewers if the wind is blowing in the right direction.

Hongbinlou (☎ 65 5691) *(hóngbīnlóu fànzhuāng)* at 82 Xi Chang'an Jie, just east of the Xidan intersection, serves shashlik (kebabs), Beijing Duck and Mongolian hotpot. Lamb banquets can be ordered in advance.

Shoudu Kaorouji (☎ 44 5921) at 37 Shichahai is difficult to find but worth it in summer. Go to the Drum Tower *(gǔlóu)* area, turn into a hutong to the left immediately before the Drum Tower as you go north, and follow it down to the lakeside. The dowdy interiors of most Chinese restaurants make you feel boxed in – they often have no windows – but here you've got a view of the lake, the alleys and the activity in the area. In summer tables are moved onto the balcony. This is a place for potless hotpot and Muslim barbecues.

Shanghainese

If this greasy cuisine appeals to you, try *Laozhengxing* (☎ 511 2148) *(lǎozhèngxīng fàndiàn)* at 46 Qianmen Dajie. This place serves the whole range of Shanghai-style seafood including fish, eel, and hairy crabs when in season.

Cantonese

Guangdong Restaurant (☎ 89 4881) *(guǎngdōng cāntīng)* in the Xijiao market opposite the zoo serves up Beijing Duck and Cantonese-style cuisine, including turtle and snake.

Vegetarian

The Yangzhou-style *Gongdelin Vegetarian Restaurant* *(gōngdélín sùcàiguǎn)* at 158 Qianmen Dajie is probably the best in the city. It gets rave reviews and serves up wonderful veggie food with names to match. How about the 'peacock in pride' or 'the fire is singeing the snow-capped mountains'? The helpings are generous, the prices low and the staff friendly.

Other Chinese Restaurants

Just across the street from the Confucius Temple is a restaurant called – you guessed it – the *Confucius Restaurant*. It looks like it would bankrupt any budget traveller and is crawling with staff, but a meal for four people with dessert and tea costs around Y120, or Y30 per person.

Huaiyang Fanzhuang at 217 Xidan Beidajie has a Jiangsu-cuisine section serving hairy crab in season.

Shaguoju Restaurant (☎ 66 1126) *(shāguōjū fànzhuāng)*, in a tacky building at 60 Xisi Nandajie, is further north toward the Xisi intersection. Pork is served in many forms, some dishes in earthenware pots; the food is cheap.

Kangle Restaurant (☎ 44 3884) *(kānglè fàndiàn)* at 259 Andingmennei is further east of the Drum Tower near the Jiaodaokou intersection. This place serves up Fujian and Yunnan styles of food. Expensive 'across-the-bridge noodles' must be ordered in advance for a minimum of four people. Also try Yunnan-style steamed chicken, seafood and *san bu zhan* (sweet sticky pudding).

NON-CHINESE FOOD

All the large tourist hotels serve Western food of varying quality and price. Travellers pining for a croissant or strong coffee will be pleased to know that Beijing is the best place in China to find such delicacies.

Good bets for Western meals are the *Beijing* and *Minzu* hotels. The *Jianguo Hotel* serves Holiday Inn, California home-style cooking at greater than Californian prices. Check the ads in the China Daily for novelty events; anyone for a Texas spare-rib barbecue at the *Great Wall Sheraton Hotel*?

German

Within the caverns of the enormous Lufthansa Centre (just north of the Great Wall Sheraton) is *Paulaner Bräuhaus*, an excellent German restaurant. This place brews its own genuine German beer! Don't confuse this place with the other Bräuhaus in the China World Trade Centre, because the latter is a bar only, not a restaurant.

French

Maxim's of Paris (☎ 512 2110) *(bālí mǎkèxīmǔ cāntīng)* is not just in Paris – a branch can be found within the precincts of the Chongwenmen Hotel. The joint China-French venture initiated by Pierre Cardin opened in October 1983 with the understanding that the Chinese would take it over after 10 years. Now that the deadline has passed, the place has gone sharply downhill and it is not recommended. The deteriorating standard of food and service has *not* been accompanied by a commensurate drop in price. Dinner for two – *sacré bleu* – is a cool Y200 or so excluding that Bordeaux red or the Alsatian Gewürztraminer.

Mexican

Alfredo's in the Sara Hotel *(huáqiáo dàshà)* at 2 Wangfujing Dajie is a Mexican restaurant by day. In the evening, there are often live bands and loud music – especially on Monday after 10 pm – and the place becomes more of a dance bar. Otherwise, it's sedate enough and the food is fine. The cook is indeed from Mexico, but the prices are Beijing luxury hotel-style.

Similar fare can be had at *Mexican Wave* (☎ 506 3961) on Dongdaqiao Lu near the intersection with Guanghua Lu. Dongdaqiao Lu is the major north-south road between the Friendship Store and the Jianguo Hotel on Jianguomenwai. Mexican Wave serves set lunches (Western not Mexican food) from noon until 2.30 pm and dinners (Mexican style) are from around 6 pm onwards. The prices are definitely not for backpackers.

The *Holiday Inn Lido* also has a Mexican restaurant.

Russian

Overall not too good, but you may find it a welcome break from the noodle and rice dishes. The *Moscow Restaurant* (☎ 89 4454) *(mòsīkē cāntīng)* is on the west side of the Soviet-designed Exhibition Centre in the zoo district. The vast interior has chandeliers, a high ceiling and fluted columns. Foreigners are shuffled to a side room overlooking the zoo (which has, by the way, no connection with the menu). The food gets mixed reviews, but it's definitely Russian – borsch, cream prawns au gratin, pork à la Kiev, beef stroganoff, black bread, soups and black caviar, moderately priced.

Indian

This style of cooking hasn't yet taken Beijing by storm, but there is at least one decent restaurant serving subcontinent cuisine. The *Holiday Inn Downtown (jīndū jiàrì fàndiàn)* at 98 Beilishi Lu in the Xicheng District is where you can get your chappatis and tandoori chicken. The tariff will run to about Y100 per person. The food is outstanding, the service rotten.

Muslim Food

This type of cuisine is not only excellent but dirt cheap, if you know the right place to look for it. The right place is a little street called Baiwanzhuangxi Lu in a neighbourhood known as Ganjiakou (not far south of the zoo). This is where Beijing's Uigur minority congregates; if you didn't know better you'd swear you were walking down a side street in Ürümqi. Restaurants here are very specialised: the way to eat is to collect some Uigur bread (outstanding stuff!) from the stalls, then sit down in a tea shop or restaurant and order Uigur tea (contains sugar and salt plums), some vegetable dishes, noodles and shashlik. You'll probably have to collect your meal from several proprietors, because one restaurant won't have the full range of goodies. It's often best to eat with a small group (two to four persons) so you can get several dishes and sample everything. Alternatively, you can just drift from stall to stall sampling as you go.

This is a true haven for budget travellers, as prices in this neighbourhood are dirt cheap.

Fast Food

From the day of its grand opening in 1992, *McDonald's (màidāngláo)* has been all the rage with Beijingers who easily outnumber the foreigners eating here. Though prices are low, this is one of Beijing's most prestigious restaurants, the venue for cadre birthday parties and a popular hang-out for the upper crust. There are separate lines for RMB and FEC, but everyone can pay with RMB. Not surprisingly, there's no waiting at the FEC counter. A plastic Ronald McDonald sits on a bench just outside the door and Chinese queue up to be photographed with him. McDonald's occupies a prime piece of real estate on the corner of Wangfujing and Dongchang'an Jie, just east of the Beijing Hotel. Business has been so good that a second (but smaller) branch opened in 1993 at the

Chang'an Market on Fuxingmenwai Dajie near the Yanjing Hotel.

By comparison, *Kentucky Fried Chicken (kěndéjī jiāxiāng jī)* enjoys a much longer history in Beijing, having spread its wings in 1987. At the time of its opening, it was the largest KFC in the world. The colonel's smiling face is just across the street from Mao's mausoleum in Tiananmen Square. If this doesn't make the late Chairman turn over in his grave, nothing will. A smaller Kentucky Fried has hatched one block east of Wangfujing on the southwest corner of Dongsi Xidajie and Dongsi Nan Dajie.

Pizza Hut (bìshèngkè) has arrived on the Beijing fastfood scene, with two branches. One is on Dongzhimenwai Dajie in the Sanlitun area (next to the Australian Embassy). The other hut is less conspicuous, at 33 Zhushikou Xi Dajie, which is the second major road south of Qianmen (first big road south of Dazhalan Dajie).

Shakey's Pizza (xīkè měishì cāntīng) has entered the pizza war with a branch on Dongchang'an Jie just east of the Wangfujing McDonald's.

Carl's Jr (kèlì hànbǔbāo) and *Dairy Queen (dílì bīngqílín)* occupy the same building on the south-east corner of Wangfujing and Jinyu Hutong near the Taiwan Hotel. On Sunday, Chinese dressed as clowns are hired to draw in business.

Uncle Sam's is on the south side of Jianguomenwai. It's just east of CITS but don't let that ruin your appetite; this place seems to do a pretty good business. The food is mixed Western and Chinese and not bad, although it gets mixed reviews from travellers.

You've heard of Maxims – Beijing's fast-food equivalent is *Minim's*. No joke; it's one door down from its famous big sister in the Chongwenmen Hotel. Lots of tin-foil and surly staff, but for a few yuan they'll put a burger, pizza or sandwich into the microwave oven for you. Mediocre coffee, OK chocolate mousse, and the tomato soup in a cup is not bad.

SELF-CATERING

Supermarkets

Despite the abundance of cheap Chinese restaurants, self-catering in the capital is certainly a reasonable idea. There's no other way to satisfy those sudden urges for peanut butter, Dutch cheese and Vegemite on French rolls. Or whatever.

Beijing has several notable supermarkets, the best being Hong Kong or Japanese joint-ventures, and at

McDonald's, Beijing-style (RS)

most of them you can pay in RMB. The 'express FEC line' is for suckers. The best of the bunch is *Yaohan* on the south side of Jianguomenwai, across the street from the CITIC building and adjacent to Scite Tower. The supermarket is in the basement.

On the eastern fringe of Jianguomenwai is the China World Trade Centre. Go down into the basement to find a fully-fledged *Wellcome* supermarket, imported lock, stock and shopping carts from Hong Kong. The Wellcome slogan 'low everyday prices' doesn't quite describe the situation in Beijing, but you'll find all the familiar goodies right down to the 'No Frills Dried Lemon Peel'.

Just next to the CITIC building is the *Friendship Store*; when you enter the building turn sharp right to find the food section. The supermarket is decidedly mediocre, but new competition may force an improvement soon.

If you're out in Sanlitun embassyland, there's a small *Friendship Supermarket* serving the diplomatic (and not so diplomatic) crowd. Selection is limited but you can score chocolate chip cookies and other imported delicacies. The store is at 5 Sanlitun Lu. In the same neighbourhood just north of the Great Wall Sheraton Hotel is the enormous *Lufthansa Centre* – yes, it is a ticket office for a German airline, but also a multistorey shopping mall. There is a supermarket of sorts in here, but you may have a hard time finding the food amongst the personal stereos, computers and colour TVs.

Bakeries

Chinese bread is about as tasty as a wet sponge, but a few entrepreneurs in Beijing have started to introduce edible baked goods to the masses. Most of the customers are foreigners, but some of the locals are beginning to catch on and you can expect the number of European-style bakeries to multiply.

One fine effort in this direction is *Vie de France (dà mòfáng miànbāo diàn)*, which boasts genuine croissants and prices a fraction of what you'd pay in Paris. This bakery currently has two branches; one is at the Qianmen Zhengyang Market, just south-west of Chairman Mao's mausoleum and adjacent to the enormous Kentucky Fried Chicken. The other branch is on the south-east corner of Xidan and Xichang'an Dajie, across the street from the CAAC office.

Within the confines of the *Friendship Store*, there is a bakery off to the right as you enter the store. Prices here are also very low but selection is limited.

Other places to look are some of the big hotels, a few of which have sent their staff off to Europe for a wintertime crash course in making German black bread and Danish pastries. Unfortunately, hotel prices tend to be outrageous. The deli in the *Holiday Inn Lido* is a good example; you'll pay Y20 or so for a slice of delectable chocolate cake.

Entertainment

AFTER DARK

To locate the venues for most forms of entertainment mentioned here, refer to Map Nos 1, 10 and 12; you'll find the first of these on the inside front cover and the others at the end of the book.

Discos

Alfredos in the Sara Hotel *(huáqiáo dàshà)* at 2 Wangfujing Dajie is normally a mellow Mexican restaurant, but on Monday nights after 9 pm or so, the heavy metal is rolled out and the volume is turned up loud enough to shatter a taco chip, not to mention eardrums. The foreign bands (Filipino, American and who knows?) keep the disco floor thumping until the wee hours of the morning. This is mostly a hang-out for Westerners and Chinese are few in number here, although you do see the odd Hong Konger or Beijing trendy. There is no cover charge but you are expected to buy a couple of pricey drinks.

The *Harmony Club (xìngfú jùlèbù)* is a sort of Chinese and foreign counter-culture club offering hard rock music on Saturday nights. It's an unusual place, built in a former bomb shelter which at leasts solves problems with noise and neighbours. This place attracts a lot of young people despite the Y30 cover charge. The Harmony Club is in a hutong just south of the East Gate of Tiantan Park; go down the stairs to enter.

Bars

The *Bräuhaus* in the China World Trade Centre on Jianguomenwai is a small bar with occasional live rock bands. There are just a few tables and drinks are expensive, but there's no cover charge and it is popular with the foreign community. This place shouldn't be mistaken for the Paulaner Bräuhaus in the Lufthansa Centre, which is a German restaurant.

The *Pig & Whistle* (☎ 500 6688 ext 1976) on the ground floor of the Holiday Inn Lido is the most British thing in Beijing besides the UK Embassy. Operating hours are from 5 pm until 1 am on weekdays, or noon until 1 am on weekends and holidays.

CINEMA *(diànyǐng)*

Film is out of the boring stage and starting to delve into some contemporary issues, even verging on Cultural Revolution aftershock in a mild manner. Altogether there are about 50 cinemas in the capital, showing a mix of Chinese and foreign films. The International Club near the Friendship Store shows Chinese films with English subtitles or simultaneous translation into English, every Saturday night at 7 pm. The Rainbow Hall in the International Hotel (☎ 512 9960 ext 1883) also has Chinese films with English subtitles, but only shows these once every two weeks on Saturday night. Ditto for the Great Wall Sheraton Hotel (☎ 500 5566 ext 2280). The Friendship Hotel shows old foreign and Chinese films (with simultaneous translation) every Friday night.

Or you can just dive in with the locals at the Dahua Cinema *(dàhuá diànyǐng yuàn)* at 82 Dongdan Beidajie. One of Beijing's trendy movie houses is the Shoudu Cinema *(shǒudū diànyǐng yuàn)* at 46 Xichang'an Dajie (near Xidan and CAAC). Another very fashionable place is the Dizhi Cinema Hall *(dìzhì lǐtáng)* at 30 Yangrou Hutong, which is just west of Xisi Nandajie (the northern end of Xidan). This place also has a dancehall, karaoke bar and hall for playing snooker. Less trendy but perhaps more educational is the Tuxin Cinema (☎ 841 5566 ext 5727), actually inside the National Library *(běijīng túshūguǎn)*, which is just north of Zizhuyuan Park in north-west Beijing.

Some other good bets are the Dazhalan Cinema *(dàzhàlán xìyuàn)* on Dazhalan Jie; the Jixiang at 14 Jinyu Hutong, off Wangfujing; and the Chaoyang *(cháoyáng xìyuàn)*, on the corner of Dongsanhuan Beilu and Chaoyang Beilu out in the eastern part of the city.

CLUBBING

Sporting, recreational and club facilities are to be found in the Friendship Hotel and the International Club. The International Club can be dull during the daytime – a place with signs telling you what not to do – but livens up in the evening. There are tennis courts, billiard tables, a full-sized swimming pool, a bowling alley (a bummer – you have to set up your own pins) and a bar/restaurant (it's debatable whether the chef isn't in fact a can opener).

Major hotels have swimming pools, tennis courts and other amenities which are open to non-guests who pay the requisite fees. Many places charge daily admission fees, but others offer discounts if you pay on a monthly

Cinema advertising (RS)

basis. The Shangri-la Hotel, for example, charges Y450 per month for the use of the pool and exercise rooms.

CULTURAL SHOWS

Back in the days of Mao, 'cultural events' often meant revolutionary operas featuring evil foreign and Kuomintang devils who eventually were defeated by heroic workers and peasants inspired by the Little Red Book. Fortunately, performances have improved considerably. The China Daily carries a listing of cultural evenings recommended for foreigners; also worth checking is the Beijing Weekend which is published once a week. Offerings include concerts, theatre, minority dancing and some cinema. You can reserve ahead by phoning the box office via your hotel, or pick up tickets at CITS (for a surcharge) – or take a risk and just roll up at the theatre.

Theatre

Entertainment is cheap compared to the West, but prices are rising. Beijing is on the touring circuit for foreign troupes, and these are also listed in the China Daily. They're somewhat screened for content, but they've been beefing up what's available. When Arthur Miller's *Death of a Salesman* was acted out by Chinese at the

Capital Theatre, it was held over for two months by popular demand.

The same theatre staged some avant-garde Chinese theatre. It put on two plays by Gao Zingjian, incorporating theatre of the absurd and traditional Chinese theatrical techniques. One of the plays, *Bus-stop*, is based on eight characters who spend 10 years at a bus stop, only to discover that the service was cancelled long ago. That's either a vicious comment on the Beijing bus service, or a sly reference to Gao's stint in re-education camp during the Cultural Revolution. Or maybe it's a direct steal from Samuel Beckett or Luigi Pirandello.

Something closer to the Western version of tragicomic theatre enjoys a small but dedicated following in Beijing. There are performances almost every night at the Qingyi Theatre (☎ 55 3672, 55 6029) *(qīngyì jùchǎng)* at 15 Dongchang'an Jie in the Dongcheng District. Shows get under way around 7 pm. Check the China Daily for the current schedule.

Concerts

In the concert department they've presented Beethoven's Ninth played on Chinese palace instruments, such as tuned bells copied from those found in an ancient tomb. Other classical instruments are being revived for dance-drama backings. Bizarre performances are often staged for foreign tour groups and some of these have to be seen to be believed. Perhaps trial runs before touring overseas with cultural shows tailored to Western tastes? Some of this stuff would go down great in Las Vegas.

Song & Dance Shows

These come in different varieties, from Western style to Chinese or occasionally in the style of China's ethnic minorities. They advertise in the China Daily, but may be cancelled despite being advertised in the newspapers.

One likely venue for song & dance shows is the Capital Theatre *(shǒudū jùchǎng)* (☎ 55 0978) at 22 Wangfujing Dajie. There is another Capital Theatre (☎ 512 3492) *(shǒudū tǐyùguǎn)* which has a different name in Chinese and is on Baishiqiao Lu. Both places are worth checking out.

There are also song & dance shows at the Gloria Plaza Hotel (☎ 515 8855) *(kǎilái dàjiǔdiàn)* at 2 Jianguomennan Dajie (not far from the Friendship Store).

Karaoke

As elsewhere in China, karaoke has had a heavy impact. There's no need to list the karaoke venues here, because there are so many that you'll have a hard enough time avoiding them. Remember that some of the karaoke places try to cheat foreigners in a big way, with outrageous service charges for 'talking to the hostesses'. Some of the hostesses hang out on the street near their place of employment and try to trick unsuspecting males (even domestic tourists) into going inside for 'a few drinks'. The bill for a couple of Cokes could amount to six months in wages for the average Chinese worker.

Other Entertainment

As for other events, you might like to delve into items listed in the local newspapers. If you can read Chinese or get a translation you can find out about sporting events, puppet theatre, storytelling and local cinema. These may be sold out, but scalpers do a roaring trade.

You can even set yourself up as an English teacher at the Beijing 'English corner' in Purple Bamboo Park, near the Capital Stadium in the Haidian District. Students come here to practise their English and foreigners come to meet the locals – a fair exchange.

Television, if you're that kind of addict, brings a lot of different types of entertainment directly into your hotel room, if you have the right kind of room, that is. There are a number of satellite channels, and if you have the proper electronic hookups you can enjoy Western movies and perhaps some naughty Japanese videos. Programmes (not the naughty ones) are listed in the China Daily. CCTV and Beijing TV are the two local stations, which broadcast mostly in Chinese except for daily English and Japanese lessons. TV is actually a good way of studying Chinese, especially the kids' programmes with fascinating forms of Chinese animation.

OPERA *(píngjù)*

Earlier in the century teahouses, wine shops and opera were the main nightlife in Beijing; of these, only the opera has survived (just). The opera bears little resemblance to its European counterpart. The mixture of singing, dancing, speaking, mime, acrobatics and dancing can go on for five or six hours; an hour is usually long enough for a Westerner. Plots are fairly basic so the language barrier is not really a problem. The problems are the music, which is searing to Western ears, and the heavy and stylised acting.

When you get bored after the first hour or so, and are wearying of the high-pitched singing, the local audience is with you all the way – spitting, eating apples, breast-feeding an urchin on the balcony, or plugging into a transistor radio (important sports match?). It's a lively prole audience viewing entertainment fit for kings.

Another problem is trying to find a performance that really is Beijing opera. All you can do is patiently troop around the theatre circuit until you hit the one that's still dishing up the real thing. Most performances start around 7 or 7.30 pm.

The most reliable (but most expensive) performances are put on for foreigners nightly at the Liyuan Theatre (☎ 301 6688 ext 8860 or 8986). This theatre is in fact inside the Qianmen Hotel (*qiánmén fàndiàn*) at 175 Yong'an Lu. Ticket prices depend on seat location, starting at Y8. For Y20 you can sit at a table and enjoy snacks and tea while watching the show. For Y40 you get better snacks and a table with a superior location. Performances here last just one hour with sporadic translations into English flashed on an electronic signboard; these translations can sometimes be funnier than the dialogue.

At other theatres, performances are less regular and attempts at translation usually nonexistent, but tickets typically cost only around Y5 depending on seat location. A good place to try is the Jixiang Theatre (*jíxiáng guānyuàn*) on Jinyu Hutong, just east of Wangfujing. It's next to Carls Jr and Dairy Queen, and across the road from the Taiwan Hotel. In the same neighbourhood is the Capital Theatre (*shǒudū jùcháng*) on the north end of Wangfujing, just south of the Sara Hotel. Also worth trying is the Tianqiao Theatre (*tiānqiáo jùcháng*) at 30 Beiwei Lu just west of Tiantan Park. The largest opera hall in the city is the China Grand Theatre (*zhōngguó jùyuàn*), just north of the Shangri-La Hotel in north-west Beijing.

ACROBATICS (*tèjì biǎoyǎn*)

Two thousand years old, and one of the few art forms condoned by Mao, acrobatics is the best deal in town. Acts take place in various locations, normally advertised in the China Daily. The International Club (☎ 532 2188) (*guójì jùlèbù*) at 21 Jianguomenwai Dajie (west of the Friendship Store) has performances for Y15. Another venue for acrobatics is the Chaoyang Theatre (*cháoyáng xìyuàn*) on the corner of Dongsanhuan Beilu and

Chaoyang Beilu out in the eastern part of the city. Shows start around 7 pm and acts change nightly.

SPORTS

Golf

The art of poking a white ball around a lawn enjoys considerable prestige value in face-conscious China. If your face needs a lift, check out the Beijing International Golf Course (☎ 974 6388) *(běijīng guójì gāo'ěrfū qiú cháng)*. This Chinese-Japanese joint venture opened in mid-1986. The 18-hole golf course is 35 km north of Beijing close to the Ming Tombs in Changping County, and the course was used during the 1990 Asian Games. Pushing that little ball around is not cheap, but the course is in good condition and the scenery is spectacular. Visitor fees are Y250 on weekdays and Y300 on weekends and public holidays. You can rent a set of golf clubs for Y70 and spiked golf shoes for Y50.

There is another golf course *(jīcháng gāo'ěrfū qiú cháng)* just north of Capital Airport, known in English as the Airport Golf Links.

Horse Riding

Several horse-riding parks *(qímǎ cháng)* have opened to the north-west of Beijing in the Western Hills. The nearest is at the Fragrant Hills, but the best of the lot is Kangxi Grasslands (see the Excursions section). Prices are reasonable, especially the further out you get from the city.

Hash House Harriers

This is mainly for foreign residents of Beijing, so if you're just passing through you might not be enthusiastically welcomed. Hash House Harriers is a loosely-strung international club with branches all over the world. It appeals mainly to young people, or the young at heart. Activities typically include a weekend afternoon easy jogging session followed by a dinner and beer party which can extend until the wee hours of the morning.

Beijing's Hash is very informal. There is no club headquarters and no stable contact telephone or address. Nonetheless, finding the Hash is easy. Some embassy employees know about it, otherwise ask at the Mexican Wave (☎ 506 3961) bar and restaurant on Dongdaqiao Lu (east of the Friendship Store). Various bars and beer houses are also likely places to find Hash members;

simply ask any likely-looking foreign resident of Beijing. The usual meeting time and place for the Hash is on Sunday afternoons at 3 pm in front of the Jianguo Hotel, but this is certainly not engraved in stone so don't be surprised if no one is there on the day you go.

Shopping

The Chinese produce some interesting items for export – tea and clothing being just two of them. Within China the consumer boom has arrived, and gone are the ration cards and the need for intermediaries with influence to buy TV sets and refrigerators. Chinese department stores are like Aladdin's Caves stocked to the rafters with goodies, and are tourist attractions in themselves.

Unfortunately, quality has not kept pace with quantity. There is an awful lot of junk on sale, such as zips which break literally the first time you use them, imitation personal stereos which last a week, electrical appliances which go up in smoke the first time they're plugged in. Given this state of affairs, you might wonder how China manages successfully to export so much. The simple fact is that export items are made to a much higher standard than items for the local markets. Always test zips, examine stitching and, in the case of electrical appliances, plug them in and make sure they won't electrocute you before handing over the cash. Chinese sales clerks expect you to do this; they'll consider you a fool if you don't.

WHERE TO SHOP

There are several notable Chinese shopping districts offering abundant goods and low prices: Wangfujing, Qianmen (including Dazhalan hutong) and Xidan. Pricier but more luxurious shopping areas can be found in the embassy areas of Jianguomenwai and Sanlitun. There are also some specialised shopping districts – Liulichang, Hongqiao Market and Zhongguancun.

Tourist attractions like the Forbidden City, as well as major hotels, have garish souvenir shops stocking arts & crafts. Otherwise, speciality shops are scattered around the city core. Stores are generally open from 9 am to 7 pm seven days a week; some are open from 8 am to 8 pm. Bargaining is not a way of life in the stores, but on the free market it certainly is.

Down jackets are one of the best bargains you can find in Beijing and are essential survival gear if you visit northern China during winter. Good buys are stationery (chops, brushes, inks), prints, handicrafts, clothing and antiques. Small or light items to buy are silk scarves and underwear, T-shirts, embroidered purses, papercuts,

Shopping Guide	
Antiques	Hongqiao Market
	Liulichang
Arts & Crafts	Wangfujing
Books	Jianguomenwai
	Wangfujing
Chinese Herbal Medicines	Dazhalan
	Wangfujing
Clothing	Dazhalan
	Jianguomenwai
	Qianmen
Department Stores	Dazhalan
	Jianguomenwai
	Sanlitun
	Wangfujing
	Xidan
Fabrics	Dazhalan
	Jianguomenwai
Musical Instruments	Qianmen
Photographic Film/Processing	Jianguomenwai,
	Wangfujing
Pottery	Qianmen
Technology	Zhongguancun

wooden and bronze buddhas, fold-up paper lanterns and kites.

A description of the shopping districts and bargains to be had is as follows:

Wangfujing
(wángfújǐng)

This prestigious shopping street is just east of the Beijing Hotel. It's a solid block of stores and a favourite haunt of locals and tourists seeking bargains. Westerners now call it 'McDonald's St' due to a certain well-known restaurant which occupies the south-east corner of the main intersection. In pre-'49 days it was known as Morrison St, catering mostly to foreigners. The name Wangfujing derives from a 15th-century well, the site of which is now occupied by the offices of the People's Daily.

Wangfujing's biggest emporium is the Beijing Department Store (*běijīng bǎihuò dàlóu*). It was once the city's largest and has been surpassed in size by some of the new tourist palaces, but you can't beat this place for price and variety.

For Chinese herbal medicines, try the Wangfujing Medicine Shop (☎ 553 775) at 214 Wangfujing Dajie. Of prime interest to foreign travellers is the Foreign Languages Bookstore at No 235 Wangfujing Dajie. This is not

---

Name Chops

The traditional Chinese name chop or seal has been used for thousands of years. It is quite likely that people began using name chops because Chinese characters are so complex and few people in ancient times were able to read and write. In addition, chops date back to a time when there was no other form of identification such as fingerprinting, picture ID cards or computer files.

A chop served both as a form of identification and as a valid signature. All official documents in China needed a chop to be valid. Naturally, this made a chop quite valuable, for with another person's chop it was possible to sign contracts and other legal documents in their name.

Today, most Chinese are literate, but the tradition lives on. In fact, without a chop it is difficult or impossible to enter into legally-binding contracts in China. A chop is used for bank accounts, entrance to safe-deposit boxes and land sales. Only red ink is used for a name chop.

If you live in China for work or study, you will almost certainly need to have a chop made. If you're staying a short time, a chop makes a great souvenir. A chop can be made quickly, but first you will need to have your name translated into Chinese characters.

There are many different sizes and styles of chops. Inexpensive small chops can be carved from wood or plastic, while expensive ones can be carved from ivory, jade, marble or steel. Most Chinese people have many chops to confuse a possible thief, though they run the risk of confusing themselves as well. One chop might be used for their bank account, another for contracts and another for a safe-deposit box. Obviously, a chop is important and losing one can be a big hassle.

Since the people who carve chops don't check your ID, it might occur to you that obtaining a fake or forged chop would be very easy. Indeed, it is. It's also a very serious crime in China. ■

Shop front (JO)

only *the* place in China to buy English-language books, but has a good music tape section upstairs which you should check out. There is also a Xinhua Bookstore at No 212 next to McDonald's. Most of the books are in Chinese but the map department upstairs is well worth your attention.

Wangfujing is the place to go to buy film (although the Friendship Store also offers very competitive prices). You can even find slide film here, but check the expiry dates before you hand over your money. It's also a good place to go for photo processing. Print film can be processed in one hour and the quality isn't bad. The Beijing Hotel and International Club also do processing, but at a higher price. Slides can also be developed but quality varies from acceptable to abysmal. If your slides mean anything to you, wait until you get home to have them processed. Wangfujing is also a good place to obtain passport-type photos of yourself in a hurry.

If you're into arts & crafts, it's worth looking into the Beijing Arts & Crafts Service Department at 200 Wangfujing.

If there's anything you think that is impossible to buy in Beijing, check out Watson's (*qūchénshì*), in the basement of the Palace Hotel on Jinyu Hutong (east of Wangfujing). This place sells every vitamin known to humanity, as well as sunscreen (UV lotion), beauty creams, tampons and the widest selection of condoms in China. Prices are in FEC but you can use RMB for a surcharge (sometimes this works out cheaper depending on the current black-market rate).

To find your way around this area, refer to the Wangfujing Area Map (No 17) at the back of this book.

Xidan
(*xīdān*)

Officially known as Xidan Beidajie (see Central Beijing map, No 15), this street aspires to be a little Wangfujing. There are fewer foreign tourists here and the shops tend to cater mainly to the local market. The biggest of the bunch is the Xidan Shopping Centre (*xīdān gòuwù zhōngxīn*), offering everything from imported Swiss chocolate to fashionable hairdos.

Qianmen & Dazhalan
(*qiánmén hé dàzhàlán*)

If Wangfujing is too organised for you, the place to go and rub shoulders with the proletariat is Dazhalan, a hutong running west from the top end of Qianmen. It's a heady jumble of silk shops, department stores, theatres, herbal medicine, food and clothing specialists and some unusual architecture. The hutong is really more of a sight than a place to shop, but you might find something that catches your eye.

Dazhalan has a definite medieval flavour to it, a hangover from the days when hutongs sold specialised products – one would sell lace, another lanterns, another jade. This one used to be called Silk Street. The name

Dazhalan refers to a wicket-gate that was closed at night to keep undesirable prowlers out.

In imperial Beijing, shops and theatres were not permitted near the city centre, and the Qianmen-Dazhalan District was outside the gates. Many of the city's oldest shops can be found along or near this crowded hutong.

Just off the beginning of Dazhalan at 3 Liangshidian Jie is Liubiju, a 400-year-old pickle & sauce emporium patronised by discriminating shoppers. Nearby is the Zhimielou Restaurant, which serves imperial snacks. On your right as you go down Dazhalan is a green concave archway with columns at No 5; this is the entrance to Liufuxiang, one of the better-known material and silk stores and a century old.

Dazhalan at one time had five opera theatres. The place used to be thronged with theatre-goers both by day (cheap rehearsals) and by night (professionals). The nightlife lingers on with two performing theatres, and pedicab men wait for the post-theatre crowds as the rickshaw drivers did many years ago. No 1 Dazhalan was once a theatre.

Another famous shop is the Tongrentang at No 24, selling Chinese herbal medicines. It's been in business since 1669, though it doesn't appear that way from the renovations. It was a royal dispensary in the Qing Dynasty, and creates its pills and potions from secret prescriptions used by royalty. All kinds of weird ingredients – tiger bone, rhino horn, snake wine – will cure you of anything from fright to encephalitis, or so they claim. Traditional doctors are available on the spot for consultation; perhaps ask them about fear of railway stations (patience pills?).

Dazhalan runs about 300 metres deep off the western end of Qianmen. At the far end where the hubbub dies down is a bunch of Chinese hotels. Dazhalan was once the gateway to Beijing's redlight district; the brothels were shut down in 1949 and the women packed off to factories. Towards the western end of Dazhalan is one of the best department stores on the whole street. It's called Sun City (*tàiyáng chéng*), but the sign is in Chinese characters only.

Qianmen Dajie, and Zhushikou Xidajie leading off to the west, are interesting places in which to meander. On Qianmen Dajie there are pottery stores at Nos 99 and 149, ethnic minority musical instruments at Nos 18 and 104, and a nice second-hand shop at No 117. At 190 Qianmen Dajie is the Army Store, just the place to stock up on green PLA overcoats and Snoopy hats. You'll find the two areas of Dazhalan and Qianmen shown on the Central Bejing Map No 10, given at the back of this book.

Liulichang
(líulíchǎng)

Not far to the west of Dazhalan is Liulichang, Beijing's antique street. Although it's been a shopping area for quite some time, only recently has it been dressed up for foreign tourists. The stores here are all designed to look as if they're straight out of an ancient Chinese village, and this makes for good photography even if you don't buy anything. Plenty of the entrepreneurs hang out a sign in English advising you that they accept American Express, JCB and so on. Almost everything on sale looks antique, but most are fakes. There is, of course, nothing wrong with buying fakes as long as you're paying the appropriate prices. Overall, you'll probably do better antique-hunting in Hongqiao Market or, better yet, the antique market in Tianjin which is particularly impressive at weekends.

Jianguomenwai
(jiànguóménwài)

The Friendship Store *(yǒuyí shāngdiàn)* at 17 Jianguomenwai (☎ 500 3311) is the largest in the land, and stocks both touristy souvenirs and everyday useful items. Not long ago it was *the* place to shop in Beijing, so exclusive that only foreigners and cadres were permitted inside. These days anyone can go in, and for good reason – business is fading fast due to competition from the Yaohan department store, Lufthansa Centre and Chinese department stores which offer a wider selection of goods at the same or lower prices. As a result, the Friendship Store is increasingly trying to appeal to the local market, and its prices have dropped. The top floor carries furniture, carpets, arts & crafts – in short, the overpriced touristy junk. On the middle floor are clothing items, fabrics, cosmetics, toys and appliances. The ground floor is where the really useful items are found: tinned and dried foods, tobacco, wines, spirits, coffee, Chinese medicines and film. The book and magazine section is a gold mine for travellers long starved of anything intelligent to read. To the right are a supermarket and deli. There is a café on the ground floor, where the atmosphere is fine but prices are too high, and business is being siphoned off by nearby competitors. Chinese-made goods can be paid for with RMB but imports require FEC. The demand for FEC is the main reason why this store is losing business, but the management seems indifferent.

Street scene, Dazhalan (RS)

Yaohan (*bābaǐbàn*) is a huge Japanese department store on the south side of Jianguomenwai, opposite the CITIC building, and has an enormous selection of goods. The best deals are to be found in the supermarket and restaurant in the basement. There are, of course, lots of pricey luxuries on offer such as the latest fashions, makeup and perfumes; kitchenware is in basement No 2. Everything can be purchased in RMB.

The Xiushui Silk Market (*xiùshuǐ dōngjiē*) is on the north side of Jianguomenwai between the Friendship Store and the Jianguo Hotel. Because of the prestigious location amidst the luxury hotels, this place is filled elbow-to-elbow with foreign tourists at times. Go early to avoid crowds and forget it on Sunday. This market is one of the best places to pick up good deals in upmarket clothing, everything from silk panties and negligees to leather moneybelts. Bargaining is expected here, though it's sometimes difficult because of all the foreign tourists willing to throw money around like water.

Ritan Park is north of the Friendship Store, and on the west side of the park and intersecting with it at a 90° angle is Yabao Lu Clothing Market. This place is enormous and no Beijing department store could hope to match the variety and low prices on offer here, but bargaining is *de rigueur*. To borrow a slogan from American country stores, 'If you don't find it here, you don't need it.'

Refer to the map of Central Beijing (Map No 10) at the back of this book to find the location of the above-mentioned places.

Sanlitun
(sānlǐtún)

The Sanlitun Embassy Compound (see Map No 19 at the back of the book) is in north-east Beijing, close to the Great Wall Sheraton Hotel. Like Jianguomenwai, the stores here are decidedly upmarket, but almost everything can now be bought with RMB and prices are not too outrageous.

The Lufthansa Centre *(yānshā shāngchéng)*, also known as the Kempinski Hotel *(kǎibīnsījī fàndiàn)*, falls into a category by itself, being Beijing's first flashy multi-storey shopping mall. You can buy everything here from computer floppy disks to bikinis (but who in China wears the latter?). A supermarket is in the basement.

Hongqiao Market
(hóngqiáo shìchǎng)

This very interesting market is the place to look for antiques, both real and fake. Most of the goods are under 100 years old, so they may not meet the textbook definition of 'antique'. This is no big deal as long as you're not paying antique prices. There are plenty of reasonably priced second-hand goods here.

Besides the old stuff, there are intriguing speciality items; for example, you can buy a Little Red Book for Y20 (be sure to bargain). One favourite among foreigners is a 'youth of China' alarm clock with a picture of a rosy-cheeked female Red Guard enthusiastically waving the Little Red Book.

Hongqiao Market is at the north-east corner of Tiantan Park across from the Yuanlong Silk Shop – you'll find it on the Central Beijing map (Map No 10) at the back of this book.

Zhongguancun
(zhōngguāncūn)

This is Beijing's hi-tech district, but unless you're stocking up on laser eye-surgery equipment, the real attraction here are the computer shops. However, it's not recommended that you buy a computer here unless you are going to live in Beijing for a while. You'll find lower prices, better quality and a wider selection in Hong

Kong. On the other hand, foreigners living in Beijing report that most of the shops here are good about honouring their warranties, an important consideration because sending a machine to Hong Kong for service is a time-consuming and expensive procedure.

All this having been said, Zhongguancun has a few specialised items to interest computer freaks. Much of the world's Chinese-language software originates in this neighbourhood, including that which was used to produce this book. Pirating software is a big local industry too but if you're interested, be aware that most Chinese software is copy-protected and many of the pirated programmes are infected with computer viruses.

Zhongguancun is in Haidian District in the north-west part of Beijing, not far from the Summer Palace – see Map No 1 on the inside front cover. Just off Zhongguancun is the shopping district for low-tech consumer goods (music tapes, clothing, food, etc), known as Haidian Tushucheng.

Excursions

All the places in this chapter can be visited as day trips from Beijing, although in several cases you might find it worth staying overnight. You might also like to plan an itinerary taking in more than one place of interest on the same trip out of the city. To help you plan, refer to Map No 23 at the back of the book, which gives an overview of the sites mentioned here, their relative distance from each other and from Beijing.

THE GREAT WALL

(chángchéng) 长城

Construction began 2000 years ago during the Qin Dynasty (221-207 BC) when China was unified under Emperor Qin Shihuang. Separate walls, built by independent kingdoms to keep out marauding nomads, were linked up. The effort required hundreds of thousands of workers, many of them political prisoners, and 10 years of hard labour under General Meng Tian. An estimated 180 million cubic metres of rammed earth was used to form the core of the original wall, and legend has it that among the building materials used were the bodies of dead workers.

The wall never really did perform its function as a defence line to keep invaders out. As Genghis Khan supposedly said, 'The strength of a wall depends on the courage of those who defend it.' Sentries could be bribed. However, it did work very well as a kind of elevated highway, transporting men and equipment across mountainous terrain. Its beacon tower system, using smoke signals generated by burning wolves' dung, transmitted news of enemy movements quickly back to the capital. To the west was Jiayuguan Pass, an important link on the Silk Road where there was a Customs post of sorts, and where unwanted Chinese were ejected through the gates to face the terrifying wild west.

Marco Polo makes no mention of China's greatest public works project. Both sides of the wall were under the same government at the time of his visit, but the Ming Great Wall had not been built. During the Ming Dynasty (1368-1644) a determined effort was made to rehash the whole project, this time facing it with bricks and stone slabs, some 60 million cubic metres of them.

This created double-walling running in an elliptical shape to the west of Beijing, and did not necessarily follow the older earthen wall. This Ming project took over 100 years, and costs in human effort and resources were phenomenal.

The wall was largely forgotten after that, but now it's reached its greatest heights as a tourist attraction. Lengthy sections of it have been swallowed up by the sands, claimed by the mountains, intersected by road or rail, or simply returned to dust. Other bits were carted off by local peasants to construct their own four walls, a hobby that no-one objected to during the Cultural Revolution. The depiction of the wall as an object of great beauty is a bizarre one, since until recent times it symbolised tyranny.

Badaling Great Wall
(bādálǐng chángchéng) 八达岭长城

Most foreigners see the wall at Badaling, 70 km north-west of Beijing at an elevation of 1000 metres. It was restored in 1957 with the addition of guard rails. The section is almost eight metres high with a base of 6½ metres and a width at the top of almost six metres. It runs for several hundred metres after which, if you keep going, are the unrestored sections where the crowds peter out. Originally the wall here could hold five horsemen riding abreast; nowadays it's about 15 tourists walking abreast.

Unfortunately, if you take a tour bus or train from Beijing you hit peak hour, and you only get a touch over an hour at the wall. Many are dissatisfied with such a paltry stretch of time at one of the most spectacular sights in the PRC. The solution is to take one-way tours or public transport, spend the time you want, and then figure out a way to get back (you can negotiate a minibus ride for around Y10).

The Great Wall Circle Vision Theatre was opened in 1990 and is a 360° amphitheatre showing 15-minute films about the wall. You hear about the wall's history and legends via a narration in English or Chinese; other languages may be added later.

To get up on top of the wall, there is an admission fee of Y15. The wall also has a cable car, which costs Y55 for foreigners (only Y5 with student card).

You can spend plenty more on a trashy 'I Climbed the Great Wall' T-shirt, a talking panda bear doll, a cuckoo clock that plays 'The East is Red' or a plastic reclining buddha statue with a lightbulb in its mouth. For an

MAP 4

1 North No 8 Tower
2 Fort
3 North No 4 Tower
4 Car Park
5 Yanshan Restaurant
6 Industrial & Commercial
  Administrative Office
7 Reclining Dragon
  Restaurant
8 Tourist Shop
9 Restaurant
10 Tourist Shop
11 North Gate Lock & Key
12 Foreigners' Restaurant
13 Outer Town of Juyyong
  Pass
14 South Fourth Tower
15 Qinglongqiao Station
16 Zhan Tianyou Statue
17 Qinglongqiao Village
18 Qinglongqiao New
  Station

1 北八楼
2 炮台
3 北四楼
4 停车场
5 燕山餐厅
6 工商所
7 卧龙餐厅
8 商店
9 餐厅
10 商店
11 北门锁钥
12 外宾餐厅
13 居庸外镇
14 南四楼
15 青龙桥站
16 詹天佑像
17 青龙桥村
18 青龙桥新站

八达岭长城

Badaling Great Wall

additional fee you can get your snapshot taken aboard a camel and pretend to be Marco Polo.

If you're hungry, you won't have to look far for food – everything from yoghurt to Beijing Duck is available.

Getting There & Away There are cheapie Chinese tours departing from a number of venues. Some depart from the south side of Tiananmen Square (near Kentucky Fried Chicken). Others depart from the car park in front of the Beijing railway station (west side of station), but don't get confused with the buses heading for Tianjin (which depart from the exact same spot). You can also catch buses from the car park of the Workers' Stadium (*gōngrén tǐyùguǎn*) which is on Gongren Tiyuchang Beilu next to the Beijing Asia Hotel and the Dongsishitiao subway station. Departures are only in the morning, around 7.30 to 8 am. Tours cost about Y15 or so, but you often have to bargain and there is sometimes the sickening tendency to try raising the price after you're halfway to the wall. Make sure you understand just what time the tour returns to Beijing unless you want to find another way back. Some tour operators have nice air-con buses; others have older vehicles which appear to date back to the Qing Dynasty.

CITS, CTS, big hotels and everyone else in the tourist business offer tours to Badaling. Prices border on the ridiculous, with some hotels asking over Y300 per person.

Local buses also ply the route to the wall but it's slow going. Take bus Nos 5 or 44 to Deshengmen, then No 345 to the terminal (Changping), then a numberless bus to the wall (alternatively, bus No 357 goes part way along the route and you then hitch). Another route is bus No 14 to Beijiao long-distance bus station, which is north of Deshengmen, then a numberless bus to the wall. Going on local buses saves some money but it's a headache even if you speak Chinese, and if you don't it's a migraine.

You can reach the wall by express train from Beijing main railway station, getting off at Qinglongqiao. There are actually three stations within one km of the wall – Qinglongqiao, New Qinglongqiao and Badaling – but the first is by far the closest to your destination. Qinglongqiao station is notable for the statue of Zhan Tianyou, the engineer in charge of building the Beijing to Baotou line. No trains stop at all three stations and many only stop at Qinglongqiao. If you're coming from the direction of Hohhot or Datong you could get out at Qinglongqiao, look around the wall and then continue on to Beijing on the same day. Your ticket will still be

Badaling Great Wall (JO)

valid for the last stretch to Beijing and you can safely
dump your bags in the left-luggage room at
Qinglongqiao station while you look around.

There's another approach by slower local trains from
Xizhimen (north railway station) in Beijing which stops
at Badaling or Qinglongqiao and continues to
Kangzhuang. There are several trains on this route with
different departure times, so check times at the station.
One train leaves Xizhimen around 8.10 am and arrives
at Badaling at 10.50 am. It leaves Badaling around 2.11
pm and arrives at Beijing at 4 pm. The return fare is about
Y20. At Xizhimen station there is a special booking office

for this train; tickets are sold only on the day of departure. It is also possible to catch train No 527 at 9.40 am from Yongdingmen (south railway station) and get off at Juyongguan station, but then you'll have to walk several (pleasant) km to the wall. Badaling station is one km from the wall and the Badaling line is quite a feat of engineering, built in 1909, It tunnels under the wall.

A microbus-style taxi to the wall and back will cost at least Y250 for an eight-hour hire with a maximum of five passengers; you are expected to buy lunch for the driver. Considering that this works out to less than Y60 per person, it's certainly not unreasonable.

Mutianyu Great Wall
(mùtiányù chángchéng) 慕田峪长城
To take some of the pressure off crowded Badaling, a second site for Great Wall viewing has been opened at Mutianyu, 90 km north-east of Beijing. This part of the wall is less of a carnival than Badaling, but the recent addition of souvenir shops and a cable car is starting to attract the armadas of Japanese tour buses. Nevertheless, Mutianyu is the place most preferred by individual travellers and is still much less crowded than Badaling.

Getting There & Away The Qiaoyuan Hotel operates a minibus directly to the wall at Mutianyu for Y40, which is about the easiest way to get there. A small number of Chinese tour buses also go to Mutianyu. Look for them near the Kentucky Fried Chicken close to

Great Wall at Mutianyu (RS)

MAP 5

慕田峪长城

Mutianyu
Great Wall

Scale Unknown

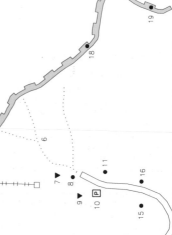

1 Pearl Spring
2 Dragon Pool
3 Cable Car
4 Beacon Tower
5 Lotus Pond
6 Footpath to Wall
7 Foreigners' Restaurant
8 Yanjing Studio
9 Locals' Restaurant
10 No 1 Car Park
11 Ticket Office
12 Ticket Office
13 No 2 Car Park
14 Tourist Office
15 Mandarin Duck Pine
16 Guest-Welcoming
   Pine Tree
17 Mutianyu Village
18 Zhengguan Tower
19 Stone Mortar

1 珍珠泉
2 龙潭
3 缆花车池
4 烽火台
5 莲花池
6 登城步道
7 外宾餐厅
8 燕京书画社
9 内宾餐厅
10 第一停车场
11 售票处
12 第二售票处
13 第二停车场
14 旅游区办事处
15 鸳鸯松
16 迎客松
17 慕田峪村
18 正关台
19 石臼

Tiananmen Square, at the Beijing railway station, or at the Workers' Stadium on Gongren Tiyuchang Beilu next to the Beijing Asia Hotel. Entrance to the wall at Mutianyu costs Y15. The cable car ride costs Y30 one way or Y40 for the return trip.

To go by yourself is complicated and doesn't save much money. If you're starting from the Qiaoyuan Hotel area, take bus No 106 (from Yongdingmen) to Dongzhimen (last station). From there walk across the street to the long-distance bus station and take a bus to Huairou, then it's another 20 km by local minibus (these are scarce), taxi or bicycle.

Simatai Great Wall

(sīmǎtái chángchéng) 司马台长城

If you prefer your wall without the benefit of handrails, cable cars and tacky souvenir shops, Simatai is the place to go. Of all the parts of the wall near Beijing which are open to tourism, the 19-km section at Simatai is the least developed (for now). Many consider this part of the wall to be the most beautiful.

This section of the wall dates from the Ming Dynasty and has some unusual features like 'obstacle-walls', which are walls-within-walls used for defending against enemies who'd already scaled the Great Wall. There are 135 watchtowers at Simatai, the highest being Wangjinglou. Small cannon have been discovered in this area, as well as evidence of rocket-type weapons such as flying knives and flying swords.

Simatai is not for the chicken-hearted because this section of the wall is very steep. A few slopes have a 70° incline and you need both hands free, so bring a daypack to hold your camera and other essentials. One narrow section of footpath has a 500-metre drop-off, so it's no place for acrophobiacs.

An early Western visitor was Lord Macartney, who crossed nearby Gubei Pass on his way to Chengde in 1793. His party made a wild guess that the wall contained almost as much material as all the houses in England and Scotland.

In the early 1970s a nearby PLA unit destroyed about three km of the wall to build barracks, setting an example for the locals who likewise used parts of the wall to build their houses. The story goes that in 1979 the same PLA unit was ordered to rebuild the section which had been torn down.

A small section of the wall at Simatai has already been renovated, but most of it remains in its non-commercialised, crumbling condition. Seeing the wall in its undisturbed state is a sharp contrast to Badaling and Mutianyu, which are so well restored that you may get the impression the wall was built just yesterday to serve CITS tour groups. Perhaps it was.

There is a small restaurant at the car park near the base of the wall, and at the present time prices are still reasonable, although it's not a bad idea to come prepared with some snacks and water. There is a Y10 admission charge.

Besides those already mentioned, other parts of the wall open to foreigners are those stretches at Jiayuguan in Gansu Province, Shanhaiguan in Hebei Province and Huangyaguan in Tianjin municipality.

Getting There & Away Simatai is 110 km north-east of Beijing, and due to the distance and lack of tourist facilities, getting there is not particularly convenient unless you arrange your own transport. Hiring a microbus taxi for the day would cost at least Y300, but getting a group together makes it more affordable. Buses to Simatai cost Y20 for the round-trip and depart just once daily from the Dongzhimen bus station at 7 am. The journey takes two to three hours, and the bus departs from Simatai for Beijing at 3 pm (but ask to be sure).

TOMBS
(líng) 陵

Dying is a big deal in China, especially if you're an emperor. Since they had to go, the royal families decided to go in style. Around Beijing are three major tomb sites, and each tomb holds (or held) the body of an emperor, his wives, girlfriends and funerary treasures. All of the tombs have been plundered at one time or other, but recent efforts at restoration have benefitted China's cultural pride, not to mention the tourist industry.

The three tomb sites around Beijing open to tourists are the Ming Tombs, Western Qing Tombs and Eastern Qing Tombs. Of the three, the Ming Tombs are by far the most frequently visited.

Ming Tombs
(shísān líng) 十三陵

The general travellers' consensus on the tombs is that you'd be better off looking at a bank vault which is, roughly, what the tombs are. However, the scenery along the way is charming. See Map No 13 at the back of the book for details of the site.

Stone figure at Ming Tombs (RS)

Aware of the fact that many visitors have found the tombs disappointing, the Beijing municipal government is busy dressing up the area. New facilities include a golf course, the Dingling Museum (with a wax Genghis Khan), the Nine Dragons Amusement Park, an archery and rifle range, shops, cafés, a 350-room hotel, swimming pool, aquarium, camp site, picnic area, fountain (with 200-metre waterjet), fishing pier (on the Ming Tombs Reservoir) and a bicycle racing velodrome. There are also helicopter rides over the tombs and the nearby Great Wall. Plans call for the construction of additional facilities, including a horse race track, cross-country skiing area and Mongolian yurts for use as a summer hotel.

The seven-km 'spirit way' starts with a triumphal arch then goes through the Great Palace Gate, where officials had to dismount, and passes a giant tortoise (made in 1425) bearing the largest stele in China. This is followed by a guard of 12 sets of stone animals. Every second one is in a reclining position, legend has it, to allow for a 'changing of the guard' at midnight. If your tour bus driver whips past them, insist on stopping to look – they're far more interesting than the tombs – because the drivers like to spend half an hour at the Ming Tombs Reservoir which is dead boring. Beyond the stone animals are 12 stone-faced human statues of generals, ministers and officials, each distinguishable by headgear. The stone figures terminate at the Lingxing Gate.

Dingling was the first of the tombs to be excavated

and opened to the public. In total, 13 of the 16 Ming emperors are buried in this 40-sq-km area which is why another name for this site is the Thirteen Tombs. Besides Dingling two other tombs, Changling and Zhaoling, are open to the public.

Dingling, the tomb of Emperor Wan Li (1573-1620), is the second largest tomb. Over six years the emperor used half a million workers and a heap of silver to build his necropolis and then held a wild party inside the completed chambers. It was excavated between 1956 and 1958 and you can now visit the underground passageways and caverns. The underground construction covers 1195 sq metres, is built entirely of stone, and is sealed with an unusual lock stone. The tomb yielded 26 lacquered trunks of funerary objects, some of which are displayed on site, while others have been removed to Beijing museums and replaced with copies.

Wan Li and his royal spouses were buried in double coffins surrounded by chunks of uncut jade. The jade was thought to have the power to preserve the dead (or could have bought millions of bowls of rice for starving peasants), so the Chinese tour literature relates. Meanwhile experts on cultural relics as well as chefs are studying the ancient cookbooks unearthed from Dingling with a view to serving Wan Li's favourite dishes to visitors, using replicas of imperial banquet tableware.

Another tomb, Changling, was started in 1409 and took 18 years to complete. This is the final resting place of Emperor Yong Le. According to the story, 16 concubines were buried alive with his corpse. This was the second of the Ming Tombs to be excavated and opened to the public.

Zhaoling is the ninth of the Ming Tombs and was opened to visitors in 1989. This is the tomb of Emperor Longqing, who died in 1572, and three of his wives. Admission to the Ming Tombs costs Y15 for foreigners, but a student card reduces it to Y2.

Getting There & Away The tombs lie 50 km northwest of Beijing and four km from the small town of Changping. The tour buses usually combine them with a visit to the Great Wall. You can also get there on the local buses. Take bus Nos 5 or 44 to Deshengmen terminal. West of the flyover is the terminal of bus No 345 which you take to Changping, a one-hour ride. Then take bus No 314 to the tombs (or hitch the last stretch).

Changping main railway station is on the main Beijing to Baotou train line. There is another station, Changping north, which is closer to the Ming Tombs but relatively few trains stop there.

Western Qing Tombs

(qīng xī líng) 清西陵

These tombs are in Yixian County, 110 km south-west of Beijing. If you didn't see enough of Dingling, Yuling, Yongling and Deling, well, there's always Tailing, Changling, Chongling and Muling, the latter four being part of Xiling.

The tomb area is vast and houses the corpses of the emperors, empresses and other members and hangers-on of the royal family. The tomb of Emperor Guangxu (Chongling) has been excavated. His was the last imperial tomb and was constructed between 1905 and 1915.

Eastern Qing Tombs

(qīng dōng líng) 清东陵

The Eastern Qing Tombs area is Death Valley, housing five emperors, 14 empresses and 136 imperial consorts. In the mountains ringing the valley are buried princes, dukes, imperial nurses, and so on.

The approach to the tomb area is a common 'spirit way', similar to that of the Ming Tombs but with the addition of marble-arch bridges. The materials for the tombs come from all over China, including 20-tonne logs which were pulled over iced roads, and giant stone slabs.

Two of the tombs are open; Map No 14 at the back of the book shows their location. Emperor Qianlong (1711-99) started preparations when he was 30, and by the time he was 88 the old boy had used up 90 tonnes of his silver. His resting place covers half a sq km. Some of the beam less stone chambers are decorated with Tibetan and Sanskrit sutras; the doors bear bas-relief bodhisattvas.

Empress Dowager Cixi also got a head start. Her tomb, Dingdong, was completed some three decades before her death. The phoenix, symbol of the empress, appears above that of the dragon (the emperor's symbol) in the artwork at the front of the tomb – not side by side as on other tombs. Both tombs were plundered in the 1920s.

In Zunhua County, 125 km east of Beijing, the Eastern Qing Tombs have a lot more to see in them than the Ming Tombs, although you may be a little jaded after the Forbidden City.

Getting There & Away The only way to get there is by bus and it's a long ride. Tour buses are considerably more comfortable than the local rattletraps and take three or four hours to get there; you have about three hours on site.

WESTERN HILLS

(xī shān) 西山

Within striking distance of the Summer Palace and often combined with it on a tour are the Western Hills, another former villa-resort area. The part of the Western Hills closest to Beijing is known as the Fragrant Hills – see Map No 15 at the back of the book. This is the last stop for the city buses, so if you want to get further into the mountains you'll have to walk, cycle or take a taxi.

Fragrant Hills Park

(xiāngshān gōngyuán) 香山公园

You can scramble up the slopes to the top of Incense-Burner Peak, or take the crowded cable car. From the peak you get an all-embracing view of the countryside. The cable car is a good way to get up the mountain, but it tends to spray you with black grease so an umbrella might be helpful! Starting from the Fragrant Hills, you can hike further into the Western Hills and leave the crowds behind.

The Fragrant Hills area was razed by foreign troops in 1860 and 1900 but a few bits of original architecture still poke out. A glazed-tile pagoda and the renovated Temple of Brilliance *(zhāo miào)* – a mock-Tibetan temple built in 1780 – are both in the same area. The surrounding heavily wooded park was a hunting ground for the emperors, and once contained a multitude of pavilions and shrines, many of which are now being restored. It's a favourite strolling spot for Beijingers and destined to become another Chinese Disneyland – the cable car is probably a sign of things to come. It's possible to stay here at the pricey *Xiangshan Hotel*.

A bicycle trip to the Fragrant Hills is beautiful but exhausting. There are a couple of ways of getting to the Fragrant Hills by public transport: bus No 333 from the Summer Palace, bus No 360 from the zoo, and bus No 318 from Pingguoyuan (the last stop west on the subway).

Azure Clouds Temple

(bìyún sì) 碧云寺

Within walking distance of the North Gate of Fragrant

Hills Park is the Azure Clouds Temple, whose landmark is the Diamond Throne Pagoda. Of Indian design, it consists of a raised platform with a central pagoda and stupas around it. The temple was first built in 1366, and was expanded in the 18th century with the addition of the Hall of Arhats, containing 500 statues representing disciples of Buddha. Dr Sun Yatsen's coffin was placed in the temple in 1925 before being moved to Nanjing. In 1954 the government renovated Sun's memorial hall, which has a picture display of his revolutionary activities.

Temple of the Sleeping Buddha
(wòfó sì) 卧佛寺

About halfway between the Fragrant Hills and the Summer Palace is the Temple of the Sleeping Buddha. During the Cultural Revolution the buddhas in one of the halls were replaced by a statue of Mao (since removed). The draw card is the huge reclining buddha, 5.2 metres long and cast in copper; its weight is unknown but could be up to 50 tonnes. The history books place it in the year 1331 but it's most likely a copy. Pilgrims used to make offerings of shoes to the barefoot statue.

Xiangshan Botanical Gardens
(xiāngshān zhíwù yuán) 香山植物园

About two km east of Fragrant Hills Park and just to the south of the Temple of the Reclining Buddha is the new Botanical Gardens. Presently, the gardens are under development and it's hard to say if it's worth your trouble to visit. Seeing that this is Beijing and the government is determined to make it a showcase, the gardens could be turned into something spectacular.

BADACHU
(bādàchù) 八大处

Directly south of the Fragrant Hills is Badachu, the Eight Great Sites, also known as Eight Great Temples *(bādà sì)*. It has eight monasteries or temples scattered in wooded valleys; see Map No 16 at the end of this book. The Second Site has the Buddha's Tooth Relic Pagoda, built to house the sacred fang and accidentally discovered when the Allied army demolished the place in 1900.

Take bus No 347, which runs there from the zoo (it crosses the No 318 route). Alternatively, you could take the east-west subway line westwards to the last stop at Pingguoyuan and catch a taxi from there.

TANZHE TEMPLE

(tánzhè sì) 潭柘寺

About 45 km directly west of Beijing is Tanzhe Temple, the largest of all the Beijing temples, occupying an area 260 by 160 metres. The Buddhist complex has a long history dating as far back as the 3rd century (Jin Dynasty). Structural modifications date from the Liao, Tang, Ming and Qing dynasties. It therefore has a number of features – dragon decorations, mythical animal sculptures and grimacing gods – no longer found in temples in the capital.

Translated literally, 'Tanzhe' means 'Pool Cudrania'. The temple takes its name from its proximity to the Dragon Pool *(lóng tán)* and some rare Cudrania *(zhè)* trees. Locals come to the Dragon Pool to pray for rain during droughts. The Cudrania trees nourish silkworms and provide a yellow dye and the bark of the tree is believed to cure women of sterility, which may explain why there are so few of these trees left at the temple entrance.

The temple complex is open to the public daily from 8.30 am until 6 pm. To get there, one option is to take bus No 336 from Zhanlanguan Lu, which runs off Fuchengmenwai Dajie north-west of Yuetan Park, to the terminal at Mentougou and then hitch or take a taxi. A direct route is bus No 307 from Qianmen to the Hetan terminal and then a numberless bus to the temple. Alternatively, take the subway to Pingguoyuan, bus No 336 to Hetan and the numberless bus to the temple.

JIETAI TEMPLE

(jiètái sì) 戒台寺

About 10 km south-east of the Tanzhe Temple is a similar but smaller compound, Jietai Temple. The name roughly translates as Temple of Ordination Terrace. The temple was built around 622 AD, during the Tang Dynasty, with major improvements made by later tenants during the Ming Dynasty. The main complex is dotted with ancient pines, all of which have quaint names. Nine Dragon Pine is claimed to be over 1300 years old.

It's roughly 35 km from Jietai Temple to Beijing, and a journey out here is usually combined with a visit to Tanzhe Temple.

MARCO POLO BRIDGE

(lúgōuqiáo) 卢沟桥

Publicised by the great traveller himself, the Reed Moat Bridge is made of grey marble, is 260 metres long, and has over 250 marble balustrades supporting 485 carved stone lions. First built in 1192, the original arches were washed away in the 17th century. The bridge is a composite of different eras and was widened in 1969. It spans the Yongding River near the little town of Wanping.

Long before CITS, Emperor Qianlong also did his bit to promote the bridge. In 1751 he put his calligraphy to use and wrote some poetic tracts about Beijing's scenic wonders. His 'Morning Moon Over Lugou Bridge' is now engraved into stone tablets and placed on steles next to the bridge. On the opposite bank is a monument to Qianlong's inspection of the Yongding River.

Despite the publicity campaign by Marco and Qianlong, the bridge wouldn't rate more than a footnote in Chinese history were it not for the famed 'Marco Polo Bridge Incident' which ignited a full-scale war with Japan. On the night of 7 July 1937, Japanese troops illegally occupied a railway junction outside Wanping, which prompted Japanese and Chinese soldiers to start shooting at each other, and that gave Japan enough of an excuse to attack and occupy Beijing. The Chinese were more than a little displeased, especially since Japan had already occupied Manchuria and Taiwan. The Marco Polo Bridge Incident is considered by many as the date of China's entry into WW II.

A relatively recent addition to this ancient site is the 'Memorial Hall of the War of Resistance Against Japan', built in 1987. Besides Qianlong's Morning Moon stele, there is also a stele commemorating his inspection of the Yongding River. Also on the site is the Wanping Castle, the Daiwang Temple and a tourist hotel.

You can get to the bridge by taking bus No 109 to Guang'anmen and then catching bus No 339. By bicycle it's about a 16-km trip one way.

PEKING MAN SITE

(zhōukǒudiàn) 周口店

Site of those primeval Chinese, the Peking Men, Zhoukoudian Village is 50 km south-west of Beijing. There's an 'Apeman Cave' here on a hill above the village, several lesser caves and some dig sites. There is also a fossil exhibition hall – you'd have to be a fossil to

MAP 6

1 Beijing First Waterfall
  & Black Dragon Pool
2 Fengjiayu
3 Cloud Peak (Yunfengshan)
4 Banchengzi
5 Lupi Pass
6 Bulaotun
7 Taishitun
8 White Dragon Pool
  (Bailongtan)
9 Holiday Resort Village
10 In Front of the Dam Park
11 Xiwengzhuang
12 Miyun International
   Amusement Park
13 Baihe Outskirts Park
14 Mujiayu
15 Miyun Railway Station
16 Dachengzi

1 京都第一瀑布和黑龙潭
2 冯家峪
3 云峰山子关屯
4 云半城皮
5 鹿皮老师屯
6 不老师龙潭
7 太白度假村前
8 白度假前翁公园
9 坝前翁庄
10 坝庄
11 溪云
12 密云国际游乐场
13 白河郊野公园
14 穆家峪
15 密云火车站
16 大城子

密云水库
Miyun
Reservoir

0   4   8 km

To Tongliao

To Tianxian
Waterfall

To Simatai
Great Wall
(12 km)

● 1   ● 2   ▲ 3   ● 4

● 6

5

● 7

Miyun
Reservoir

■ 9   ● 8

10 ●

● 11

12 ●

13 ●

● 14

To Chengde

Chaohe

15

● 16

Miyun

River

River

Baihe

To Beijing
(70 km)

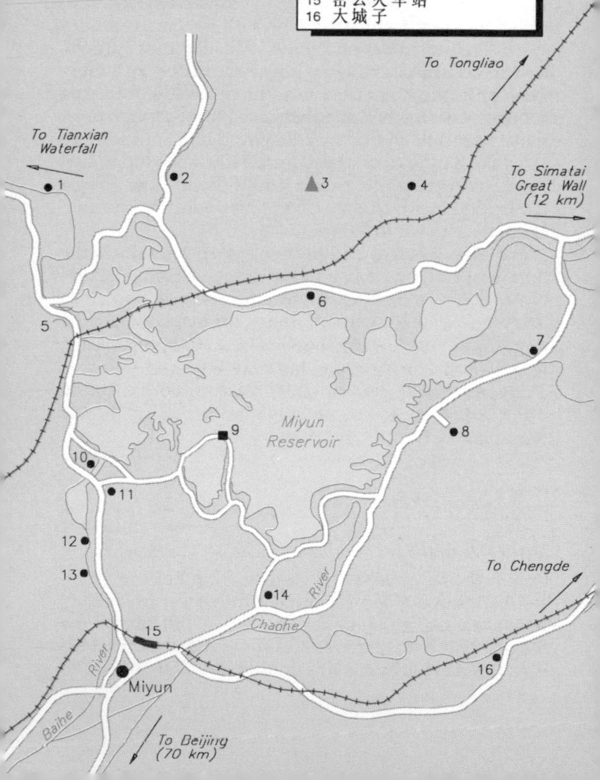

stay here for more than 15 minutes. There are three sections to the exhibition hall: pre-human history, the life and times of Peking Man, and one dealing with recent anthropological research. There are ceramic models, stone tools and the skeletons of prehistoric creatures.

The exhibition hall (☎ 931 0278) is open daily from 9 am to 4 pm, but check before you go. You could get a suburban train from Yongdingmen station and get off at Zhoukoudian. Another possibility is a bus from the Haihutun bus station (on the corner of Nansanhuan Zhonglu and Nanyuan Lu). If combined with a trip to Tanzhe Temple and Marco Polo Bridge, approaching the site by taxi is not unreasonable. Pricey CITS or CTS tours to the site are available according to demand.

There is a *guesthouse* on the site, though it seems to be intended more for locals than foreign tourists. Map No 17 at the back of this book shows details of the site.

KANGXI GRASSLANDS

(kāngxī cǎoyuán) 慷西草原

The grasslands are actually in a beautiful hilly region 180 km north-west of the city. This is considered the best place in Beijing municipality for horse riding. It is possible to spend the night there in a Mongolian yurt.

MIYUN RESERVOIR

(mìyún shuǐkù) 密云水库

Some 90 km north-east of Beijing is Miyun Reservoir, the city's water supply and largest lake in Beijing municipality. Since this is drinking water, swimming is prohibited, but the lake is impressive for its scenery.

Chinese entrepreneurs know a good thing when they see it, and Miyun Reservoir has now acquired a number of commercial recreation sites. Most important is the Miyun International Amusement Park *(mìyún guójì yóulè cháng)*, not on the lake itself but 20 km to the south-east, about seven km outside of Miyun town. Facilities include a merry-go-round, monorail, automobile race track, souvenir shops – just about everything you could possibly want in life.

If the carnival atmosphere gets to be too much, there are less touristy scenic sites around the reservoir. On the east side of the lake is White Dragon Pool *(bái lóng tán)*. While also being developed for tourism, it retains much of its former charm. During the Qing Dynasty, emperors on their way to Chengde would drop in for a visit, so the area is dotted with temples and pavilions which recently have been renovated.

Right in front of the dam is the In Front of the Dam Park (*bàqián gōngyuán*), though this is mainly just a place for Chinese tourists to get their pictures taken. On the shores of the reservoir itself is a Holiday Resort Village (*dùjià cūn*). North-west of Miyun Reservoir are less visited scenic spots, including Black Dragon Pool (*hēi lóng tán*), Beijing First Waterfall (*jīngdū dìyī pùbù*), Tianxian Waterfall (*tiānxiān pùbù*); due north is Cloud Peak (*yúnfēng shān*).

Trains running to Chengde stop at Miyun. Buses to Miyun depart from the car park of the Workers' Stadium on Gongren Tiyuguan Beilu near the Dongsishitiao subway station.

HAIZI RESERVOIR

(*hǎizi shuǐkù*) 海子水库

At the far eastern end of the Beijing municipality is Haizi Reservoir, a relatively recent artificial creation hardly ever visited by tourists. Not that there is all that much to see here. The reservoir is distinguished by the fact that it was the site of the aquatic sports (waterskiing, etc) during the 1990 Asian Games.

Due to the games (which were poorly attended), the area has decent recreation facilities, though it's hard to say if everything will be kept in good nick or be allowed to become dilapidated. At the present time, modern amenities include the *Jinhai Hotel* (*jīnhǎi bīnguǎn*) and *Jinhai Restaurant* (*jīnhǎi cāntīng*). There is a pier (*yóuchuán mǎtóu*) where you can sometimes catch a cruise across the lake to the aquatic sports area (*shuǐshàng yùndòng cháng*). The shore of the reservoir is dotted with a few recently-constructed pavilions to remind you that this is indeed China. Nearby is Jinghaihu (Golden Sea Lake) Park.

Not being next to any railway line, getting here requires a substantial detour for most travellers. It would be conceivable for tour groups heading out to the Eastern Qing Tombs to make a stopoff at Haizi Reservoir along the way.

SHIDU

(*shídù*) 十渡

This is Beijing's answer to Guilin. The pinnacle-shaped rock formations, small rivers and general beauty of the place make it a favourite spot with expatriates like foreign students, diplomats and business people.

Situated 110 km south-west of central Beijing, Shidu means '10 ferries' or '10 crossings'. At least before the new road and bridges were built, it was necessary to cross the Juma River 10 times while travelling along the gorge between Zhangfang and Shidu village.

Places to Stay

The *Longshan Hotel (lóngshān fàndiàn)* is opposite the railway station and is the relatively upmarket place to stay in Shidu itself (but that will change soon!). Another place in Shidu is simply called the *Shidu Lüguan* but doesn't take foreigners – at least not until the renovations are complete.

Down near Jiudu (the 'ninth ferry') there is a camp site, conveniently located on a flood-plain.

There is a *cheap hotel (liùdù lüguǎn)* in Liudu which will probably not take foreigners until it becomes renovated and pricey.

Getting There & Away

This is one of the few scenic areas outside of Beijing which can be easily reached by train. Departures are from the south railway station (Yongdingmen) near the Qiaoyuan Hotel, not to be confused with Beijing's main railway station. If you take the morning train, the trip can be done in one day. The schedule is as follows:

No	From	To	Depart	Arrive
595	Yongdingmen	Shidu	6.07 am	8.40 am
597	Yongdingmen	Shidu	5.40 pm	8.00 pm
596	Shidu	Yongdingmen	6.41 pm	9.03 pm
598	Shidu	Yongdingmen	10.41 am	1.05 pm

YUNSHUI CAVES

(yúnshuǐ dòng) 云水洞

The caves are in the Shangfang Mountains, not far north of the highway between the Peking Man Site and Shidu. Don't expect to be the first human to explore these depths because you'll find coloured lights, souvenir shops and snack bars. About one km to the east of the cave entrance is the Doulü Temple, a large monastery complex in the foothills.

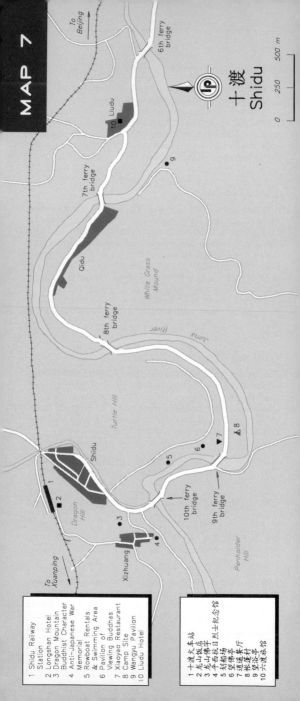

MAP 7

0   250   500 m

十渡
Shidu

1 Shidu Railway
    Station
2 Longshan Hotel
3 Dragon Mountain
4 Anti-Japanese War
    Memorial
5 Rowboat Rentals
    & Swimming Area
6 Pavilion of
    Viewing Buddhas
7 Xiaoyao Restaurant
8 Camp Site
9 Wangyu Pavilion
10 Liudu Hotel

1 十渡火车站
2 龙山饭店
3 龙山佛字
4 平西抗日烈士纪念馆
5 划船场
6 望佛亭
7 逍遥素厅
8 帐篷村
9 望谷亭
10 六渡旅馆

To Beijing

6th ferry
bridge

Liudu

7th ferry
bridge

Qidu

8th ferry
bridge

White Grass
Mound

Juma River

Turtle Hill

Shidu

To Xuanping

Dragon Hill

Xizhuang

10th ferry
bridge

9th ferry
bridge

Penholder Hill

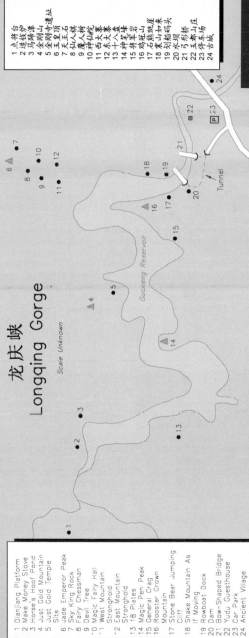

龙庆峡
Longqing Gorge

Scale Unknown

Guicheng Reservoir

Tunnel

MAP 8

1 点将台
2 造钱炉
3 马蹄潭
4 金刚山
5 金刚寺遗址
6 玉皇顶
7 天王石
8 仙人棋
9 魔人树
10 神仙院
11 西大寨
12 东大寨
13 十八盘
14 神笔峰
15 将军岩
16 鸡冠山
17 石熊乐窿
18 蛇山如来
19 划船码头
20 水坝
21 弓形桥
22 玉渡山庄
23 停车场
24 古城

1 Dianjiang Platform
2 Make Money Stove
3 Horse's Hoof Pond
4 Just Gold Mountain
5 Just Gold Temple Site
6 Jade Emperor Peak
7 Sky King Rock
8 Fairy Chessman
9 Devil Tree
10 Magic Fairy Hall
11 West Mountain Stronghold
12 East Mountain Stronghold
13 18 Plates
14 Magic Pen Peak
15 General Crag
16 Rooster Crown Mountain
17 Stone Bear Jumping Cliff
18 Snake Mountain As If Moving
19 Rowboat Dock
20 Dam
21 Bow-Shaped Bridge
22 Yudu Guesthouse
23 Car Park
24 Ancient Village

LONGQING GORGE

(lóngqìngxiá) 龙庆峡

About 90 km north-west of Beijing is Longqing Gorge, a canyon in Yanqing County. The gorge was probably more scenic before the dam and consequent reservoir flooded out the area. Rowing and hiking are the big attractions during summer. From mid-December to the end of January this is the site of Beijing's Ice Lantern Festival (bīngdōng jié). Similar to the more well-known and longer-lasting festival at Harbin, the 'lanterns' are huge ice carvings into which coloured electric lights are inserted. The effect (at least during the night) is stunning. Children (including adult children) can amuse themselves on the ice slide.

This being a night-time event, there are tactical problems with getting there and staying there during the Ice Lantern Festival. The ride takes two hours each way and chartering a taxi is expensive, but the cost can be divided amongst a group of travellers. Most visitors go and return the same day. The one hotel in Longqing Gorge packs out during festival time, though this situation might improve with time if new places are built.

TIANJIN

(tiānjīn) 天津

Tianjin is a major port city about two hours by bus or car to the south-east of Beijing. For centuries, it has served as Beijing's outlet to the sea and has often been referred to as 'the Shanghai of the north'.

For the sea-dog Western nations of the 19th century, Tianjin was a trading bottleneck too good to be passed up. British gunboats persuaded the Chinese to sign the Treaty of Tianjin (1858) which opened the port up to foreign trade. The Brits were soon joined by the French, Japanese, Germans, Austro-Hungarians, Italians and Belgians. The era of foreign concessions has left Tianjin with much old European architecture which you can see today.

Since 1949 Tianjin has been a focus for major industrialisation. Plans call for opening China's third stock market in Tianjin, the first and second being in Shanghai and Shenzhen respectively.

Tianjin is a popular day trip for Beijingers. Spending the night is certainly possible, but hotels in Tianjin are absurdly expensive.

Antique Market
(gǔwán shìcháng) 古玩市场

Just the sheer size and variety of this market makes it fascinating to stroll through. Amongst the many items on sale include stamps, silver coins, silverware, porcelain, clocks, photos of Mao, Cultural Revolution exotica and old books.

The market runs seven days a week, on weekdays only occupying a section of Shenyang Dao in the centre of town. On weekends it expands enormously, spilling out into side streets in every direction. Operating hours are from 7.30 am until around 3 pm – it's best to arrive around 8 am for the widest selection. Sunday morning is best.

Ancient Culture Street
(gǔ wénhuà jiē) 古文化街

The Ancient Culture Street is an attempt to recreate the appearance of an ancient Chinese city. Besides the traditional buildings, the street is lined with vendors plugging every imaginable type of cultural goodies from Chinese scrolls, paintings and chops to the latest heavy metal sounds on CD. During certain public holidays, street operas are staged here.

Within the confines of the street is the small Tianhou Temple (tiānhòu gōng). Tianhou (Heaven Queen) is the goddess of the sea, and is known by various names (Matsu in Taiwan, Tin Hau in Hong Kong). It is claimed that Tianjin's Tianhou Temple was built in 1326, but it has seen a bit of renovation work since then.

The Ancient Culture Street is a major drawcard for tourists, both foreigners and Chinese. The street is in the north-west part of town (see Tianjin map).

Confucius Temple
(wén miào) 文庙

On the north side of Dongmennei Dajie, one block to the west of the Ancient Culture Street, is Tianjin's Confucius Temple. It was originally built in 1463 during the Ming Dynasty. The temple, and Confucianists in general, took a beating during the Cultural Revolution. By 1993 the buildings had been restored and opened to the public.

Tianjin (RS)

Grand Mosque

(qīngzhēn sì) 清真寺

Although it has a distinctly Chinese look, this large mosque is an active place of worship for Tianjin's Muslims. The mosque is on Dafeng Lu, not far to the south of the west railway station.

Dabeiyuan Monastery

(dàbēiyuàn) 大悲院

This is one of the largest and best-preserved temples in the city. Dabeiyuan was built between 1611 and 1644,

Tianjin Antique Market (RS)

was expanded in 1940, battered during the Cultural Revolution and finally restored in 1980. The temple is on Tianwei Lu in the northern part of the city.

Catholic Church
(xīkāi jiāotáng) 西开教堂

This is one of the most bizarre looking churches you'll see. Situated on the southern end of Binjiang Dao, the twin onion domes form a dramatic backdrop to the 'Coca-Cola Bridge' (a pedestrian overpass crossing Nanjing Lu). It's definitely worth a look. Church services are now being permitted again on Sunday, which is about the only time you'll have a chance to look inside.

Earthquake Memorial
(kàngzhèn jìniàn bēi) 抗震纪念碑

Just opposite the Friendship Hotel on Nanjing Lu is a curious pyramid-shaped memorial. Though there's not much to see here, the memorial is a pointed reminder of the horrific events of 28 July 1976, when an earthquake registering eight on the Richter scale struck north-east China.

It was the greatest natural disaster of the decade. Tianjin was severely affected and the city was closed to tourists for two years. The epicentre was at Tangshan – that city basically disappeared in a few minutes.

Hai River Park
(hǎihé gōngyuán) 海河公园

Stroll along the banks of the Hai River (a popular pastime with the locals) and see photo booths, fishing, early-morning taiji, opera-singer practice and old men toting bird cages. The Hai River esplanades have a peculiarly Parisian feel, in part due to the fact that some of the railing and bridge work is French.

Tianjin's sewage has to go somewhere and the river water isn't so pure that you'd want to drink it. It's not Venice, but there are tourist boat cruises on the Hai River which start not far from the Astor Hotel.

TV Tower
(diànshì tái) 电视台

The pride and joy of Tianjin residents, the TV Tower dominates the horizon on the south side of town. Besides its functional purpose of transmitting TV and radio broadcasts to the masses, tourists can go upstairs for a whopping Y80 fee. While the tower looks impressive from the ground, views from the top aren't spectacular in the daytime. After all, Tianjin's flat landscape of old buildings isn't exactly the eighth wonder of the world. However, things get better at night, as long as the weather cooperates by giving good visibility.

The TV Tower is also topped by a revolving restaurant, but you're liable to get indigestion when you see the bill.

Shuishang Park
(shuǐshàng gōngyuán) 水上公园

This large park is in the south-west corner of town, not far from the TV Tower. The name in Chinese means 'Water Park' and over half the surface area is a lake. The major activity here is renting rowing boats and pedalboats.

It's one of the more relaxed places in busy Tianjin, except on weekends when the locals descend on the place like cadres at a banquet. The park features a Japanese-style floating garden and a decent zoo.

Getting to the park from the railway station requires two buses. Take bus No 8 to the terminus and from there hop onto bus No 54, also to the terminus which is just outside the park entrance.

Art Museum
(yìshù bówùguǎn) 艺术博物馆

This museum is easy to get to and is pleasant to stroll around. It's at 77 Jiefang Beilu, one stop from the main railway station.

Zhou Enlai Memorial Hall
(zhōu ēnlái jìniàn guǎn) 周恩来纪念馆

Zhou Enlai grew up in Shaoxing in Zhejiang Province but he attended school in Tianjin, so his classroom is enshrined and there are photos and other memorabilia from his time there (1913-17). The memorial is on the western side of the city in the Nankai District, occupying the eastern building of Nankai School.

天津
Tianjin

0   0.5   1 km

1 North Railway Station
2 West Railway Station
3 Dabeiyuan Monastery
4 Zhongshan Park
5 Grand Mosque
6 Eardrum Fried Spongecake Shop
7 North-East Bus Station
8 Ancient Culture Street
9 Confucius Temple
10 5th Subway Exit
11 Zhou Enlai Memorial Hall
12 Food Street
13 Yanchunlou Restaurant
14 Quanjude Restaurant
15 Buses to Beijing
16 Main Railway Station
17 Antique Market
18 International Market
19 Catholic Church
20 Kiessling's Bakery
21 Tianjin No 1 Hotel
22 Furama Hotel
23 Tianjin University
24 Nankai University
25 South Bus Station
26 Foreign Languages Bookstore
27 TV Tower
28 Natural History Museum & Cadre Club
29 18th Street Dough-Twists
30 Sheraton Hotel
31 Friendship Store
32 Crystal Palace Hotel
33 Tianjin Grand Hotel
34 Geneva Hotel
35 Park Hotel

1 北火车站
2 西火车站
3 大悲院
4 中山公园
5 清真寺
6 耳朵眼炸糕店
7 东北角汽车站
8 古文化街
9 文庙
10 地下铁第五站
11 周恩来纪念馆
12 食品街
13 燕春楼饭庄
14 全聚德烤鸭店
15 往北京汽车站
16 天津火车站
17 古玩市场
18 国际商场
19 西开教堂
20 起士林餐厅
21 天津第一饭店
22 富丽华大酒店
23 天津大学
24 南开大学
25 八里台发车站
26 外文书店
27 电视台
28 自然博物馆/干部俱乐部
29 桂发祥麻花店
30 喜来登大酒店
31 友谊商店
32 水晶宫饭店
33 天津利华大酒店
34 日内瓦大酒店
35 乐园饭店

Beilu

Jinzhong Dajie

Zhenli Dao

Huoxing Lu

To Airport

Zhangguozhuang Lu

Shiyijing Lu

To Harbin

Jieyang Beilu

Hai River

To Tanggu

Dagu Nanlu

Renmu Park River

Dongxing Lu

29

35

Jianshan Lu

Dagu Nanlu

Places to Stay

There are heaps of decent hotels of high standard which have been placed off-limits to foreigners. Those which do permit foreigners charge ridiculous prices. So unless you've got a Chinese ID card, real or fake, and heaps of money, or ingratiate yourself into one of the university residences, you'll probably end up back at the station.

The only mid-range place accepting foreigners is the *Tianjin Grand Hotel* (☎ 35 9000; fax 35 9822) *(tiānjīn bīnguǎn)* on Youyi Lu, Hexi District. And grand it is: 1000 beds in two high-rise blocks built in 1960, but now showing signs of age. No doubt the day of renovation (and higher prices) will come, but at present doubles cost Y120, Y150 and Y240. Take bus No 13 from the main railway station. But because of the 'cheap' prices, it's often full, many of the rooms being permanently occupied by foreigners and locals setting up 'temporary' offices.

Also on the cheaper end by Tianjin standards is the *Park Hotel* (☎ 80 9818; fax 80 2042) *(lèyuán fàndiàn)*, 1 Leyuan Lu, east of the Friendship Store and, as the name implies, near a park. Doubles are Y253, Y297 and Y417. Rooms are very comfortable.

The *Tianjin No 1 Hotel (tiānjīn dìyī fàndiàn)* (☎ 31 0707; fax 31 3341) is at 158 Jiefang Beilu. It's got a bit of old world charm, which perhaps will make you feel better about having to fork out Y380 for a double. Some travellers have managed to negotiate the tab down to Y190 after exhaustive bargaining and poverty-pleading sessions. Take bus No 13 three stops from the main railway station and walk south.

The *Friendship Hotel* (☎ 31 0372) *(yǒuyí bīnguǎn)* charges rather unfriendly prices, with doubles at Y402 and Y460. The hotel is at 94 Nanjing Lu.

One of the most glamorous places in town is the 346-room *Crystal Palace Hotel* (☎ 31 0567; fax 31 0591) *(shuǐjīnggōng fàndiàn)* on Youyi Lu. Doubles start at Y575. Facilities include a swimming pool, tennis court, health club and French restaurant.

Also in the neighbourhood is the *Geneva Hotel* (☎ 34 2222; fax 34 9854) *(jīnlìhuá dàjiǔdiàn)*, 30 Youyi Lu, where doubles cost Y383.

Somewhat peculiar-looking is the *Hyatt Hotel* (☎ 31 8888; fax 31 0021) *(kǎiyuè fàndiàn)* at 219 Jiefang Beilu overlooking the Hai River. Superior/deluxe rooms cost Y632/690 and suites begin at Y805, plus 10% service charge.

The *Astor Hotel* (☎ 31 1112; fax 31 6282) *(lìshùndé fàndiàn)*, at 33 Tai'erzhuang Lu, dates from early this century but has been completely refurbished. Doubles cost from Y440 to Y505. The hotel is near the Hyatt.

On the east bank of the Hai River not far from the Astor is the fancy new *Furama Hotel (fúlìhuá dàjiǔdiàn)*. Rooms at this luxury tower start at Y690.

The *Sheraton Hotel* (☎ 34 3388; fax 35 8740) *(xǐláidēng dàjiǔdiàn)* on Zijinshan Lu in the south of Tianjin offers a special price of Y545 (plus 15% service charge), which includes accommodation, buffet breakfast, laundry service and airport shuttle service (for international flights only).

Places to Eat

The place to go is *Food St (shípǐn jiē)*, a covered alley with two levels of restaurants. Old places close and new ones open all the time here, but there are approximately 40 to 50 restaurants on each level. You need to check prices, because some of the food stalls are dirt cheap but a few upmarket restaurants are almost absurdly expensive. You can find some real exotica here like snake (expensive), dogmeat (cheap) and eels (mid-range). Mexican food fans take note, this is the only place in China where we found bags of nacho chips for sale! Food St is a couple of blocks south of Nanma Lu, about one km west of the centre.

Rongji Dajie is an alley just one block north of Food St and also boasts a fair share of restaurants. The *Quanjude* (☎ 75 0046) is at 53 Rongji Dajie. Upstairs are banquet rooms with moderate to expensive prices. Seafood is expensive (such as sea-cucumber, a delicacy that chefs love to serve up to foreigners). Beijing Duck and Shandong food are also served.

Directly opposite the Quanjude is the *Yanchunlou* (☎ 75 2761) at 46 Rongji Dajie. It serves Muslim food, lamb dishes and hotpot in winter.

Brownies (bāngní zhàjī) doesn't sell brownies; it's a Canadian-built fast-food restaurant, Tianjin's answer to Kentucky Fried Chicken. It's proven popular with both Chinese and foreigners and is at the northern end of Binjiang Dao near Quanyechang Department Store.

Just down the street from Brownies is *Franco's Italian Fast Food (yìqílín)*. Specialities here include pizza, spaghetti and real Italian ice cream. This place is doing a raging business with the foreign community in Tianjin.

The *Tianjin Roast Duck Restaurant* (☎ 70 2660) *(tiānjīn kǎoyā diàn)* is at 146 Liaoning Lu in the city centre. You can get Beijing Duck here, either the full works or a cheaper basic duck. This place has Mao Zedong's seal of approval (one doesn't really know if that's positive or

Food St in Tianjin (RS)

positively embarrassing as an advertising ploy these days) and on the restaurant walls are a couple of black & white photos of a relaxed-looking Mao talking to the chefs and autographing the visitors' book.

The *Chuansu Restaurant* (☎ 70 5142) is at 153 Changchun Dao, between Xinhua Lu and Liaoning Lu, very close to the Tianjin Roast Duck. Spicy hot Sichuan food is the speciality here but other styles are also on the menu.

King of the dumpling shops is *Goubuli* (☎ 70 0810) (*gǒubùlǐ*) at 77 Shandong Dao, between Changchun Lu and Binjiang Dao. Very crowded! 'Goubuli' has the alarming translation of 'dog doesn't care'. The most satisfying explanation of this seems to be that Goubuli was the nickname of the shop's founder, a man with such an extraordinarily ugly face that even dogs were turned off by him.

The Eardrum Fried Spongecake Shop (*ěrduǒyǎn zhàgāo diàn*) takes its name from its proximity to Eardrum Lane. This shop specialises in cakes made from rice powder, sugar and bean paste, all fried in sesame oil. These special cakes have been named (you guessed it) 'eardrum fried spongecake'.

Another Tianjin speciality that takes its name from a shop's location is 18th Street dough-twists (*máhuā*). The street seems to have been renamed 'Love Your Country St' (*àiguó dào*), and the famous shop also seems to have a new label (*guìfā xiáng máhuā diàn*). However, the dough-twists (made from sugar, sesame, nuts, vanilla) still taste the same. This is one form of Chinese junkfood worth trying. *Kiessling's Bakery* (*qǐshílín cāntīng*), built by the Austrians back in foreign concession days (1911), is a Tianjin institution. It's at 33 Zhejiang Lu, west of the Astor Hotel. From the railway station it's the fourth stop on the No 13 bus route.

Foreign residents of Tianjin with a bit of cash like to pig out every Sunday at the *Sheraton Hotel* which does a mean buffet from 11 am until 2 pm. It costs Y90 FEC (no student cards accepted), so don't eat breakfast if you want to get the maximum benefit. On other days there are also lunch and dinner buffets with prices ranging from Y30 to Y60, and sometimes they serve pizza!

The *Hyatt Hotel* also does a memorable breakfast buffet. This one costs Y40 and can fill you up for the rest of the day.

Should you wish to fortify a main meal, an ice cream or a coffee, Tianjin produces a variety of liquid substances. There's *kafeijiu* which approximates to Kahlua, and *sekijiu*, which is halfway between vodka and aviation fuel.

Getting There & Away

Air CAAC (☎ 70 4045, 70 5888) is at 242 Heping Lu. Tianjin has daily flights to Beijing, though it seems crazy to fly since the time spent getting to and from the airport on either end plus airport check-in and security procedures (and CAAC's typical delays) means that flying is usually slower than a direct Beijing to Tianjin bus trip. There are also international flights from Tianjin and flights to numerous domestic destinations.

Bus Buses to Beijing depart from in front of the Tianjin main railway station. Costs depend on bus size, but average around Y15. In Beijing, catch the bus to Tianjin from the west side of the car park in front of the Beijing main railway station. The great advantage the bus has over the train is that there are no hassles in buying a ticket and you are guaranteed a seat.

Train For Beijing trains you'll want the main station in Tianjin. Some trains stop at both main and west, and some go only through the west station (particularly those originating in Beijing and heading south). Through trains to north-east China often stop at the north station.

The main station is one of the cleanest and most modern in China. Foreigners can avoid the horrible queues by purchasing tickets on the second floor at the soft-seat ticket office.

Express trains take just under two hours for the trip between Tianjin and Beijing. Local trains take about 2½ hours.

Boat Tianjin's harbour is Tanggu, 50 km (30 minutes by train) from Tianjin proper. This is one of China's major ports, offering a number of possibilities for arriving and departing by boat. For further details, see the section headed SEA in our Getting There & Away chapter.

Map Index

MAP	1	Beijing (inside front cover)	
MAP	2	Beihai Park	pp 154
MAP	3	Tiantan Park (Temple of Heaven)	pp 159
MAP	4	Badaling Great Wall	pp 222
MAP	5	Mutianyu Great Wall	pp 226
MAP	6	Miyun Reservoir	pp 236
MAP	7	Shidu	pp 240
MAP	8	Longqing Gorge	pp 241
MAP	9	Tianjin	pp 248

Maps 10-24 appear at the back of this book

MAP 10	Central Beijing
MAP 11	Beijing Bicycle Tour
MAP 12	Wangfujing Area
MAP 13	Ming Tombs
MAP 14	Eastern Qing Tombs
MAP 15	Fragrant Hills Park
MAP 16	Badachu
MAP 17	Peking Man Site
MAP 18	Jianguomenwai Embassy Compound
MAP 19	Sanlitun Embassy Compound
MAP 20	Palace Area of the Forbidden City
MAP 21	Summer Palace
MAP 22	Old Summer Palace

Index

Accommodation, see Places
    to Stay
Acrobatics 17-20, 207-208
Air Travel 102-113
    Baggage Allowance 113
    Departure Tax 113
    Domestic 111
    International 104-111
Airline Offices 111-113
Airport 127
Ancient Culture Street,
    Tianjin 243
Antique Market, Tianjin 243
Antiques 216
Art Gallery, China 151
Art Museum, Tianjin 247
Avoiding Offence 23-25
    Deadly Chopsticks 25
    Face 23-24
    Passion Prohibited 25
    Personal Questions 25
    Red Ink 25
    Speaking Frankly 24
Azure Clouds Temple 232-233

Badachu 233-234, **Map 16**
Badaling Great Wall 221-225,
    Map 4 (222)
Bargaining, see Money
Bars, see Entertainment
Beihai Park 153-156, **Map 2
    (154)**
Beijing Amusement Park 164
Beijing Department Store 212
Beijing Duck, see Places to
    Eat
Beijing University 172
Bell Tower 177
Bicycle 129-130, 173-178
Black Market, see Money
Black Temple 169
Blockbuster Bicycle Tour 173-
    178, **Map 11**
Books 72-74
Bookshops 74-75, 212-213
Botanical Gardens, Xiangshan
    233
Bus Travel 114, 127
    Local 127

Long-distance 114
Business Hours 61
Business, see Work

Capital Museum & Library
    152, 167
Car Travel 131
Cathedrals 169-170
Chinese herbal medicines
    212, 215
Cinema 203
Climate 16-17
Clubs, see Entertainment
Coal Hill (Jingshan), see
    Parks
Concerts, see Entertainment
Confucius Temple & Imperial
    College 167
Confucius Temple, Tianjin 243
Cultural Shows, see Entertain-
    ment
Currency, see Money
Customs 45-46

Dabeiyuan Monastery, Tianjin
    244
Dangers & Annoyances 83-86
Department Stores
    Beijing 212
    Friendship Store 216
    Lufthansa Centre 218
    Sun City 215
    Xidan Shopping Centre 214
    Yaohan 217
Discos, see Entertainment
Ditan Park 162
Documents 43-45
    Chinese 44
    Foreign 43-44
    Travel Permit 45
Drinks 99-101
    Alcoholic 100-101
    Non-alcoholic 99
    Vocabulary 101
Drum Tower 177

East Cathedral 169
Eastern Qing Tombs 231-232,
    Map 14

Eight Great Sites, see
    Badachu
Electricity 71
Embassies 40-43
    Chinese 40-41
    Foreign 41-43
Entertainment 202-209
    Acrobatics 207-208
    Bars 202
    Cinema 203
    Clubs 203-204
    Concerts 205
    Cultural Shows 204
    Discos 202
    Karaoke 206
    Opera 206-207
    Other 206
    Song & Dance Shows 205
    Sports 208-209
    Theatre 204-205
Exchange Rates, see Money
Excursions 220-254

Fayuan Temple 169
Festivals 62
Food 89-99, 199-201
    Bakeries 201
    Beijing & Shandong 89-90
    Cantonese & Chaozhou 91
    Menus 91-99
    Self-catering 199-201
    Shanghainese 90
    Sichuan & Hunan 91
Forbidden City 140, **Map 20**
Fragrant Hills Park 232,
    Map 15

Gongfu 20
Grand Mosque, Tianjin 244
Grand View Garden 164
Great Bell Temple 167-168
Great Hall of the People 138
Great Wall, The 220-228
    Mutianyu 225-227, **Map 5**
    (226)
    Simatai 227-228
    Badaling 221-225, **Map 4**
    (222)
Guangji Temple 168

Hai River Park, Tianjin 246
Haizi Reservoir 238
Health 81-83
History 12-15
Hitching 132-133

Holidays 61
Hongqiao Market 218
Hutongs 175, 214-215

Imperial College 167

Jietai Temple 234
Jingshan Park 152-153

Kangxi Grasslands 237
Karaoke, see Entertainment
Kungfu, see Gongfu
Kunming Lake 146

Lake District 174-175
Lama Temple 165-167
Language 25-38
    Written 29-30
    Gestures 28
    Grammar 26
    Pinyin 26-27
    Studying Chinese 38
    Tones 26
    Vocabulary 30-38
    Vowels 27-28

Laundry 71
Leaving Beijing 126
Libraries 151-152
Longqing Gorge 242, **Map 8**
    (241)
Longtan Park 163
Lu Xun Museum 150

Mao Zedong Mausoleum 138-
    139
Maps 75, 213
Marco Polo Bridge 235
Markets
    Hongqiao 218
    Tianjin Antique 243
    Xiushui Silk 217
    Yabao Lu Clothing 217
Media 75-79
    Chinese-Language
        Publications 76
    Foreign-Language
        Publications 76-78
    Imported Publications 78
    News Agencies 75-76
    Radio & TV 78-79
Military Museum 150
Ming Tombs 228-230,
    Map 13

Miyun Reservoir 237-238, **Map 6 (236)**
Money 46-53
　Bank Accounts 51
　Bargaining 52-53
　Black Market 49-50
　Changing Money 48-49
　Consumer Taxes 53
　Costs 51
　Credit Cards 50
　Currency 46-48
　Exchange Rates 48
　Price Hikes 51-52
　Telegraphic Transfers 50
　Tipping 52
　Travellers' Cheques 50
Monument to the People's Heroes 138
Museum of the Revolution 149
Museums 149-152
　Capital Museum & Library 152
　History Museum & Museum of the Revolution 149-150
　Lu Xun 150
　Military 150
　Natural History 150
　Song Qingling 151
　Xu Beihong 151
Music 21-22
Mutianyu Great Wall 225-227, **Map 5 (226)**

National Library 151
Natural History Museum 150
Niujie Mosque 169
North Cathedral 170

Observatory, Ancient 171-172
Old Summer Palace 147-149, **Map 22**
Opera 18-19, 206-207
Orientation 15-16

Parks 142, 152-164, 232, 237, 246-247
　Beihai 153-156, **Map 2 (154)**
　Beijing Amusement 164
　Ditan 162
　Fragrant Hills 232, **Map 15**
　Grand View Garden 164
　Hai River, Tianjin 246
　Jingshan 152-153
　Longtan 163

Miyun International Amusement 237
Ritan 162
Shuishang, Tianjin 247
Taoranting 163
Tiantan 157-162, **Map 3 (159)**
Yuetan 162
Yuyuantan 163
Zhongshan 142
Zizhuyuan 163
Pedicab 131
Peking Man Site 235-237, **Map 17**
Photography 79-81, 213-214
Pinyin, see Language
Places to Eat 191-201
　Beijing Duck 192-193
　Cantonese 195
　Cheap Eats 191-192
　Fast Food 198-199
　Hunanese 194-195
　Mongolian Hotpot & Muslim Barbecue 195
　Non-Chinese Food 196-198
　Other Chinese Restaurants 196
　Shanghainese 195
　Sichuan 194
　Tianjin 251-253
　Vegetarian 195
Places to Stay 179-190
　Bottom End 179-183
　Long Term 189-190
　Middle Range 183-185
　Tianjin 250-251
　Top End 185-189
Population 17
Post 62-65
Prince Gong's Residence 174
Public Security Bureau (PSB) 59-61

Qianmen 137-138
Qigong 20-21
Qinglongqiao 223-224

Religion 23
Restaurants, see Places to Eat
Ritan Park 162

Sea Travel 113-114
Shangfang Mountains 239
Shidu 238-239, **Map 7 (240)**
Shopping 210-219

Antiques 216, 218, 243
Arts & crafts 214
Books 212-213, 216
Chinese herbal medicines
212, 215
Clothing 217
Fabrics 215
Film & Photography 213-214
Hutongs 214-215
Shopping guide 211
Technology 218-219
Shuishang Park, Tianjin 247
Song & Dance Shows, see
Entertainment
Song Qingling Museum 151
South Cathedral 170
Sports 208-209
Studying Chinese, see Lan-
guage
Subway 128-129, **Map 24**
Summer Palace 144-147,
Map 21
Supermarkets 199-201

Taichi, see Taijiquan
Taijiquan 20
Tanzhe Temple 234
Taoranting Park 163
Taxi 131
Telephone 65-70
Area Codes 67-68
Essential Numbers 68
Temple of Heaven, see
Tiantan Park
Temple of the Sleeping
Buddha 233
Temples 165-169, 232-234,
239, 243
Azure Clouds 232-233
Badachu 233-234, **Map 16**
Black 169
Confucius 167
Confucius (Tianjin) 243
Doulü 239
Fayuan 169
Great Bell 167-168
Guangji 168
Jietai 234
Lama 165-167
Sleeping Buddha 233
Tanzhe 234
White Cloud 169
White Dagoba 168
Wuta 168

Theatre, see Entertainment
Tiananmen Gate 136-137
Tiananmen Square 135
Tianjin 242-254, **Map 9 (248-249)**
Tiantan Park 157-162, **Map 3 (159)**
Time 71
Tipping, see Money
Tombs 228-232
Changling 230
Dingdong 231
Dingling 229 230
Eastern Qing 231-232,
Map 14
Ming 228-230, **Map 13**
Western Qing 231
Zhaoling 230
Tourist Offices 55-59
Tourist Sites 134-178
Admission Fees 134-135
Tours 126, 133, 173-178
Bicycle 173-178, **Map 11**
Train Travel 114-125
Domestic Train 121-125
International Train 114-121
Trans-Siberian Railway 114-
121
Travellers' Cheques, see
Money
TV, see Entertainment (Other)

Underground City 170-171
University of Beijing 172

Visas 39 40, 60 61, 119 121
Extensions 40, 60-61
Re-entry 40
Requirements 39-40
Trans-Siberian Railway Route
119-121

Western Hills 232-233
Western Qing Tombs 231
White Cloud Temple 169
White Dagoba Temple 168
Women Travellers 83
Work 86-89
Doing Business 87-89
Workers' Cultural Palace 142
Wuta Temple 168

Xu Beihong Museum 151

Yuetan Park 162

Yunshui Caves 239
Yuyuantan Park 163

Zhongguancun 218-219
Zhongnanhai 144
Zhongshan Park 142

Zhou Enlai Memorial Hall,
    Tianjin 247
Zhoukoudian Village 235-237
Zizhuyuan Park 163
Zoo, Beijing 164

MAP LEGEND

BOUNDARIES

— ‒ · — · — ..... International ⎯ ⎯ · · ⎯ .... Regional

SYMBOLS

✈	.... Airport	Ⓟ	.... Parking
⊖	.... Bus Station	) (	.... Pass
⚊	.... Camping Area	⊠	.... Post Office
♣ ⚱	.... Church, Cathedral	⊶⊣⊢⊶	.... Railway Bridge
⌒	.... Cave	⊶▬⊶	.... Railway Station
✚	.... Hospital	→⊶⊷←	.... Railway Tunnel
⚑	.... Tourist Information	∴	.... Ruin
☪ ⚲	.... Mosque, Temple	�	.... Spring
▲	.... Mountain	⊓	.... Tomb

ROUTES

════	.... City Street	⊹⊹⊹⊹⊹⊹	.... Railway
▬▬▬	...... Major Road	⊣⊢⊣⊢⊣⊢	.... Cable Car
⎯ ⎯ ⎯	...... Ferry Route	⎯ ⎯ ⎯ ⎯	.... Bicycle Path
▬ ▬ ▬	.... Subway	⋯⋯⋯	.... Walking Path

HYDROGRAPHIC FEATURES

⌒	..... River, Creek	⌒	.... Coastline
⬭	.... Lake	⌇	.... Waterfall

OTHER FEATURES

▦	.... Park, Garden	▦	.... Place to Shop
▦	.... Urban Area	▢ ■	.... Place to Stay
▦	.... Building	▢ ▼	.... Place to Eat

Note: not all symbols displayed above appear in this book

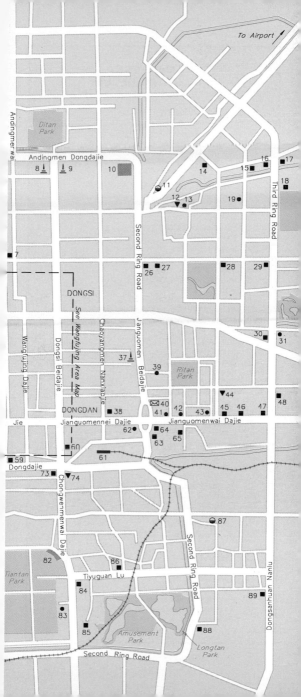

MAP 10 KEY
CENTRAL BEIJING

■ PLACES TO STAY

4 Bamboo Garden Hotel/Restaurant
7 Lüsongyuan Hotel
14 Yuyang Hotel
15 Huadu Hotel
16 Kunlun Hotel
17 Lufthansa Centre & Kempinski Hotel
18 Great Wall Sheraton
20 Holiday Inn Downtown
26 Swissôtel
27 Beijing Asia Hotel
28 Chains City Hotel
29 Zhaolong Hotel
30 Jingguang New World Hotel
32 Minzu Hotel
38 International Hotel & CITS
45 Jianguo Hotel
46 Hotel Beijing Toronto
47 China World Trade Centre & Hotel
48 Guanghua Hotel
53 Yuexiu Hotel
59 Capital Hotel
60 Jinlang Hotel
63 Gloria Plaza Hotel & CITS
64 Hotel New Otani
65 CVIK Hotel & Yaohan
   Department Store
68 Qiaoyuan Hotel
69 Far East Hotel
73 Chongwenmen Hotel
75 Qianmen Hotel
76 Dongfang Hotel
78 Rainbow & Beiwei Hotels
84 Tiantan Sports Hotel & Shanghai
   Jakarta Restaurant
85 Traffic Hotel
86 Parkview Tiantan Hotel
88 Longtan Hotel
89 Leyou & Hua Thai Hotels

▼ PLACES TO EAT

12 Pizza Hut
33 Quyuan Restaurant
44 Mexican Wave
49 Vie de France Bakery
51 Kaorouwan Restaurant
56 Kentucky Fried Chicken & Vie de France
   Bakery

71 Pizza Hut
72 Qianmen Roast Duck Restaurant
74 Bianyifang Duck Restaurant
77 Gongdelin Vegetarian Restaurant

OTHER

1   Xizhimen Railway Station
2   Song Qingling Museum
3   Prince Gong's Residence
5   Bell Tower
6   Drum Tower
8   Confucius Temple
9   Lama Temple
10 Russian Embassy
11 Dongzhimen Long Distance
    Bus Station
13 Australian Embassy
19 Friendship Supermarket
21 Lu Xun Museum
22 White Dagoba Temple
23 Guangji Temple
24 Dizhi Cinema Hall
25 North Cathedral
31 Chaoyang Theatre
34 Aviation Building
    (CAAC & Airport Bus)
35 Forbidden City
36 Tiananmen Gate
37 Black Temple
39 Yabao Lu Clothing Market
40 International Post &
    Telecom Office
41 International Club
42 Friendship Store & CITIC
43 Xiushui Silk Market
50 Shoudu Cinema
52 South Cathedral
54 Great Hall of the People
55 Tiananmen Square
57 Qianmen
58 History Museum &
    Museum of the Revolution
61 Beijing Railway Station
62 Ancient Observatory
66 Niu Jie Mosque
67 Fayuan Temple
70 Sun City Department Store
79 Friendship Hospital
80 Tianqiao Theatre
81 Natural History Museum
82 Hongqiao Market
83 Harmony Club
87 Majuan Long Distance Bus Station

MAP 10 CHINESE KEY
CENTRAL BEIJING

■ PLACES TO STAY

4　竹园宾馆
7　侣松园宾馆
14　渔阳饭店
15　华都饭店
16　昆仑饭店
17　燕沙商城/凯宾斯基饭店
18　长城饭店
20　金都假日饭店
26　北京港澳中心
27　亚洲大酒店
28　城市宾馆
29　兆龙饭店
30　京广新世界饭店飙
32　民族饭店
38　国际饭店/中国国际旅行社
45　建国饭店
46　京伦饭店
47　国际贸易中心/中国大饭店
48　光华饭店
53　越秀大饭店
59　首都宾馆
60　金朗大酒店
63　凯莱大酒店/旅游大厦/国际旅行社
64　长富宫饭店
65　赛特饭店/八佰伴
68　侨园饭店
69　远东饭店
73　崇文门饭店
75　前门饭店
76　东方饭店
78　天桥宾馆/北纬饭店
84　天坛体育宾馆
85　交通饭店
86　天坛饭店
88　龙潭饭店
89　乐游饭店/华泰饭店

▼ PLACES TO EAT

12　必胜客
33　曲园坡沙
44　墨西哥波波涛
49　大磨坊面包
51　烤肉宛饭庄
56　肯德基家乡鸡/大磨坊面包
71　必胜客
72　前门全聚德烤鸭店
74　便宜坊垦
77　功德林素菜馆

OTHER

1 火车居
2 门故
3 西直门
5 宋庆龄府
6 恭王楼
8 钟鼓楼
9 孔庙
10 雍和宫
11 苏联大使馆
13 东直门长途汽车站
19 澳大利亚大使馆
21 友谊超级商场
22 鲁迅博物馆
23 白塔寺
24 北京百货大楼
25 地质礼堂
31 北朝阳剧场
34 民航营业大厦
35 紫禁城
36 天安门
37 安化寺
39 智化寺
40 雅宝路
41 国际邮局
42 国际俱乐部
43 友谊商店/国际大厦
50 秀水东街
52 首都电影院
54 南堂
55 人民大会堂
57 天安门广场
58 中国革命历史博物馆
61 北京火车站
62 古观象台
66 牛街礼拜寺
67 法源寺
70 太阳城百货
79 友谊医院
80 天桥剧场
81 自然博物馆
82 红桥商场
83 幸福俱乐部
87 马圈长途汽车站

1 Song Qingling Museum
2 Bamboo Garden Hotel
3 Bell Tower
4 Drum Tower
5 Kaorouji Restaurant
6 Prince Gong's Residence
7 Confucius Temple
8 Lama Temple
9 Confucius Restaurant
10 Beihai Park Main Entrance
11 Forbidden City Rear Gate
12 China Art Gallery
13 Kentucky Fried Chicken
14 Tiananmen Gate
15 Great Hall of the People
16 History Museum & Museum of the Revolution
17 McDonald's
18 Qianmen

1 宋庆龄故居
2 竹园宾馆
3 钟楼
4 鼓楼
5 北京烤肉季
6 恭王府
7 孔庙
8 雍和宫
9 孔子餐厅
10 北海公园北门
11 故宫北门
12 中国美术馆
13 肯德基家乡鸡
14 天安门
15 人民大会堂
16 中国革命历史博物馆
17 麦当劳
18 前门

MAP 12

王府井地区

Wangfujing Area

0   250   500 m

To Lama
Temple

To Jingshan
Park

Wusi   Dajie   Dongsi Xidajie

1

2

3

4

5

6

Beichizi

Dajie

Donghuangchenggen Nanjie

Beihean Dajie

Qihelou Jie

Forbidden
City

7

Dongsi Nan Dajie

8

Dengshihou Jie

Dengshihou Xijie

9   10

Dongdan Beida Jie

Donghuamen Dajie

Dong'anmen Dajie

11

12   13

Jinyu   Hutong

14

18

17 16 15

Chenguang Jie

Nanchizi

19

20

Wangfujing

Dajie

21

22

23   24

Raise the
People's
Consciousness
Cultural Palace

Nanheyan Dajie

31

29   28

30

Clothing Market

27   26   25

Dongchang'an   Jie

To Tiananmen

32

To Friendship
Store

Tajichang Dajie

Chongwenmennei Dajie

Dongdan
Park

33

	PLACES TO STAY	2	CAAC Booking Office
5	Sara Hotel	4	Mosque
8	Holiday Inn Crowne Plaza	6	Capital Theatre
9	Tianlun Dynasty Hotel	7	PSB Foreign Affairs Branch (Visa Extensions)
10	Novotel Hotel	11	Bank of China
12	Taiwan Hotel	15	Jixiang Theatre
13	Peace Hotel	18	Foreign Languages Bookstore
14	Palace Hotel & Watson's	19	Pudu Temple
22	Central Institute of Fine Arts	20	Beijing Department Store
30	Beijing Hotel	21	Dong'an Bazaar
		23	Beijing Union Medical College
▼	PLACES TO EAT	24	Dahua Cinema
		25	Dongdan Vegetable Market
3	Kentucky Fried Chicken	28	Xinhua Bookstore
16	Carls Jr	29	China Photo Studio
17	Dairy Queen	31	Huangshicheng Temple
26	Shakey's Pizza	32	Shanghai Airlines
27	McDonald's	33	History Museum & Museum of the Revolution
	OTHER		
1	China Art Gallery		

■ PLACES TO STAY

5 华侨大厦
8 国际艺苑皇冠假日饭店
9 天伦王朝酒店
10 松鹤大饭店
12 台湾饭店
13 和平饭店宾馆
14 王府饭店 / 屈臣氏
22 中央美术学院
30 北京饭店

▼ PLACES TO EAT

3 肯德基家乡鸡
16 克力汉堡包
17 迪利冰淇淋
26 喜客美式餐厅
27 麦当劳

OTHER

1 中国美术馆
2 中国民航售票处
4 清真寺
6 首都剧场
7 公安局外事科
11 中国银行
15 吉祥戏院
18 外文书店
19 普渡寺
20 北京百货大楼
21 东安市场
23 协和医院
24 大华电影院
25 东单菜市场
28 新华书店
29 中国照相
31 皇史宬寺
32 上海航空公司售票处
33 中国历史革命博物馆

1 Tailing Tomb
2 Kangling Tomb
3 Maoling Tomb
4 Yuling Tomb
5 Qingling Tomb
6 Xianling Tomb
7 Changling Tomb
8 Jingling Tomb
9 Dingling Tomb
10 Zhaoling Tomb
11 International
   Friendship Forest
12 Heliport
13 Yongling Tomb
14 Deling Tomb
15 Golf Course
16 North New Village
17 Seven Arch Bridge
18 Siling Tomb
19 Small Palace Gate
20 Lingxing Gate
21 Stone Statues
22 Great Palace Gate
23 Dragon Hill
24 Fairy Cave
25 Shisanling
   Reservoir Memorial
26 Changping North
   Railway Station
27 Changping Village

MAP

十三陵

Ming Tombs

0   1.5   3 km

Tianshou Mountains

1

2

3 4

5 6

7

8

9

10

11

12

13

14

16

15

17

18

19

20

21

Shisanling Reservoir

25

22

24

23

26

27

To Beijing   To Tongliao

1 泰陵
2 康陵
3 茂陵
4 裕陵
5 庆陵
6 献陵
7 长陵
8 景陵
9 定陵
10 昭陵
11 国际友谊林
12 空中旅游机场
13 永陵
14 德陵
15 北京国际高尔夫球场
16 北新村
17 七孔桥
18 思陵
19 小宫门
20 棂星门
21 石像生
22 大宫门
23 龙山
24 仙人洞
25 十三陵水库纪念碑
26 昌平北火车站
27 昌平

MAP 14

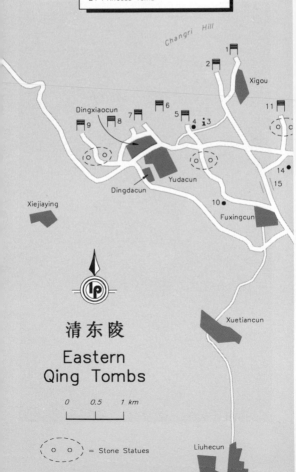

1 Xiaodong Tomb
2 Xiaoling Tomb
3 Tourist Office
4 Foreign Guest Reception Centre
5 Yuling (Emperor Qianlong) Tomb
6 Yufei Tomb
7 Dingdong (Empress Cixi) Tomb
8 Dingfei Tomb
9 Dingling Tomb
10 Stele Tower
11 Jingling Tomb
12 Jingfei Tomb
13 Taifei (Two Imperial Concubines
   of Emperor Kangxi) Tombs
14 Stele Tower
15 Seven-Arch Bridge
16 Longfeng (Dragon-Phoenix) Gate
17 Stele Tower
18 Robing Hall
19 Dagong Gate
20 Stone Archway
21 Zhaoxi Tomb
22 Huiling Tomb
23 Huifei Tomb
24 Princess Tomb

Changri Hill

Xigou

Dingxiaocun

Dingdacun

Yudacun

Xiejiaying

Fuxingcun

Xuetiancun

清东陵

Eastern
Qing Tombs

0   0.5   1 km

(o o) = Stone Statues

Liuhecun

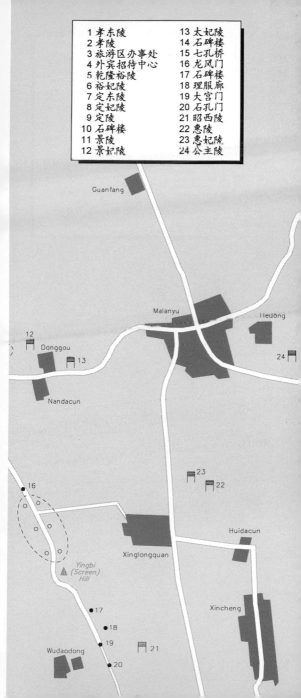

1 孝东陵	13 太妃陵
2 孝陵	14 石碑楼
3 旅游区办事处	15 七孔桥
4 外宾招待中心	16 龙凤门
5 乾隆裕陵	17 石碑楼
6 裕妃陵	18 理服廊
7 定东陵	19 大宫门
8 定妃陵	20 石孔门
9 定陵	21 昭西陵
10 石碑楼	22 惠陵
11 景陵	23 惠妃陵
12 景妃陵	24 公主陵

Guanfang

Malanyu

Hedong

12
Donggou
13
24

Nandacun

23
22

16

Huidacun

Yingbi
(Screen)
Hill

Xinglongquan

Xincheng

17

18

19
Wudaodong
21

20

MAP 15

1 Vajra Throng Pagoda	19 Hibiscus Hall
2 Sun Yatsen Memorial Hall	20 Glazed Tile Pagoda
3 Temple of Azure Clouds	21 Temple of Brilliance
4 North Gate	22 Pine Forest Restaurant
5 Spectacles Lake	23 Xiangshan Villa
6 Unbosoming Chamber	24 Administrative Office
7 Incense Burner Peak	25 Peak Viewing Pavilion
8 Middle Station	26 Pavilion of Scattered Clouds
9 Cable Car	27 East Gate
10 Stele of Western Hills Shimmering in Snow	28 Botanical Gardens
11 Platform	29 Jade Fragrance Hall
12 Sun Facing Cave	30 White Pine Pavilion
13 Jade Sceptre Cliff	31 Xiangshan Temple Site
14 Moonlight Villa	32 Halfway Pavilion
15 Tiered Cloud Villa	33 Temple of Red Glow
16 Fourth Jade Flower Villa	34 Eighteen Turns
17 Pavilion of Varied Scenery	35 Xiangshan Hotel
18 Jade Flower Villa	36 Jingcui Lake
	37 Red Leaf Forest
	38 Twin Lakes Villa
	39 See Clouds Rise

香山公园

Fragrant Hills Park

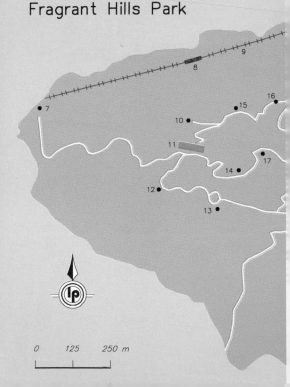

0   125   250 m

1 金刚宝座塔	21 昭庙
2 孙中山纪念堂	22 松林餐厅
3 碧云寺	23 香山别墅
4 北门	24 管理处
5 眼镜湖	25 望峰亭
6 见心斋	26 多云亭
7 香炉峰	27 东门
8 中站	28 植物园
9 登山览车	29 玉香馆
10 西山晴雪	30 白松亭
11 平台	31 香山寺遗址
12 朝阳洞	32 半山亭
13 森玉笏	33 洪光寺
14 栖月山庄	34 十八盘
15 梯云山馆	35 香山宾馆
16 玉乳四院	36 静翠间
17 多景亭	37 红叶林
18 玉花山庄	38 双清别墅
19 芙蓉馆	39 看云起
20 琉璃塔	

MAP 16

八大处

Badachu

0   150   300 m

1	宝珠洞
2	香界寺
3	冰川漂砾
4	证果寺
5	大悲寺
6	龙泉庵
7	八大处别墅
8	三山庵
9	佛牙舍利塔
10	长廊
11	金鱼池
12	餐厅
13	灵光寺
14	售票处
15	长安寺

1 Precious Pearl Cave (Baozhudong)
2 Fragrant World Temple (Xiangjiesi)
3 Glacial Drift Boulder (Bingchuan Piaoli)
4 Temple of Rewards Attainment (Zhengguosi)
5 Great Mercy Temple (Dabeisi)
6 Dragon-Spring Nunnery (Longquan An)
7 Badachu Villa (Bieshu)
8 Three Mountain Nunnery (Sanshan An)
9 Buddha's Tooth Relic Pagoda (Foyashe Lita)
10 Long Corridor (Changlang)
11 Goldfish Pond (Jinyuchi)
12 Restaurant
13 Divine Light Temple (Linguangsi)
14 Ticket Office
15 Eternal Peace Temple (Chang'ansi)

1 第二地点
2 北京猿人館
3 招待所
4 外宾接待室
5 停车场
6 大门
7 鸽子堂洞
8 猿人洞
9 山顶洞
10 第十五地点
11 第四地点
12 第十二地点
13 第三地点
14 周口店火车站

MAP 18

5
6 P
7 Pi
8 Ape
9 Uppe
10 No 15
11 No 4 D
12 No 12 D
13 No 3 Dig
14 Zhoukoudia
   Railway Stat

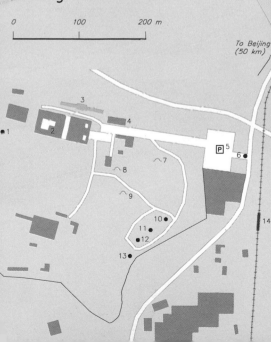

周口店
Peking Man Site

0   100   200 m

To Beijing
(50 km)

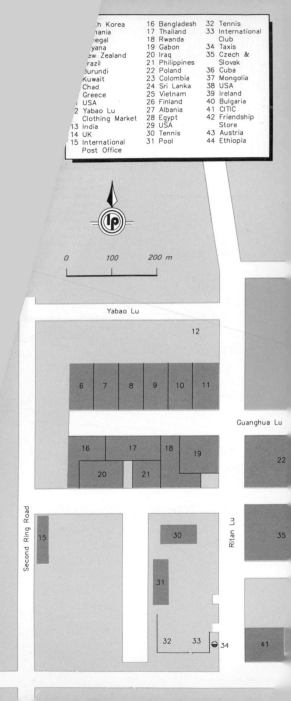

h Korea 16 Bangladesh 32 Tennis
ania 17 Thailand 33 International
egal 18 Rwanda Club
yana 19 Gabon 34 Taxis
ew Zealand 20 Iraq 35 Czech &
razil 21 Philippines Slovak
Burundi 22 Poland 36 Cuba
Kuwait 23 Colombia 37 Mongolia
Chad 24 Sri Lanka 38 USA
Greece 25 Vietnam 39 Ireland
USA 26 Finland 40 Bulgaria
2 Yabao Lu 27 Albania 41 CITIC
Clothing Market 28 Egypt 42 Friendship
13 India 29 USA Store
14 UK 30 Tennis 43 Austria
15 International 31 Pool 44 Ethiopia
Post Office

0   100   200 m

Yabao Lu

12

6 7 8 9 10 11

Guanghua Lu

16 17 18 19

20 21

22

Second Ring Road

15

30

31

Ritan Lu

35

32 33 34

41

1 北朝鲜	16 加拿大	31 游泳池
2 罗马尼亚	17 孟加拉国	32 网球场
3 塞内加尔	18 泰国	33 国际俱乐部
4 圭亚那	19 加蓬	34 出租汽车
5 新西兰	20 卢旺达	35 捷克斯洛伐克
6 巴布亚	21 加纳	36 古巴
7 科威特	22 伊拉克	37 蒙古
8 乍得	23 菲律宾	38 美国
9 布隆迪	24 波兰	39 爱尔兰
10 希腊	25 哥伦比亚	40 保加利亚
11 美国(房子)	26 斯里兰卡	41 国际大厦
12 雅宝路	27 越南	42 友谊商店
13 印度	28 芬兰	43 奥地利
14 联合王国	29 阿尔及利亚	44 埃塞俄比亚
15 国际邮电局	30 埃及	

建国门外大使馆区
Jianguomenwai
Embassy
Compound

1

Ritan Beilu

Ritan Dong 1-Jie

2 | 3
2 | 4
2 | 5

Ritan Dong 2-Jie

13 | 14

Ritan Park

23 | 25
24 | 25

26 | 27
28 | 29

Xiushui Beijie

36 | 37
36 | 37

38 | 40
39 | 40

Ritan Dongjie

Xiushui Dongjie

Xiushui Nanjie

43 | 44

42

Jianguomenwai Dajie

MAP 19

Sanlitun
Embassy
Compound

0   250   500 m

三里屯大使馆区

1 斋尔里亚
2 味泊比京国际商店
3 多尼利
4 北京朗巴桑尼亚
5 伊黎坦
6 阿新尼加嫩尼亚
7 八约利坡尔那法索
8 南甩几
9 肯友索店
10 阿土喀里廷
11 墨璃丹麦其隆哥
12 阿班牙及利亚
13 澳马大来西亚
14 多比利那时
15 加纳
16 加东埔寨
17 坡尔那法索

33 利昂
34 拉伊尼斯加岛
35 尔斯加达
36 突乌德干国日基
37 马乌德尼巴璃巴
38 亚坦
39 利斯
40 大利亚
41 拿牙合封
42 加匈利合联老国儿童基金会
43 比汗门
44 阿南刚国亚
45 利赞智委
46 内兰哥璃拉
47 摩洛里亚
48 马叙也尼亚
49 法利门
50 中巴苏丹非斯和国放党
51 意勒丹利
52 斯大威利
53 三里屯百货商场
64 三里屯百货商场

Canal

Mahe Nanlu

Great Wall Hotel

Sanlitun Dong 6-Jie

Sanlitun Xi 6-Jie

Sanlitun Dong 5-Jie

Sanlitun Beixiao Jie

Sanlitun Xi 5-Jie

Sanlitun Lu

Sanlitun Dongjie

No 110 Bus Stop

Agricultural Exhibition Centre

Dongzhimenwai Dajie

Xindong Lu

Sanlitun Zhongjie

Sanlitun Dong 4-Jie

Sanlitun Dong 3-Jie

Dongsanhuan Beilu (Ring Road)

Sanlitun Dong 2-Jie

Sanlitun Dong 1-Jie

Gongren Tiyu Chang Beilu

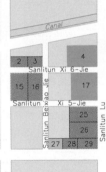

1	Duoweizhai Restaurant	33	Sierra Leone
2	Nepal	34	Zaire
3	Liberia	35	Tunisia
4	Beijing International Store	36	Madagascar
5	Iran	37	Uganda
6	Lebanon	38	Germany
7	Tanzania	39	Nigeria
8	Oman	40	Pakistan
9	Singapore	41	Sweden
10	Niger	42	Canada
11	Burkina Faso	43	Hungary
12	Jordan	44	UNICEF
13	Libya	45	Laos
14	Yugoslavia	46	Afghanistan
15	Guinea	47	South Yemen
16	Kenya	48	Congo
17	Friendship Store	49	Zambia
18	Somalia	50	Chile
19	Argentina	51	Venezuela
20	Turkey	52	Holland
21	Cameroon	53	Morocco
22	Mexico	54	Mauritania
23	Switzerland	55	Mali
24	Denmark	56	Syria
25	Algeria	57	Yemen
26	Spain	58	France
27	Australia	59	Central African Republic
28	Malaysia	60	PLO
29	Togo	61	Sudan
30	Belgium	62	Italy
31	Ghana	63	Norway
32	Cambodia	64	Sanlitun Department Store

Outdoor Barber Shop (RS)

MAP 20

1 神武门
2 钦安殿
3 千秋亭
4 明清工艺美术馆
5 御花园
6 宫廷史迹陈列
7 长春宫
8 坤宁宫
9 陶瓷馆
10 交泰殿
11 珍馆
12 养性殿
13 绘画馆
14 青铜器馆
15 乾清宫
16 养心殿
17 乾清门
18 九龙壁
19 保和殿
20 中和殿
21 太和殿
22 太和门
23 午门

紫禁城的宫殿地区

Palace Area of Forbidden City

0   150   300 m

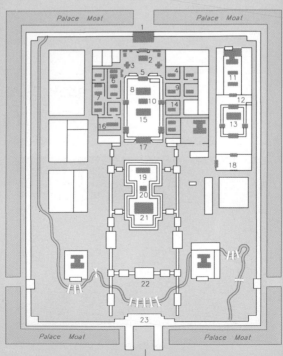

Palace Moat   Palace Moat

Palace Moat   Palace Moat

To the Gate of Heavenly Peace (Tiananmen)

1 Gate of Divine Military Genius
  (Shenwumen)
2 Hall of Imperial Peace
3 Thousand Autumns Pavilion
4 Exhibition of Ming &
  Qing Dynasty Arts & Crafts
5 Imperial Garden (Yuhuayuan)
6 Western Palaces Nos 16, 17 & 18
  (residential palaces now used as museums)
7 Palace of Eternal Spring
  (Changchungong)
8 Palace of Earthly Tranquillity
  (Kunninggong)
9 Exhibition of Ceramics
10 Hall of Union (Jiaotaidian)
11 Exhibition of Jewellery (Hall of the
   Cultivation of Character)
12 Hall of the Cultivation of Character
13 Exhibition of Paintings (Hall of Imperial
   Supremacy)
14 Exhibition of Bronzes
15 Palace of Heavenly Purity (Qianqinggong)
16 Hall of Mental Cultivation (Yangxindian)
17 Gate of Heavenly Purity (Qianqingmen)
18 Nine Dragon Screen
19 Hall of Preserving Harmony (Baohedian)
20 Hall of Middle Harmony (Zhonghedian)
21 Hall of Supreme Harmony (Taihedian)
22 Supreme Harmony Gate (Taihemen)
23 Meridian Gate (Wumen)

Rubbish Bin (RS)

MAP 21

颐和园
Summer Palace

0   150   300 m

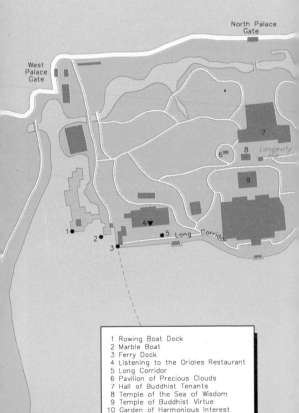

North Palace Gate

West Palace Gate

7

8 *Longevity Hill*

6

9

1

2

3

4 ▼

5 Long Corridor

1 Rowing Boat Dock
2 Marble Boat
3 Ferry Dock
4 Listening to the Orioles Restaurant
5 Long Corridor
6 Pavilion of Precious Clouds
7 Hall of Buddhist Tenants
8 Temple of the Sea of Wisdom
9 Temple of Buddhist Virtue
10 Garden of Harmonious Interest
11 Hall of Benevolence & Longevity
12 Rowing Boat Dock
13 Jade Belt Bridge
14 Pavilion of Knowing in the Spring
15 Bronze Ox

Long Corridor

See Enlargement

13

15

14

10

Long Corridor

11

East
Palace
Gate

*Kunming
Lake*

12

1 划船码头
2 清晏船
3 码头
4 听鹂馆
5 长廊
6 排云殿
7 香崇宗印之阁
8 智慧海
9 佛香阁
10 谐趣园
11 仁寿殿
12 划船码头
13 玉带桥
14 知春亭
15 铜牛

MAP 22

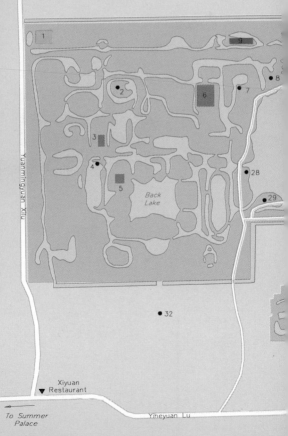

1 紫碧山房	21 蓬岛瑶台
2 文源阁	22 瀛海仙山亭
3 武陵春色	23 接秀山房
4 万方安和	24 海岳开襟
5 杏花春馆	25 思永斋
6 舍卫城	26 含经堂
7 鱼然大公	27 玉玲珑馆
8 平湖秋月	28 澡身浴德
9 北远山村	29 湖山在望
10 藏密楼	30 广育宫
11 方壶胜境	31 别有洞天
12 万花阵	32 大宫门
13 海宴堂	33 松月亭
14 展览馆	34 涵秋馆
15 大水法残迹	35 凤麟洲
16 线法山	36 宫门
17 狮子林	37 船台
18 船台	38 槛碧亭
19 福海酒家	39 正觉寺
20 涵虚朗鉴	40 宫门

1 Purple Blue Lodge
2 Library Pavilion
3 Wuling Spring Beauty
4 Universal Peace
5 Lodge of Apricot Blossoms in Spring
6 Citadel of Guards
7 Open World to the Public
8 Autumn Moon Over the Calm Lake
9 Far North Mountain Village
10 Collecting Mysteries Tower
11 Wonderland of Square Pots
12 Flowers Maze
13 Oceanic Banquet Hall
14 Exhibition Hall
15 Great Fountains Ruins
16 Racecourse
17 Lion's Forest
18 Rowboat Dock
19 Fuhai Restaurant
20 Clear Reflection of the Void

21 Jade Terraces on Penglai Isles
22 Blessing Sea Fairy Hill Hall
23 Lodge of Grace & Beauty
24 Open Sea Hill
25 Studio of Everlasting Thoughts
26 Containing Scriptures Hall
27 Exquisite Jade Hall
28 Body Bathed in Virtue
29 Lakes & Hills View
30 Palace of Broad Nutrient
31 New Fairyland
32 Great Palace Entrance Gate
33 Nine Moon Pavilion
34 Contain Autumn Hall
35 Phoenix & Unicorn Isles
36 Entrance Gate
37 Boat Dock
38 Pavilion of Enjoying Jasper
39 Temple of Awareness
40 Entrance Gate

圆明园

Old Summer Palace

0   150   300 m

To Beijing Zoo

MAP 23

北京地区

Beijing
Municipality

0   25   50 km

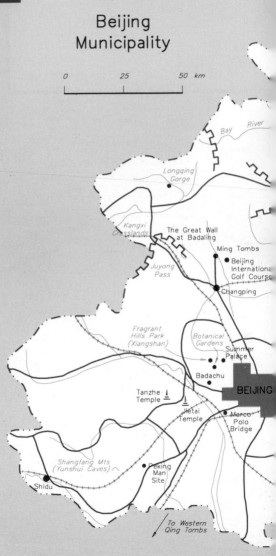

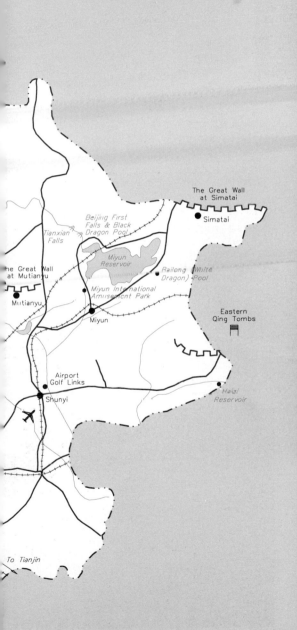

The Great Wall
at Simatai

● Simatai

Beijing First
Falls & Black
Dragon Pool

Tianxian
Falls

Miyun
Reservoir

Railong (White
Dragon) Pool

he Great Wall
at Mutianyu

Miyun International
Amusement Park

■ Mutianyu

Eastern
Qing Tombs

■ Miyun

● Miyun

Airport
Golf Links

Haizi
Reservoir

◆ Shunyi

To Tianjin

MAP 24

To Summer Palace
& Fragrant Hills

Baishiqao Lu

Zizhuyuan
Park

Xizhimen
Railway
Station

Zoo

Xizhimenwai Dajie

10

Chegongzhuang Dajie

11

北京地铁站和路线

Beijing Subway
Stations

*Dots indicate the location of
stops underground, not exits*

Fuchengmenwai Dajie

Yuetan Bejie

12

Yuetan
Park

Yuetan Nanjie

E   D   C   B

13

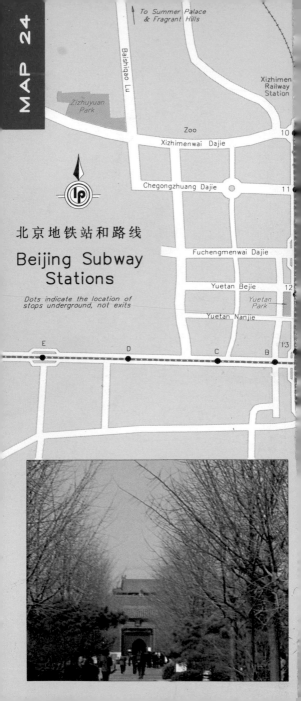